NONPROFITS &BUSINESS

Also of interest from the Urban Institute Press:

Contemporary U.S. Tax Policy, second edition, by C. Eugene Steuerle
The Nonprofit Almanac 2008, by Kennard T. Wing, Thomas H. Pollak,
   and Amy Blackwood
Nonprofits and Government: Collaboration and Conflict, second edition,
   edited by Elizabeth Boris and C. Eugene Steuerle

NONPROFITS &BUSINESS

Edited by Joseph J. Cordes and C. Eugene Steuerle

THE URBAN INSTITUTE PRESS
WASHINGTON, DC

THE URBAN INSTITUTE PRESS
2100 M Street, N.W.
Washington, D.C. 20037

Library of Congress Cataloging-in-Publication Data

Nonprofits and business / edited by Joseph J. Cordes and C. Eugene Steuerle.
    p. cm.
  Includes index.
  ISBN 978-0-87766-741-4
  1. Nonprofit organizations—United States—Finance. 2. Social entrepreneurship—United States. 3. Voluntarism—United States—Finance. 4. Corporations—Charitable contributions—United States. 5. Strategic alliances (Business)—United States. I. Cordes, Joseph J. II. Steuerle, C. Eugene, 1946-
  HD2769.2.U6N665 2008
  658.15—dc22   2008038627

Printed in the United States of America

10 09 08   1 2 3 4 5

THE URBAN INSTITUTE is a nonprofit, nonpartisan policy research and educational organization established in Washington, D.C., in 1968. Its staff investigates the social, economic, and governance problems confronting the nation and evaluates the public and private means to alleviate them. The Institute disseminates its research findings through publications, its web site, the media, seminars, and forums.

Through work that ranges from broad conceptual studies to administrative and technical assistance, Institute researchers contribute to the stock of knowledge available to guide decisionmaking in the public interest.

Contents

Acknowledgments   ix

1 Nonprofits and Business: A New World
of Innovation and Adaptation   1
Joseph J. Cordes and C. Eugene Steuerle

2 Alternative Perspectives on Social Enterprise   21
Dennis R. Young

3 The Changing Economy and the Scope
of Nonprofit-Like Activities   47
Joseph J. Cordes and C. Eugene Steuerle

4 Business Activities of Nonprofit Organizations:
Legal Boundary Problems   83
Evelyn Brody

5 The Strategic and Economic Value
of Hybrid Nonprofit Structures   129
Howard P. Tuckman

6 Cross-Sector Marketing Alliances: Partnerships, Sponsorships, and Cause-Related Marketing   155
Alan R. Andreasen

7 Innovative Foundation Financing: The Annie E. Casey Foundation   193
Burton Sonenstein and Christa Velasquez

8 Nonprofit Labor: Current Trends and Future Directions   217
Eric C. Twombly

9 Measuring the Nonprofit Bottom Line   239
Linda M. Lampkin and Harry P. Hatry

About the Editors   271

About the Contributors   273

Index   277

Acknowledgments

The editors gratefully acknowledge support received from the Annie E. Casey Foundation for this volume. Burton Sonenstein and Christa Velasquez of the Annie E. Casey Foundation additionally provided quite useful comments and feedback in the early stages of the volume, not to mention their own engaging chapter. We are also indebted beyond measure to Elizabeth Boris, director of the Center on Nonprofits and Philanthropy, and Janelle Kerlin of the Andrew Young School of Policy Studies, for their constant work and support on this project. We received excellent suggestions from reviewers of earlier drafts of the manuscript. Zina Poletz deserves much of the credit for the material appearing in the appendix to chapter 3. Alison Moore and Will Bradbury did their usual masterful job editing the manuscript, turning our ramblings into prose. Finally, we learned a great deal from meetings with nonprofit stakeholders and practitioners, including those who participated in a January 2006 seminar on nonprofits and business held at the Center on Nonprofits and Philanthropy.

1

Nonprofits and Business
A New World of Innovation and Adaptation

Joseph J. Cordes and C. Eugene Steuerle

In September 2006, the founders of Google, who had just made a splash with a highly successful public stock offering, garnered headlines once again by setting up a foundation, appropriately named Google.org, with about $1 billion in funding. What captured the public's attention, however, was not the creation by newly wealthy dot-com entrepreneurs of a foundation with a mission to address problems of poverty, disease, and global warming. Rather, it was that Google.org was to be established not as a traditional grantmaking foundation but as what many would regard as an organizational oxymoron: a for-profit, tax-paying charity.

Google.org was one of several examples in 2006 that led the *New York Times* to remark that "this year, as never before, the line between philanthropy and business is blurring" (Strom 2006). Although Google.org may be the most prominent recent instance of such blurring, those familiar with the recent history of the nonprofit sector in the United States will recognize it as one of many examples of how the boundaries between nonprofit and for-profit activities continue to shift, redefining what it means to be a nonprofit organization and forcing new attention to existing laws about public policy, taxation, and business regulation.

Traditionally, economists and legal scholars have argued that what differentiates nonprofit and for-profit organizations is the so-called nondistribution constraint (the lack of a formal profit function) that prevents some group of owners (but not necessarily managers and staff) of nonprofit organizations from appropriating any economic surplus a nonprofit generates. An important corollary attribute has been the privilege of tax exemption that has been accorded to entities that organize themselves as nonprofits by imposing the nondistribution constraint.

As has been noted by Weisbrod (1988), this particular set of institutional attributes creates both incentives and constraints that set nonprofits apart both from government and from for-profit enterprises. The organizational boundary associated with nonprofit status has traditionally accompanied a number of other differences between for-profits and not-for-profits, including what goods and services are produced, how goods and services are produced, and internal organization and culture. The organizational boundary has also at least implicitly if not explicitly defined what many regarded to be an appropriate relationship between for-profits and nonprofits, which typically involved grants or contributions from the former to the latter.

Although these traditional boundaries between for-profit and not-for-profit organizations continue to exist, they have never been universal, and, increasingly, they have become more permeable. Many nonprofits have found it advantageous to operate more like businesses in some respects; some for-profit businesses have adopted some nonprofit attributes; and businesses and nonprofits have discovered mutual benefit from acting as partners, both in for-profit and in not-for-profit ventures. The result is a spectrum of nonprofit organizational forms, ranging from traditional donative nonprofits that rely almost entirely on contributions and grants to for-profit enterprises with related charitable activities, such as Ben and Jerry's and Newman's Own. Between these polar cases lie a range of intermediate arrangements, including newer hybrid forms that combine charitable mission and the nondistribution constraint with business activities.

Some of these adaptations are relatively recent, such as the evolution of new institutional arrangements in the form of "double bottom-line" social ventures and nonprofits' creation of for-profit affiliates and subsidiaries that incorporate profit seeking as an integral rather than ancillary part of operations.

Adjusting to changing needs and market demands is hardly a new phenomenon. In the past, nonprofit staff and managers have shown themselves to be quite able to adapt to a changing environment (Hammack and Young 1993; Weisbrod 1998). For example, it has long been recognized that some missions, such as providing job training, can be fruitfully carried out by actively engaging in business activities, and Weisbrod (1988) cites a 1985 survey of 700 nonprofit hospitals showing that a third of respondents were involved in joint ventures with for-profit firms.

The response of traditional nonprofits and for-profits to changing circumstances takes on new salience, however, as events and forces—such as devolution of government services and the evolution from an industrial to an information economy—offer new opportunities and incentives for organizations to explore new modes of operating; new relationships between for-profit and not-for-profit organizations; and new organizational forms. Examples of such adaptations include nonprofits' creation of for-profit affiliates and subsidiaries that incorporate profit-seeking as an integral rather than ancillary part of operations, as well as new institutional arrangements in the form of "double bottom-line" social ventures, in which a nonprofit entity is organized to create economic value both through a traditional commercial bottom line, defined in terms of market revenue and cost, and a social bottom line that identifies and values mission-related outputs that have clear social value not explicitly captured in the marketplace.

In exploring these issues, this book follows and builds on prior work on the intersection of the nonprofit and for-profit sectors, including Weisbrod (1988, 1998) and Hammack and Young (1993). Our purpose is not to reexamine such issues as competition between for-profits and nonprofits or the role and tax treatment of unrelated business income earned by nonprofits. Rather, it is to consider new developments in the relationship between nonprofits and business ventures, and the adoption of business-like practices by nonprofits. In a distinctive approach, we examine the blurring of the boundaries between nonprofit and for-profit organizations from an evolutionary organizational perspective (Aldrich and Ruef 2006). A key organizing theme is that nonprofits, like other organizations, have natural tendencies to adapt to changes in their environment as well as to changes in organizational culture caused by shifts in attitudes and norms. The organizational propensity for adaptation creates a natural, dynamic process of change in the boundaries between nonprofit and for-profit sectors. Such adaptations may be inevitable and may or may not be desirable; regardless, many have interesting and important implications for public policy.

The contributing authors focus on several aspects of this process of adaptation. The first three chapters examine factors that implicitly or explicitly influence choice of organizational form: organizational identity (chapter 2); the economic environment in which nonprofit organizations operate (chapter 3); and laws and public policies that regulate use of the nonprofit form of organization (chapter 4). The discussion then turns to examples of institutional arrangements that mix and match for-profit and nonprofit elements in response to changes in the environment and organizational identity: the creation of hybrid organizational structures involving cross-ownership between nonprofit and for-profit enterprises (chapter 5); partnerships involving separate nonprofit and corporate partners (chapter 6); and double-bottom-line investment strategies of foundations (chapter 7).

Lastly, we consider how nonprofits have taken on more businesslike ways of operating while retaining the traditional nonprofit form. Calls for nonprofits to engage in more systematic and strategic assessment of performance create an environment in which they face incentives to behave more like their for-profit counterparts on decisions of allocating scarce resources internally (chapter 8), whereas competition for financing and staff means that nonprofits increasingly have to be prepared to meet a changing market when hiring employees (chapter 9).

Choice of Organizational Form

Although at any moment in time organizational form is a given that defines how an entity operates, organization theorists from disciplines as diverse as sociology, economics, and management science have long recognized that organizational behavior and form is not immutable; it is subject to change in response to a variety of external and internal forces. In chapter 2, Dennis R. Young deconstructs the concept of "social enterprise"—the type of venture many regard as symbolic of the blurring of the lines between nonprofits and business—to show how and why this broad concept may be compatible with a number of organizational forms.

Young proposes that a social enterprise be defined as "activity intended to address social goals through the operation of private organizations in the marketplace," noting that this definition is consistent with any number of private organizations, from a traditional nonprofit to a socially conscious for-profit business and a number of hybrid arrangements in between. Like the elephant in the famous story of the blind men, different insights about the concept of social enterprise emerge as it is viewed from different perspectives.

Among scholars who study the nonprofit sector, historians remind us that there has been a long-standing involvement of nonprofit organizations in commercial activity in the United States, suggesting that the blurring of the boundaries is an evolutionary development—albeit an important one—and not a discrete break with the past. Economists and management theorists emphasize the comparative benefits and costs of relying on the nonprofit and for-profit organizational forms as a means for achieving the broad aims of social enterprise as potential explanatory factors.

Among practitioners, entrepreneurs are likely to see "the mold-breaking reflected in for-profit activity within nonprofits or social ventures in for-profit form" as a "natural kind of experiment that entrepreneurs undertake in seeking new ways of doing things." From a comparative perspective, Young notes that what is viewed as social enterprise is context-dependent, so that in both Europe and the developing world, social enterprise is considered to be almost any new, nongovernmental approach to social problems, whereas in the United States the concept is somewhat less encompassing, referring instead to recent innovations in how private entities, especially nonprofits, organize to meet various social needs.

Last, but not least, Young notes that organization theorists focus on the dual importance of organizational culture and organizational identity in determining the proper match of organizational form with social mission. The concept of organizational identity is especially important because specific organizational identities are more likely to be compatible with particular organizational forms than with others.

A general implication of Young's analysis is that changes in the environment will prompt adaptations in organizational form when such changes alter organizational identities or will open up the range of possible structures that may be compatible with particular organizational identities. This general theme is developed in more detail in subsequent chapters, which examine the influence of changes in the external economic and legal environment on organizational form.

As several scholars have noted, organizing as a nonprofit and imposing the nondistribution constraint confers both advantages and disadvantages. On the plus side, accepting the nondistribution constraint provides useful

signals to potential donors that contributions will in fact be used to provide goods and services the market might otherwise not provide and to
clients or customers that the organization can be trusted to place quality
and service above profit (Bilodeau and Slavinski 1998; Cordes, Steuerle,
and Twombly 2004; Glaeser and Schleifer 1998). At the same time, reliance
on the traditional nonprofit form creates dependence on contributions
and grants, limits the ability of an organization to seek debt financing of
its activities, and rules out entirely access to equity in capital.

Conversely, the for-profit organizational form has advantages that
mirror the disadvantages of the nonprofit model. The acceptance of
owners seeking profits for themselves limits access to contributions,
donations, and grants but provides collateral for debt financing as well
as access to external equity and retained earnings. Potential customers of
certain goods and services are also less likely to trust for-profit providers
of these goods and services.

The advantages and disadvantages of the not-for-profit and for-profit
organizational forms create opportunities for what Cordes and Steuerle
describe in chapter 3 as "organizational arbitrage": the creation of formal and informal institutional arrangements that allow an entity to exploit
the best features of each type of organizational form. One important
change in the economic environment is that opportunities for such organizational arbitrage may be increasing because changes in the economy
at large make it technologically easier to blend charitable and profit-
making activities than was possible in the past.

In particular, more of the outputs and labor functions of society are
becoming common to both sectors, and, increasingly, the output of the
economy involves activities that can qualify under charitable 501(c)(3)
definitions. For example, health care and information services have been
a growing portion of the economy, so it is not surprising that opportunities for producing many types of goods and services in the nonprofit
and for-profit sectors have also increased. One also would expect to find
more overlapping organizational structures such as subsidiaries (or related
organizations) in one sector controlled by an entity in the other sector,
or nonprofit–for-profit partnerships. At the individual worker level, the
relative ease of transferring skills common to either for-profits or nonprofits facilitates ease of mobility between sectors at different points in a
worker's career or even daily.

Although a changing economy may create more opportunities for
mixing and matching of both organizational forms and those organiza-

tions to which executives and workers hold some fiduciary responsibility, what is possible in practice depends on laws and regulations attempting to govern behavior. Chapter 4, by Evelyn Brody, examines the legal framework in which nonprofit activities are defined and regulated.

Brody notes that the laws that govern business activities of nonprofits stem from several different sources. There are rules and laws that govern the operation of business activities that apply to specific sectors of the economy (e.g., hospitals) without regard to nonprofit status. A classic example is that of hospitals, where the day-to-day operations of nonprofit hospitals are governed by rules that apply to health care organizations generally, regardless of whether the entity is public, for-profit, or nonprofit.

State laws also define and regulate the formation of nonprofit organizations, but as Brody notes, these laws generally say little about whether and what business activities are acceptable for a nonprofit organization. Instead, the task of establishing and enforcing appropriate boundaries between business and other activities of nonprofit organizations usually falls to federal and state rules governing tax exemption, which provide the principal constraints on what nonprofits can and cannot do under a tax-exempt status. Strengthening such constraints reduces opportunities for nonprofit organizations to undertake business ventures in the traditional nonprofit form or in hybrid forms. Conversely, relaxing such constraints, as when nonprofits receive royalty income from corporations for using intangible assets, such as organization names and logos, has the opposite effect (Varley 2003).

In the end, Brody cautions that there is no obvious right way to allocate business activities between the for-profit and nonprofit sectors; hence, the use of the law to regulate the conduct of businesslike activities should be targeted to specific and narrow cases. Because of such limits, the law by itself cannot define completely or adequately the boundaries between the two sectors. Instead, the outcome will depend on the combined impact of legal constraints, economic opportunities, and the internal culture of nonprofits.

Crossing Boundaries

Three chapters focus on different examples of organizational arbitrage that involve combining aspects of nonprofit and for-profit structures to exploit the comparative advantages of each. In chapter 5, Howard Tuckman focuses explicitly on the role of hybrid structures consisting of at least one for-profit or equivalent entity and one nonprofit organization.

A number of nonprofits now own for-profit subsidiaries. In some cases, the subsidiary's activity is clearly unrelated to the nonprofit's mission and the main rationale for creating a separate, taxable subsidiary is to facilitate segregation of accounting for an activity that would be taxable in any case. But often the story is not so simple. A number of nonprofits are setting up profit-making organizations even when they are not required to do so.

Tuckman's essay examines why nonprofits form hybrid organizations, how these organizations can facilitate the strategies of their nonprofit parents, and how these entities operate in the real world. Echoing Young's point about the need for organizational form to match organizational identity, Tuckman notes that in successful organizations there is a match between organizational structure and strategy. An important implication is that changes in strategy may call for adaptation in organizational form.

A number of strategies consistent with the central mission of certain types of nonprofits lend themselves well to hybrid organizational forms. These strategies are conditioned in part by financing needs, legal constraints, and the opportunities for nonprofits to legally exploit their unique assets through commercialization.

Empirical evidence on the use of hybrid arrangements is limited to data reported on the Internal Revenue Service Form 990 on the ownership of for-profit subsidiaries by nonprofit organizations. As Tuckman and Chang (2006) note, creation of and participation in hybrid organizational structures may not make a great deal of sense for smaller nonprofits, and hence it is not surprising that such structures are more likely to be found among larger nonprofits.

As one would expect, the relative frequency of ownership of for-profit subsidiaries also varies with nature of the tax-exempt activity. Nonprofits with for-profit subsidiaries are more likely to be engaged in activities such as provision of health, education, and research services, where the nonprofit parent, as part of its mission-related activities, is apt to generate valuable goods or services that have the potential to be exploited profitably in the marketplace. This latter point is important, however, because it suggests that hybrid structures may become more prevalent as a changing economy creates more possibilities for nonprofits engaged in a wider range of missions to exploit potentially valuable commercial opportunities.

Despite the potential advantages of creating hybrid structures, Tuckman sounds a note of caution about potential pitfalls. Operating a hybrid properly can compete for the time and energy of the nonprofit's senior management, especially as the complexity of the hybrid relationship grows. Continuously operating a hybrid structure may alter management's ways of thinking, potentially diluting commitment to the nonprofit's original mission. Governance of a hybrid raises further questions of whether the same individuals can and should serve as directors of both the nonprofit and the for-profit entities, an issue likely to rise in importance as a consequence of such legislation as the Sarbanes-Oxley Act,[1] which has been applied by analogy from the for-profit to the nonprofit sector (Ostrower and Bobowick 2006).

A final issue is that of public perception. Tuckman notes that the public may be unaware of whether the nonprofit that receives private contributions is part of a hybrid structure. Becoming aware may influence donors' giving behavior. These effects can be positive (if donors are prompted to give more because participation in a hybrid structure is seen as a sign of innovative and effective leadership) or negative (donors may give less because participation in a hybrid is seen as diluting the central mission of the parent nonprofit).

Hybrids are just one of several ways nonprofit organizations can form partnerships with for-profit enterprises. In chapter 6, Alan R. Andreasen examines an arrangement that has become quite popular in recent years: alliances between corporations and nonprofits in the marketing arena.

The economic value of branding creates potential economic gains from trade between for-profit and nonprofit enterprises. These partnerships, which are often described under the rubric of "cause-related marketing," allow nonprofit organizations to derive economic benefits from the value that the public may attach to their charitable activities by trading with private corporations.

The corporate partner in such partnerships benefits from the ability to use its affiliation with the nonprofit organization to achieve certain specific marketing objectives and to garner economically valuable goodwill that leads to increased sales and profits that offset the cost. On the other side of the transaction, the nonprofit partner receives a number of benefits in exchange for allowing its name and reputation to be used in connection with a marketing campaign, including increased corporate contributions, sponsorship, or licensing agreements.

Andreasen identifies what he terms first-order and second-order benefits to each party from such partnerships. First-order benefits to the corporate partner include the additional sales generated from marketing goods by, for example, linking a set contribution to a charity or charities per dollar of sales. First-order benefits to nonprofits include financial payments and contributions of goods, services, and volunteers from the corporate partner.

In addition to these immediate benefits, one or both partners may also derive important second-order gains from participation. On the corporate side, being "socially responsible" may improve corporate image and branding, improve company morale, and aid in recruiting new employees. On the nonprofit side, participation may bring in additional donors (as a result of the corporate marketing campaign) and leave the impression of innovation and effectiveness.

Andreasen cautions, however, that there may also be costs to the parties on each side of the transaction. For corporations, potential buyers may view an alliance as a cynical corporate attempt to buy respectability. In the case of nonprofits, people may legitimately question whether payments from a corporate partner augment revenues or merely substitute for revenue that would otherwise have come from traditional contributions. Reduced contributions from donors who disapprove of corporate alliances with nonprofits may offset in part or entirely the increased donations from the corporate marketing effort.

Moreover, there is a question of which partner captures most of the potential gains from trade in the partnership. Andreasen summarizes the results of a financial analysis of the first- and second-order benefits accruing to Toyota and to the Sierra Club from a cause-related marketing venture. This partnership provided $12 million in benefits, of which Toyota captured $10 million and the Sierra Club $2 million. The author is careful to note that whether this division is "fair and economically favorable" to the nonprofit partner depends on a number of factors, including the portion of the alliance costs borne by each party.

Overall, Andreasen concludes that cross-sector marketing alliances can yield an important new source of revenue for the nonprofit sector. However, questions about the impact of such partnerships on the sector remain to be answered. These questions include the degree to which revenue from such arrangements simply substitutes for traditional forms of corporate philanthropy and, perhaps as important, whether some types of nonprofits benefit more than others from this organizational innovation.

A recent *New York Times* article (Santora 2006) highlights another potential dilemma that may confront some sponsorship arrangements: the possibility that the economic benefits from sponsorship may need to be weighed against potential conflicts with the stated mission of the nonprofit. Santora discusses how the American Diabetes Association has been criticized for its endorsement of certain sugar-free yet high-calorie food products. In response, the American Diabetes Association has allowed some sponsorships to expire and has turned down new sponsorship opportunities. Critics, however, maintain that the organization has not gone far enough.

Chapter 7 takes up the question of social investing by foundations. Private foundations have access to substantial pools of capital through their endowments. These endowment funds can be put in traditional investments; income from these investments may then be used to support nonprofit organizations through traditional means, such as grants. Increasingly, however, some foundations have embraced a different model in which capital from endowments is invested directly in enterprises that combine profit-making activities with social purposes, generating what is commonly described as a "double bottom line" consisting of the profit from the investment plus social benefits from the investment.

Burton Sonenstein and Christa Velasquez of the Annie E. Casey Foundation provide a case study of how a major urban foundation engages in such double-bottom-line investments. To preserve its tax-exempt status, a foundation must pay out at least 5 percent of its endowment each year on activities for its social mission. At the same time, foundations also seek to earn an investment return to grow or maintain the corpus of their endowment to increase their ability to support charitable works over time. A traditional approach has been for a foundation to separate its investment and grant-making activities by, for example, investing its endowment to maximize investment return and then distributing these earnings in the form of grants. In some cases, however, a foundation may believe that it can achieve a similar or better outcome by investing endowment funds directly in a social venture with an explicit willingness on the foundation's part to accept a below-market return on the investment in recognition of its social character. The foundation effectively makes an implicit grant by accepting a below-market return on a socially beneficial investment.

The tax law provides foundations with the opportunity to make such investments by allowing a foundation to treat program-related investments as distributions of endowment for the 5 percent distribution requirement. In the past, foundations were reluctant to take advantage of this opportunity because they considered it inappropriate to mix investment with charitable activities.

In recent years, however, there has been growth in the number of foundations making such investments. Between 1990 and 2001, the number of foundations making program-related investments increased from 57 to 205, as did the number of program-related investments by foundations, which increased from 161 in 1990 to 340 in 2001. The annual dollar amount of program-related investments grew from $91.9 million in 1990 to $246 million in 2001, which on an inflation-adjusted basis represented an increase of more than 100 percent (Foundation Center 2003). A recent Urban Institute survey of foundations found that among respondents with $50 million or more in assets, more than a quarter engaged in investments related to their mission (Ostrower 2004).

Foundations have become more open to making program-related investments for a variety of reasons. One motivation relates to the notion of organizational identity Young discussed in chapter 2. A growing number of foundations no longer see themselves simply as fiduciaries whose role is to protect and grow their endowments and to make grants. Instead, they seek to align their investment strategies more actively with their underlying social mission. They see engaging in program-related investments as accomplishing this objective in several ways.

One broad motivation is to use a larger portion of assets to directly support their philanthropic mission, beyond paying out the minimum required 5 percent of endowment in grants. Program-related investments offer an attractive mechanism by enabling a foundation to increase the dollar amount of resources made available for charitable causes without having to reduce the endowment dollar for dollar. As Sonenstein and Velasquez note, program-related investments allow a foundation to meet or exceed payout requirements while getting the money back (plus a modest return) so that it may be used again.

It should be noted that in purely financial terms, receipt of a program-related investment from a foundation (e.g., a below-market-interest-rate loan) by itself may not be of equivalent value to a grant for the affected charity. However, packaging financial support in the form of a program-related investment has the potential to draw in resources from other stakeholders, which may be more advantageous than simply receiving a traditional foundation grant. For example, a charity might have greater access to other sources of financing in private capital markets as result of receiving a below-market-interest-rate loan, a loan guarantee from a foundation, or a package of financing from a variety of stakeholders, including program-related investments from foundations.

Program-related investments may also be a potentially attractive source of financing for for-profit business ventures where a significant component of the overall economic return may include social benefits not readily captured in the marketplace (Emerson, Freundlich, and Fruchterman 2007). For example, the development of technologies to produce and use alternative, nonpolluting sources of energy has the potential to provide significant economic benefits to the overall economy, but many of these benefits may be in the form of public goods that the private market may not value. Traditional sources of private financing will not take such social benefits into account, but a foundation may consider making a program-related investment in such a venture because the social benefits would contribute to the double bottom line.

An important issue for foundations supporting the activities of nonprofits with program-related investments is that of how to measure and evaluate the effectiveness of the double-bottom-line venture. When the program-related investment invests in an activity valued in the marketplace, a portion of the double bottom line can be measured and assessed with standard business metrics such as revenue, profit, and rate of return. In many cases, the financial portion of the double-bottom-line venture may show little or no net return because the program-related investment's activity typically produces a hard-to-measure nonfinancial return (goods or services that may be of social value but that are not bought and sold in the marketplace).

Annie E. Casey and other foundations have invested resources in trying to develop metrics for documenting social outcomes of program-related investments. But there are considerable practical obstacles to translating such outcomes into measures of social return. Chapter 9 on outcome measurement discusses evaluating double-bottom-line investments as one of several challenges to undertaking more systematic evaluation of nonprofit performance.

Internal Organizational Change

Another way in which organizations can redefine their boundaries is by changing how they operate while retaining all of the organizational characteristics of a traditional nonprofit entity. The chapters by Eric C. Twombly and Linda M. Lampkin and Harry Hatry consider two important aspects of such internal change when it comes to nonprofit organizations.

In chapter 8, Twombly examines potential effects of the changing character of nonprofit organizations on the labor market for nonprofit staff. In the parlance of economists, pressures for nonprofits to operate in more businesslike ways are likely to shift labor supply upward (e.g., cause potential employees of nonprofits to expect higher wages).

An important driver of change in nonprofit labor markets is the increasing professionalization of nonprofit staff. Organizations are paying more attention to managers' professional skills. Increasing numbers of universities offer degrees and courses emphasizing skills for the nonprofit sector, and professional degrees with business and management training have become more commonplace in many nonprofit organizations. Many, though not all, of the managerial skills taught in these nonprofit management programs overlap with those taught in business management courses. In addition, the changing culture of nonprofit management places a higher premium on the ability of nonprofit management and staff to think and act in more managerial and entrepreneurial terms.

A consequence of nonprofits becoming more businesslike is that prospective employees of nonprofit organizations may become less likely to accept lower compensation in exchange for the altruistic benefits of working for a nonprofit. As Cordes and Steuerle discuss, the skills needed to work in nonprofits also can be put to use in the for-profit sector. At the same time as donors and foundations are requiring nonprofits to operate in an ever-more cost-effective manner, nonprofits' ability to meet increased demands for higher overall levels of compensation may be challenged.

Because of both the increased demands of public (or quasi-public) institutions for greater accountability and the increased openness of nonprofit staff to systematic approaches to deploying scarce resources, nonprofits are increasingly measuring and evaluating performance. In chapter 9, Lampkin and Hatry examine how nonprofits assess the effectiveness of what they do and how they set operating priorities, efforts which nonprofit donors and clients are apt to perceive as making nonprofits more businesslike.

Economists argue that competition in a variety of markets—most notably the markets for goods and capital—will generally force businesses to adopt strategies and processes that produce the greatest value at the lowest possible cost. Thus, we might say that nonprofits act more like their for-profit counterparts when they strive to produce the greatest value at the lowest cost (though social value would be defined more broadly than just what is valued in the private marketplace).

One important difference between nonprofits and for-profits is that market competition generally provides individual for-profit enterprises with the incentive to produce maximum value for minimum cost. Shareholders demand that share prices perform well, and there are incentives and mechanisms for mergers and acquisitions of noncompetitive for-profit organizations.

Nonprofits also have to compete for resources, but the actors and the venues for competition are different (e.g., stakeholders vs. stockholders, donors and individual contributors vs. financial institutions). As a result, competition among nonprofits need not create organizational incentives for nonprofits to strive to maximize value while minimizing costs. Whether nonprofits have the incentive to act in ways that approximate this operating goal depends on whether (1) key stakeholders of nonprofits—individual donors, foundations, the government, and private donors—believe it is useful to behave in this manner; (2) nonprofit managers and staff also believe this to be the case; and (3) it is possible to establish benchmarks for assessing performance on these goals.

Pressures for more systematic evaluation of performance are coming from a variety of sources, including government (which at the federal level has launched its own ambitious effort at more systematic outcome assessment), private foundations, and organizations such as the United Way. In a 1997 survey cited by Lampkin and Hatry of more than 600 nonprofits, almost half of the organizations reported that they regularly collected data on how their programs have affected clients. There was, however, a clear divide between small and large organizations in that less than one-third of small organizations reported keeping such data compared with four out of five larger organizations. Moreover, the authors note that the 1997 survey has not been updated, so there is no way of knowing whether there has been an increase in the proportion of nonprofits that make some systematic effort to measure what they are doing.

There is also relatively little evidence on the usefulness of outcome measurement. On the positive side, a survey of almost 400 health and human service managers conducted in 2000 indicated that more than four out of five respondents felt that engaging in more systematic outcome measurement and assessment provided benefits such as clarifying program purpose and improving service delivery. At the same time, many nonprofit organizations have decried the investment of dollars and staff time on outcome assessment.

Profit-making enterprises are able to use a bottom-line measure of profits, and until recently it was widely believed that there is no equivalent measure for the nonprofit sector. Recently, however, under the broad rubrics of "social impact analysis" and double-bottom-line investing, there has been a recognition of some similarities: obtaining the maximum *social* return on investment may reflect the goals of a nonprofit, and that return can be related, at least in part through a form of cost-benefit analysis, to the returns that a profit-making enterprise would produce.

A major constraint on the application of more systematic approaches to outcome measurement and assessment appears to be whether it is feasible to expect a typical nonprofit to have the resources necessary both to measure what they do and to integrate this knowledge into their operations. In this regard, Lampkin and Hatry conclude with a plea that "the best not become the enemy of the good." Even when it is not possible to devise and maintain the perfect indicator of performance, it often will be possible to develop reasonable, if imperfect, indicators of performance that can be consistently applied both to measuring and assessing performance over time.

Concluding Thoughts

A recent meeting at the Aspen Institute's Nonprofit Sector Research Fund took up the question of whether a "fourth sector" may be emerging, comprising hybrid entities that incorporate features of traditional nonprofits and for-profits, that may require creating new legal forms of organization. Although there was a range of views about whether the current legal structure offers sufficient flexibility to accommodate changing needs, or whether new forms are indeed needed, there was a consensus that separating the efforts of organizations or individuals into the neat categories of business and charity was becoming more difficult. As a consequence, organizations may adopt one form but take on multiple tasks. For instance, in some cases, a group of individuals may simply organize as a not-for-profit corporation that doesn't seek charitable status; in others, social entrepreneurs will try to run charitable and profit-making organizations separately, and in still others (e.g., in the recently highly publicized case of Google), an entity may be created that will earn profits and pay taxes like any other business but will be otherwise focused on charitable works. Indeed, it has even been suggested that the traditional link between imposition of the nondistribution constraint and the ability to accept tax-deductible contributions be replaced instead by contractual arrangements that would allow for-profit businesses to receive tax-deductible contributions in exchange for undertaking contractually specified charitable activities (Malani and Posner 2006).

In effect, in the broad area of what might be termed social enterprise, there is a continuum ranging from pure nonprofits at one end to socially motivated for-profit businesses at the other. What is novel is not the existence of nonprofits with important business features per se. Such entities have long occupied selected niches of the nonprofit community. But the expansion of economic activities that can be defined as charitable, as well as the adoption of more business-oriented approaches throughout the nonprofit sector, creates new opportunities along with new tensions and is likely to increase the number of firms and individuals who engage in both sectors, some at the same time.

Although the expansion and acceptance of more business-like models has meant that nonprofits have become more actively engaged with the marketplace as an important overall part of their strategy, an increasing number of for-profit businesses have also determined both that their human and financial assets are ripe for engagement in traditional non-profit activities and, further, that attention to social concerns can be good for their bottom line. The changing economy and the increasingly wide range of goods and services that either sector can effectively produce has led to new formal and informal arrangements that draw upon the distinctive advantages of the traditional nonprofit and for-profit forms of organization.

The laws determining nonprofit status have proved to be quite flexible and permeable in accommodating the desire to create such arrangements. But there is tension. Policymakers charged with regulating the activity of nonprofit organizations must also be on guard to ensure that charitable donations do end up going for charitable purposes, that tax-exempt status granted for public purpose does not simply lead to private enrichment, and that nonprofits be held accountable, just like profit-making institutions, if they falsely advertise to the public.

Although the emergence of hybrid forms has occurred in response to real economic incentives, there are potential downsides for nonprofits. Hybrid organizational forms are likely to be more complex and harder to govern than more traditional organizational forms. This has implications for the ability of both nonprofits and for-profits to fulfill their traditional missions. In the case of nonprofits, embracing more business-oriented models can exact a cost in staff time and energy that could be devoted to more traditional charitable activities. The concern that increased involvement in profit-making ventures will crowd out an organization's commitment to its primary charitable mission remains. As with the American Diabetes Association sponsorships discussed above, there is a risk of potential conflict with the mission—not just crowding out.

Increased interest among foundations in supporting investments with a double bottom line creates new opportunities for leveraging financial resources in capital markets. However, the double-bottom-line model does not apply as readily to nonprofits engaged in charitable activities incapable of generating enough of a private market bottom line to make a double bottom line possible, leaving such organizations at a potential disadvantage. In the case of for-profits with a social mission, there appear to be genuine examples in which it is possible to do good while doing well, but there is also the potential that a social cause can serve as a marketing ploy.

These concerns about commercialization pose significant challenges for not only external but internal regulation of the nonprofit sector. Burton Weisbrod, who has made significant contributions to understanding the commercial behavior of nonprofits, has recently expressed concern about growing commercialization of nonprofit activities and argues that policymakers should consider increasing incentives for donations while limiting the ability of nonprofits to engage in commercial activities (Weisbrod 2004). Weisbrod notes, however,

> Mechanisms to encourage donations, by altering tax law, are readily available. Mechanisms to discourage commercial activity, however, are more challenging. Outright prohibition of any activity that generates "sales" would have vast and uncertain consequences, but the use of tax instruments to discourage all commercial activity—not merely unrelated business activity which is already subject to taxation—deserves exploration. . . . But as these issues are examined, we should not forget that nonprofits require some kind of funding for their social missions; it would be counterproductive to constrain commercial revenue-producing activity without also relaxing constraints on donations. Reshaping the pattern of nonprofits revenue should not be a pretext for constricting this valuable economic sector.

As the American Diabetes Association example demonstrates, internal standards and norms can, to some extent, constrain behavior in ways that reduce the potential for individual nonprofits to lose sight of their primary mission as they pursue profit-making ventures. As Evelyn Brody emphasizes, ultimately, it is likely to be the combination of legal rules and internal norms that will define the effective limits to the pursuit of profit.

Although the pitfalls are real, the reality is that changes in the external environment, as well as changes in the internal culture of how nonprofits operate, will inevitably continue to test the traditional boundaries between the sectors. The task for policymakers and nonprofit practitioners alike is to learn when there are real rather than simply apparent benefits to integrating more businesslike features into their charitable activity's operation and to identify best practices for doing so.

NOTE

1. *Sarbanes-Oxley Act of 2002,* Public Law 107-204, *U.S. Statutes at Large* 116 (2002): 745.

REFERENCES

Aldrich, Howard, and Martin Ruef. 2006. *Organizations Evolving,* 2nd ed. London: Sage.

Bilodeau, Marc, and Al Slavinsky. 1998. "Rational Nonprofit Entrepreneurship." *Journal of Economics and Management Strategy* 7(4): 551–71.

Cordes, Joseph, C. Eugene Steuerle, and Eric Twombly. 2004. "Dimensions of Nonprofit Entrepreneurship: An Exploratory Essay." In *Public Policy and the Economics of Entrepreneurship,* edited by Douglas Holtz-Eakin and Harvey Rosen (115–51). Cambridge, MA: MIT Press.

Emerson, Jed, Tim Freundlich, and Jim Fruchterman. 2007. "Nothing Ventured, Nothing Gained." http://www.benetech.org/about/downloads/NothingVenturedFinal.pdf.

Foundation Center. 2003. *The PRI Directory: Charitable Loans and Other Program-Related Investments by Foundations,* 2nd ed. New York: Foundation Center.

Glaeser, Edward, and Andre Schleifer. 1998. "Not-for-Profit Entrepreneurs." NBER Working Paper W6810. Cambridge, MA: National Bureau of Economic Research.

Hammack, David, and Dennis Young, eds. 1993. *Nonprofit Organizations in a Market Economy: Understanding New Roles, Issues, and Trends.* San Francisco: Jossey–Bass.

Malani, Anup, and Eric Posner. 2006. "The Case for For-Profit Charities." Working Paper 304. Chicago: University of Chicago Law School.

Ostrower, Francie. 2004. "Attitudes and Practices Concerning Effective Philanthropy." Washington, DC: The Urban Institute. http://www.urban.org/url.cfm?ID=411067.

Ostrower, Francie, and Marla J. Bobowick. 2006. "Nonprofit Governance and the Sarbanes Oxley Act." Washington, DC: The Urban Institute. http://www.urban.org/url.cfm?ID=311363.

Santora, Marc. 2006. "In Diabetes Fight, Raising Cash and Keeping Trust." *New York Times,* Nov. 25.

Strom, Stephanie. 2006. "A Fresh Approach: What's Wrong with Profit?" *New York Times,* Nov. 13.

Tuckman, Howard, and Cyril Chang. 2006. "Commercial Activity: Technological Change and Nonprofit Mission." In *The Nonprofit Sector: A Research Handbook,* edited by Walter W. Powell and Richard Steinberg (629–45). New Haven: Yale University Press.

Varley, Doug. 2003. *Tax Issues to Consider.* Washington, DC: Independent Sector. http://www.independentsector.org/mission_market/tax.htm.

Weisbrod, Burton A., ed. 1998. *To Profit or Not to Profit: The Commercial Transformation of the Nonprofit Sector.* New York: Cambridge University Press.

———. 2004. "The Pitfalls of Profits." *Stanford Social Innovation Review* (Winter): 40–47.

2

Alternative Perspectives on Social Enterprise

Dennis R. Young

As other chapters in this volume make clear, nonprofits and business are highly intertwined. Nowhere is this more obvious than in discussions of social enterprise and social entrepreneurship. In fact, these phenomena tend to obfuscate the boundaries between nonprofits and business. In part, this is because these terms are ill defined and can be interpreted in several ways—some relating more closely to business and some corresponding more closely to the work of nonprofits. But even the common notions underlying such different interpretations combine elements of the social purpose of nonprofit organizations and the market orientation and financial-performance standards of business.

In this chapter, I seek to clarify the concept of social enterprise and its close relative, social entrepreneurship. The purpose of the discussion is two-fold: first, to permit more precise and productive consideration of social enterprise as a strategy for addressing social goals, and second, to offer a conceptual window through which the interactions between nonprofit organizations and business can be further understood. The approach is multidisciplinary and multi-contextual. First, social enterprise can be viewed through several disciplinary lenses, including history, economics, and organization and management theory. Second, social enterprise may be further appreciated by considering the various ways in which this concept is manifested from one national context to another, and in relation to social entrepreneurship.

This chapter gives particular emphasis to one disciplinary approach—the concept of organizational identity from organization theory, itself borrowed in part from psychology. In brief, different conceptions of social enterprise can be captured by alternative notions of organizational identity. Once these identities are understood, implications for business-related practices associated with social enterprise can be inferred, and the relationships between social enterprise, nonprofits, and business can be examined. In particular, the (for-profit, nonprofit, and mixed) legal forms that social enterprise can assume and the business-related practices that social enterprises can employ—such as outsourcing, pricing, collaboration, and institutional partnerships—are correlated with the organizational identities associated with social enterprises of different kinds. Thus, by examining a variety of identities for social enterprise, we can begin to understand various interfaces between nonprofits and business.

Defining Social Enterprise

Social enterprise—two little words interpreted in many different ways. To some, social enterprise means the undertaking of business or commercial activity by nonprofit organizations. To others, it means undertaking initiatives with social goals within the context of a for-profit corporation. To still others, especially outside the United States, social enterprise means carrying out government-encouraged services through private community-oriented organizations of various types (Kerlin 2005). And to still others, social enterprise is simply venture activity undertaken by people who call themselves social entrepreneurs. Despite the ambiguity, one thing is clear: social enterprise is thought to be something new, something important, and something distinct from classical business and traditional nonprofit activity. Indeed, new professional associations (such as the Social Enterprise Alliance) and new programs (such as social enterprise programs in American business schools) now use social enterprise as their organizing concept. It is not clear that this differentiation from traditional nonprofit and business activity is entirely justified. Both nonprofits and business need to understand and integrate social enterprise into their operations and strategies. The current situation more closely resembles the emergence of the field of public policy studies as an alternative approach to public administration. In the longer term, these two fields have absorbed important elements of each other—public administration integrating the analytical tools of policy analysis and public policy adjoining the concepts of public management from public administration—to the point where graduate programs in these fields have become fairly indistinguishable. The same kind of evolution may take place with the interrelated fields of social enterprise and nonprofit management studies.

In the end, is there a common definition that embraces all of the various conceptualizations of social enterprise? There does appear to be a central, core integrating concept that can be captured approximately as follows: *Social enterprise is activity intended to address social goals through the operation of private organizations in the marketplace.*

Note that this definition does not require profit seeking nor does it even require the participation of nonprofit organizations. It does allow a wide variety of combinations that include these elements.

Why Is Clarity in the Concept of Social Enterprise Important?

Discussion and debate are enhanced when participants share common definitions of terms. This has not generally been the case with "social enterprise," which enjoys different interpretations by different parties—business and nonprofit executives, U.S. and European scholars and policymakers, and so on (Kerlin 2005). Compounding this situation, recent waves of social enterprise advocates tend to frame social enterprise as a general panacea for addressing social problems or securing the financial stability of nonprofit organizations. Social enterprise is not such a general solution, but it is certainly important to understand where various forms of social enterprise can be helpful in these ways. Such understandings, however, require common definitions and frames of reference.

With a common framework, we could begin to answer some very important questions: In what circumstances are different forms of social enterprise appropriate and helpful? How are these different forms best managed and most effectively governed? What public policies are appropriate for regulating organizations engaged in social enterprise? How can entrepreneurs potentially engaged in social enterprise, and the public and private managers who deal with them, be best educated? What research is needed to improve our understanding of social enterprise and improve its effectiveness? This chapter concentrates mostly on developing the framework and touches only lightly on some of these other important questions.

Alternative Disciplinary Approaches to Social Enterprise

In the famous parable, several blind men offer different descriptions of an elephant, depending on what part they touch. If social enterprise is the elephant, then practitioners of various academic persuasions are the blind men trying to describe and understand it. Consider the following six professional "detectives": A *historian* sees social enterprise as part of a long-standing tradition in nonprofit commercial activity and private-sector engagement for the public good. An *economist* sees social enterprise as a component in the portfolio of a multi-product nonprofit firm attempting to maximize its mission impact, or as an input to the production function of a business corporation trying to maximize profits. A *management consultant* sees social enterprise as a key element of strategy and planning, designed to ensure the financial health and sustainability of a nonprofit organization, or as an element in the market strategy of a profit-seeking business corporation. An *organizational theorist* sees social enterprise as a reflection and manifestation of the identity and culture of the host nonprofit or for-profit organization that undertakes it. An *entrepreneur* sees social enterprise as an exercise in innovation and social change, initiated by adventurous individuals or restless organizations. An *international scholar* sees social enterprise as a diverse set of approaches to addressing social problems through engagement of nongovernmental organizations. Each one of these detectives has a good story to tell.

History

Our historian has two intertwined stories. The first has to do with the long-standing involvement of nonprofit organizations in commercial activity in the United States The historian will point out how, from the beginnings of the Republic and even in colonial times, it was not unusual for nonprofits to sell goods and services, often in quite creative ways, to sustain themselves (McCarthy 2003). Indeed, some of the more classical ventures, such as Girl Scout Cookies, products of Goodwill Industries, or church bingo games, can hardly be separated from the core traditions of the nonprofit organizations that offer them. In fact, a survey in the early 1980s demonstrated that these well-known initiatives were hardly exceptions to the general nonprofit modus operandi (Crimmins and Keil 1983). Over time, the historian would say, these commercial initiatives became more important to American nonprofits, as the sector assumed greater significance in the American political economy and as other sources of nonprofit income failed to keep pace with resource needs. In particular, the expansion of nonprofit responsibilities for social, health, educational, arts, environmental, community development, and other public services, as the Great Society programs of the late 1960s required, led to enormous growth of the sector, not all paid for by government. As philanthropy's relative share of nonprofit support declined, the role of fee income and commercial revenue grew, and the economic character of nonprofit operations became notably more businesslike (Weisbrod 1998). Explicitly commercial activity only loosely related to mission continues to constitute the minority of this growth, but the general role of earned income as a legitimate, sustaining component of nonprofit revenue has certainly become accepted. In all, the seeming pervasiveness of enterprising commercial activity by contemporary nonprofits, the historian would argue, is basically a natural extension of what has been going on in the sector all along.

The second story that the historian can tell pertains to the social role of corporate business. Here, too, there are early roots in American history dating back at least to the industrial tycoons of the 19th century— the Carnegies and Rockefellers who made fortunes in the business world and gave much away for libraries, medical research, and other public goods. Such activity continues today in the form of philanthropy by people such as Bill Gates and George Soros, who give from the personal fortunes they made in the corporate world, or by people such as Paul Newman, whose corporate gifts are indistinguishable from his personal philanthropies. However, the real connection to social enterprise begins in the early 20th century, when debate raged around the appropriateness of corporations supporting charitable causes (Burlingame and Young 1996). Some argued that publicly owned corporations had no right to give away money belonging to stockholders, whereas others insisted that such charity was simply good business practice or was part of the social contract under which corporations derived their societal privileges. Indeed, the historian would say, the stream of reasoning that now prevails is that businesses undertake social ventures or support of nonprofits as part of their comprehensive strategies to enhance profitability.

However, there is yet another wrinkle to the historian's yarn: In the overheated economy of the 1990s, great fortunes were made and an entrepreneurial spirit was nurtured that spilled over the borders of traditional business, leading to a fundamental questioning of the boundaries between social and private initiative. Two manifestations of this development relate to social enterprise. First, some new business venturers began thinking of themselves as "social entrepreneurs" and saw no need to segment their social and material goals as they developed their businesses. Second, some who had already amassed fortunes and had turned to philanthropy began to conceive of themselves as social venture capitalists and started to think of their charitable work as "venture philanthropy" requiring adequate social returns on their investments. As a consequence, the historian would tell us, nonprofits reciprocated by behaving more like businesses, responding with business plans and earned income ventures to satisfy their new providers of capital.

In short, the historian would say that the elephant is growing up but that the developments we now call social enterprise are nothing new, just an extension of how nonprofits and businesses have naturally evolved over the past century.

Economics

The economist has both an easy and a difficult tale to tell. The easy one has to do with why a nonprofit would ever want to undertake a commercial initiative. The hard one pertains to why a for-profit business would cast itself as a social venture.

Long ago, economists figured out that many kinds of activities undertaken by nonprofit organizations had the character of a public good and were unsupportable through marketplace sales without voluntary contributions or public subsidy. Yet voluntary support is also problematic in such circumstances because of free rider problems. One solution to this problem, first articulated by Mancur Olson (1965), was to offer "selective incentives"—essentially private goods sold at a profit that could only be purchased if support were simultaneously provided for the public good. This idea explains why public radio sells coffee cups with NPR logos and museums sell art replicas in their gift shops. It also suggests that social enterprise in the form of commercial activity by non-profits will likely have a close relationship with the identity, core competencies, or mission of the organization, in order to offer a unique quality or niche, shielded from (for-profit) competition.

Estelle James (1983) supplied another piece of this puzzle. She argued that nonprofit organizations could be understood as "multi-product firms" that offered combinations of profit-making and loss-making services in order to maximize the utility of their managers (later interpreted as mission). Loss-making services contributed directly to mission while profit-making services, less preferred in and of themselves, contributed resources to subsidize those services that addressed mission directly. James suggested that when resources from other sources were abundant, a nonprofit would cut back on commercial activity, but when they were scarce, the nonprofit would increase commercial production. An alternative hypothesis was that nonprofits might decide to grow by continuing to maximize commercial initiatives no matter what the circumstances (see James in Weisbrod 1998).

In any case, our economist tells us that it is a short distance from the model of nonprofits as multi-product firms to the now-popular program portfolio map introduced by Sharon Oster (1995) that divides nonprofit services into four categories according to their (high or low) contributions to mission on the one hand and financial support on the other. The implication of Oster's tableau is that nonprofits should abandon loss-making services that fail to contribute much to mission, maintain and grow those that contribute to both, and balance cash cows that contribute to financial support but not much to mission with loss-making services that contribute strongly to mission but run a deficit.

The economist also provides insight into why foundations and some major individual donors have interests in promoting social enterprise by nonprofit organizations. Grantmaking foundations, for example, may be viewed as nonprofit organizations with their own missions, which have capital to invest, but have decided to outsource their programming to their nonprofit grantees. Similarly, major individual donors have their own personal interests in particular social causes and a sense of mission as to what they would like to achieve with some of their wealth. Such grant makers are interested in a social rather than private return on their investments. In addition, these social investors are interested in leverage—having their resources achieve maximum impact, in part by bringing other resources into play—because such investments, though often generous and impressive in absolute terms, frequently pale in comparison to the issues addressed—poverty, illiteracy, public health, or any other such major social concern. To the extent that social enterprise ventures undertaken by nonprofit organizations provide such leverage, they may become legitimate objects of these grant makers' largesse. For example, investment in ventures that produce both social good and generate some of their own revenue may increase the ultimate impact of initial grant allocations. Furthermore, social enterprise ventures can be framed as program-related investments or loans that not only produce social benefits but also provide financial returns to the funder. Such dividends can then be reinvested in other social projects. Or, in the case of individual donors, the investment can serve a dual purpose of generating social benefits and providing at least a modest personal financial return.

Although our economist detective is clear about where social enterprise fits into the logic of nonprofit operations, she is less clear about the logic of social enterprise in for-profit form. To the extent that corporations undertake social ventures—or the support of such ventures through philanthropy—as an element of corporate strategy, social enterprise fits the classical model of businesses as profit-maximizing organizations. However, our economist has some trouble with businesses that claim to be social enterprises with dual objectives of profit making and meeting social goals. The problem is less severe for closely held private businesses that do not sell stock to the general public. In this case, it is reasonable to argue that resource allocation decisions can reflect individual owner preferences, embodying their personal trade-offs between material wealth and cherished social causes, so long as they are able to survive the market competition. Problems arise even in this case, however, because owners who eventually sell their businesses cannot control what those businesses do afterwards, although they may try to impose constraints through conditions of sale. To the contrary, nonprofits can maintain their mission focus indefinitely. That is why for-profits with social objectives sometimes seek to convert to nonprofit form when their owners can no longer run the business. Still, there are some areas of service where social enterprise owners clearly feel they have more flexibility, autonomy, or access to resources by pursuing their ventures in for-profit form, despite their social goals. For example, low-cost housing or community development initiatives require capital that may be easier to attract, through lending institutions or sale of stock, if the organization is a for-profit business. For the public corporation, however, our economist friend is skeptical about social enterprise initiatives being any different from classical business corporations with an outlook of enlightened self-interest, because stock market pressures will encourage maximum profitability and discourage unprofitable diversions of resources.

Management Theory

Our management consultant and economist detectives are pretty close friends. The management consultant appreciates the argument that nonprofits will undertake commercial ventures as strategic initiatives to advance the overall mission of the organization. He also understands why for-profit corporations would pursue social ventures as a matter of clever corporate strategy. But the management consultant wants to push these arguments further, noting that nonprofits and for-profits each have competitive advantages in a variety of situations that make social enterprise initiatives compelling.

In particular, nonprofits can bank on the trust associated with their good names and particular core competencies or special capacities they may have as a result of pursuing certain kinds of missions. For example, a nonprofit dedicated to improving the health or welfare of a certain group of individuals (e.g., the visually impaired) will have a competitive advantage in a venture to sell eye protection equipment, just as an art museum gift shop will have a leg up in selling art reproductions. In these cases, consumers' trust that the products will be safe or true to form is a key to commercial success. Similarly, the particular ambience and prestige of an arboretum serve it well as an elegant setting for private parties. And periodic slack in a hospital's well-run laundry operation allows for the marketing of that capacity to smaller residential agencies requiring this service.

The essential point that our management consultant emphasizes is that it makes sense for the nonprofit organization to take advantage of these competitive advantages to bolster the resources available for pursuing the organization's mission, so long as certain conditions hold. One condition is that the organization keep its mission strongly in mind and avoid mission drift—where the venture begins to determine the organization's course of action rather than vice versa. Another condition is to avoid depleting the special assets that provide the competitive advantage in the first place. Thus, entering into ventures that would undermine trust in the organization by delivering inferior products—or that would deteriorate facilities needed for the mission—must be eschewed.

Alternatively, our management consultant argues, those commercial initiatives that actually enhance mission in a direct way should be given even closer attention. For example, if the promotion of protective eyewear effectively helps promote eye safety, or the rental of the arboretum for private parties helps generate new interest in horticulture, then nonprofits can feel even more confident in pursuing such ventures. Indeed, in the extreme, a nonprofit may decide to substitute such a venture for a more traditional activity if the former is found to be more effective. For example, if running a restaurant is a more effective way of training a challenged population to compete in the job market than a traditional job training program, perhaps the nonprofit employment readiness organization should expand the former at the expense of the latter.

Similarly, our management consultant has little trouble understanding why corporations undertake social ventures, aside from the personal motives of their executives. Association with good causes or a reputation for social responsibility helps sell products in the long run. Indeed, companies can establish themselves in unique market niches by developing such connections—for example, becoming *the* personal products company known for its responsible environmental and human resources practices or *the* socially responsible ice cream company. Moreover, initiatives such as support for community volunteering can actually make direct contributions to corporate productivity by improving the skills and morale of corporate employees. It is widely appreciated, for example, that encouraging younger employees to volunteer on boards of nonprofits offers them opportunities for leadership development that they might not receive at an early career stage within the corporation itself.

Finally, our management consultant points out that a clear strategy and business plan are important to successfully exploit an organization's competitive advantages. Thus, business planning among nonprofits has increased as they seek to pursue their competitive advantages through social enterprise ventures.

Organization Theory

Though related to the management consultant by a common education in the ways of organizations, our organizational theorist detective takes a more skeptical view of the logic of social enterprise, as simply a strategic matter for nonprofits or for-profits. She argues that issues of culture arise in organizations, and conflicts in culture can explain why social enterprise initiatives sometimes don't fit in very well. Again, there are two tales to tell.

In the nonprofit context, the danger is that a for-profit culture associated with a commercial initiative will undermine the morale and effectiveness of the nonprofit culture in which it is embedded. Alternatively, a commercial initiative introduced into a nonprofit culture hostile to market values will struggle and fail. Thus, the organization theorist's insight is that social ventures undertaken for the purpose of making money are often best organized as separate structures outside the host organizations—for example, as wholly owned for-profit subsidiaries. To the contrary, ventures that incorporate strong mission-related goals should be run internally, to ensure that they are not co-opted by the market environment.

The organization theorist's insights apply to for-profit corporations undertaking social enterprise ventures as well. Practitioners of corporate philanthropy have experienced the isolation and tension that often come with trying to run a social venture in a for-profit company (Burlingame and Young 1996; Levy 1999). The lessons in this context appear to be twofold: be sure to relate the operation of the venture to the strategy of the corporation, and where possible engage with external nonprofit partners that can help anchor the venture's social mission. A third long-run lesson is to influence the culture of the parent corporation itself, so that it becomes more sympathetic to social initiatives and values.

Finally, the organization theorist brings another important insight to the understanding of social enterprise—that such ventures cannot be properly understood without an appreciation of their organizational identities as seen by those responsible for running or maintaining them. The concept of organizational identity, as originally introduced by Stuart Albert and David Whetten (1985), suggests that organizations, or sometimes subsidiaries thereof, have an essence, defined as that which is *central, distinctive, and enduring* about them. In connection with social enterprise, identity is closely connected with purpose—whether the intent is to make money or contribute to a particular social mission or some combination thereof. Our organization theorist argues that a social enterprise can only be successful if its leaders are clear about its identity and base their strategy on it. Our organization theorist promises to elaborate on this idea later in the chapter, because it connects closely with choices about structuring and incorporating social enterprises into different legal forms as well as other operational and strategic decisions.

Entrepreneurship

Our entrepreneur detective is not quite sure what to make of his fellow detectives' fuss over social enterprise. From his viewpoint, enterprising activity is agnostic about sector and is all about innovation and change wherever it takes place. Surely, we should expect to find it as a pervasive element in all parts of a dynamic society and economy (McClelland 1973; Young 1983). It should be no surprise that new ventures appear in nonprofit as well as for-profit form. Moreover, entrepreneurship is about *new combinations in the means of production,* as Schumpeter (1949) instructed. Thus, the mold-breaking reflected in nonprofits' for-profit activity or social ventures in for-profit form are simply the natural kinds of experiments that entrepreneurs undertake in seeking new ways of doing things. If they work, fine; if not, they are swept away through creative destruction associated with enterprising activity of all kinds.

Our entrepreneur has made a connection between entrepreneurship on the one hand and social enterprise on the other. He has introduced entrepreneurship as a generic process that takes place for a variety motives and in diverse circumstances, sharing a common approach of introducing change and innovation. From that premise, it is a short step to labeling certain varieties of entrepreneurship as social entrepreneurship, that is, enterprising activity that brings about social change and innovation and is often driven by motives other than pure wealth seeking—motives such as a strong belief in causes or seeking recognition or power. So, our entrepreneur continues—what is the relationship between social entrepreneurship and social enterprise? His short answer is that social enterprise is one particular manifestation of social entrepreneurship. In particular, social entrepreneurs have a number of different outlets for their work. They can lead social movements (Zald and McCarthy 1987), become advocates for change in public policy, engage in internal reform efforts within public-sector agencies or large influential nonprofits, develop programs of various kinds within nonprofit and sometimes government organizations, or set up their own organizations (nonprofit or for-profit) with new social missions. It is the latter category, or perhaps the latter two categories, that we normally associate with social enterprise.

Two key points stand out from the perceptions of our entrepreneur detective. First, social enterprise is about innovation, not commercial or social goals alone. Second, social entrepreneurs who happen to choose nonprofit or for-profit organizational vehicles for their work are the ones who drive social enterprise. By this account, not all commercial activities of nonprofits or social programs of for-profits would qualify as social enterprise, only those associated with innovation and change. Moreover, from the entrepreneur's viewpoint, one cannot really understand the nature of social enterprises without understanding the motivations of the social entrepreneurs who pursue them—a possible connection with the organizational theorist's notion of organizational identity.

International Manifestations

"That's all well and good," says our international scholar detective, "but most of you folks have a distinctly American bias. Cross an ocean and you will see that social entrepreneurship has more to do with public policy and social context than the particular goals, motivations, or behaviors of businesses, nonprofits, or individual entrepreneurs." Again, there are two stories for our international scholar to tell. First, social enterprise in Europe arises from evolution of the welfare state and the imperative to find new ways to control public-sector costs and address unemployment of marginalized populations (Borzaga and Defourney 2001). In this context, anything that privatizes public service activity or engages nongovernmental entities in this employment issue is considered social enterprise. Thus, the contracting out of public service work to nonprofit organizations, a routine practice in the United States, would be considered social enterprise in much of Europe.

Second, the forms of social enterprise in Europe and elsewhere are often quite different from those in the United States. In the United States, we are fixated on nonprofits and for-profits, although considerable variety does exist when one looks closely (Aspen 2005). In Europe, more attention is given to worker and consumer cooperatives, which intrinsically combine elements of profit making and individual benefit with social goals. There is less concern in Europe about the strict separation of for-profit and nonprofit forms (through the non-distribution constraint) and more emphasis on governing arrangements that help ensure that an enterprise pursues the right combination of social and private goals. In much of the developing world, cooperatives and micro-enterprise, networks of nongovernmental organizations, and a variety of public–private partnerships constitute a web of activities that may be understood as social enterprise. Here, much of the focus is on economic development and poverty with less concern about whether gains are social or private in nature.

The essential lesson about social enterprise, our international scholar points out, is that it cannot be taken out of context. In Europe, this concept is intrinsically tied to welfare state policies and privatization. In the developing world, it is tied to policy initiatives for economic development and grassroots efforts to address poverty-related concerns. In both cases, social enterprise is almost anything nongovernmental that represents new initiatives in addressing social concerns.

Organizational Identity Redux

Although our six blind detectives have very different perspectives, they can agree that social enterprise is a multifaceted, complex, and diffuse beast. Although they are separated from one another in the language they speak and the particular parts of the beast they are examining, there is still some common ground and some hope of communication and consensus. Equipped with advanced cell phones that translate messages, they can still roughly agree on the common definition advanced earlier. More than that, they can find common ground with the organizational theorist's schema for classifying different forms of social enterprise, based on the concept of organizational identity. This schema helps overcome disciplinary biases because it is borrowed from another discipline and because it deals in metaphors that can be appropriated from various disciplinary sources. A conference call among our detectives, chaired and narrated by a neutral moderator of sufficient skepticism, might go as follows:

> "So, we can agree on defining social enterprise as activity that takes place outside of government but incorporates some social goals. That's pretty general. Perhaps we can also agree, to satisfy our entrepreneurial colleague, that something qualifies as social enterprise only if it is a new initiative rather than business as usual. Oh, I see we have some objections here from our historian and economist colleagues, so forget that. We're going for consensus here. But surely we need to be more specific.
>
> "I have a proposal to borrow the framework of organizational identity from our organization theory friend. Sociologists are rarely so popular, but let's give it a try. She's had help from a psychologist!

The idea here is to come up with a taxonomy of social enterprise by suggesting metaphors that capture the essence of different manifestations that social enterprise can assume. Remember, we want these to be generic, not tied to particular legal categories or structures. Any nominations?"

The result of such a conversation might be the following list of social enterprise identities:

1. *A corporate philanthropy:* a profit-seeking organization that devotes some of its resources to social programs as part of a competitive strategy
2. *A social purpose enterprise:* an organization with a social mission that operates in the marketplace to accomplish that mission most effectively
3. *A hybrid:* an organization with dual objectives to make money for its participants and address selected social goals
4. *A money-making project:* an organization's activity solely intended to produce net revenues for the organization
5. *A social purpose project:* an organization's activity solely intended to address a social mission or selected social goals
6. *A hybrid project:* an organization's activity intended both to produce net revenues and to contribute to a social mission or selected social goals

An interesting thing about this list is that it is not tied to any particular organizational form or cultural context. Hence, it enables the consideration of organizational choices, such as profit, nonprofit, or cooperative; outsourced, in-house, or independent venture; and undertaken in collaboration with, or separately from, other organizations. Perhaps, says the moderator, but surely some of these alternatives fit better with certain identities than others. Let's make that the subject of our next conference call.

Identity versus Form of Social Enterprise

The moderator asks, is everyone on the line? I see our historian is struggling with the new technology. Take a page from the economist—just assume the technology is given! Let's talk about how the legal forms fit the organizational identities of social enterprise.

Organization-Level Identities

I recall, says the moderator, that the first three alternative identities listed above conceive of a social enterprise as an organization, but they do not specify whether that organization is nonprofit or for-profit or some sort of combination. Our organizational theorist explains that organizational form is a choice about the vehicle through which the identity is manifested. So, the moderator asks the group, can you think of both nonprofit and for-profit examples of each of these identities? The detectives agree that some categories are more difficult than others. It is easy to think of for-profit corporate philanthropies. Corporate foundations come to mind, such as the AT&T Foundation or the UPS Foundation, which function within the boundaries of major corporations and dovetail with their overall strategic goals. Georgia Pacific's projects with the Nature Conservancy or Timberland's work with City Year fit the same mold.

What about nonprofit corporate philanthropies, the moderator prods? The group agrees that these are more difficult to find. One needs to examine fields such as hospital care, which features large institutions that intensively compete with one another for market share. University Hospitals of Cleveland comes to mind. Its charitable program offers assistance to other nonprofits such as the Cleveland Children's Museum, a relationship that can burnish the hospital's image and its market position. Similar examples might be found among universities that compete with each other for students, in part by enhancing their images and visibility through community projects such as assistance to local schools. The reason, our detectives argue, that it is more difficult to find corporate philanthropies in nonprofit form is that this identity is driven by economic success, not primarily social mission.

Well, what about the social purpose identity—are there nonprofit and for-profit examples of that? The group agrees that there are, but the difficulties are reversed. Nonprofit examples abound—Goodwill Industries, Vocational Guidance Services in Cleveland, and the Atlanta Community Food Bank engage in market-based ventures for the explicit purpose of advancing their social missions. For-profit examples are more difficult. Perhaps Newman's Own, because it sells foods for the sole purpose of raising money for charity, or Shore Bank, which is dedicated to community renewal and takes advantage of the for-profit form for raising capital. In fact, Newman's Own seems to be a model for the prospective "B Corp" or "for-benefit corporation," which would enjoy tax privileges in exchange for devoting profits to charitable causes (Aspen 2005). But then, the moderator asks, how would this be different from a nonprofit foundation that just happens to be invested in a single company? Good question, our detectives agree, but beside the point. Let's continue.

What about the hybrid identity? Here's where it's easiest to identify both nonprofit and for-profit examples. Mostly these are closely held businesses or small nonprofits headed by founder-leaders—entrepreneurs, our entrepreneur detective exclaims. On the for-profit side we're talking about small businesses whose leaders try to balance their own social and material interests, like the classical radio station WCLV in Cleveland or Gallery North, an arts gallery on Long Island (Legoretta and Young 1986). In these cases, the proprietors made a good living from their businesses but constrained their profit maximizing by adhering to social goals such as maintaining classical music on the radio or promoting the work of local artists. Much the same could be said on the nonprofit side, for organizations such as the Chartwell School, a headmaster-led private school in New York, or Apollo's Fire, a baroque chamber orchestra established by a conductor entrepreneur in Cleveland. The latter are organized as nonprofits because it would be difficult for these organizations to survive without donations or government funds that are contingent on nonprofit status.

Well then, the moderator observes, some identities seem to fit certain legal forms better than others. Do you agree? The group seems to go along with this. Corporate philanthropy is a natural in for-profit form because the overall objective is market success. Putting a corporate philanthropy into nonprofit form seems to risk eroding the integrity of that form. Perhaps that's why hospitals are periodically challenged on their qualifications for nonprofit status.

Similarly, the nonprofit form seems a natural fit for a social purpose enterprise. In for-profit form, the risk of mission drift seems a serious one. What if the enterprise is sold? Will the new owners continue to pursue the social mission? That seems to be why WCLV converted part of its operation to nonprofit status, to preserve the social mission in perpetuity.

What then of the hybrid identity? More trouble here, the group agrees. In nonprofit form, there is a risk of mission drift and corrupting the nonprofit so that it functions as a for-profit wolf in nonprofit sheep's clothing. A delicate balance is required to avoid "self-inurement" (self-benefit) while satisfying the material wants of the founders. Can the governance and regulatory machinery of the nonprofit form keep this risk in check?

In for-profit form, the hybrid identity risks serious instability. What prevents a slide into for-profit competition and neglect of the social purpose over time?

Project-Level Identities

What are the organizing choices for the three social enterprise projects that we've identified? Well, the management consultant suggests, one could have an in-house project or an outsourced project. If outsourced, one could set up a separate nonprofit corporation or a separate for-profit corporation. The parent organization would control these outsourced entities. We've already talked about the identity of social enterprise in the form of separate organizations, so there's no need to consider the option of spin-offs here. Also, I'm assuming that the parent organization is nonprofit, though we could also consider how a parent for-profit corporation might organize its social enterprise ventures.

OK, the moderator replies, how about some examples again? Money-making projects? The group offers the following:

- The Cleveland Botanical Garden rents out its facilities for private parties, as an in-house operation.
- The Win-Win Cleaning service is a for-profit subsidiary of Viet-AID.
- The catering service of the Boomtown Café is a separate nonprofit organization.

The primary purpose of each of these ventures is to raise money for the parent organization but with various nuances. The Botanical Garden case is the most straightforward. Managing its grounds is part of its core competence and consistent with its mission, so there is little need to segregate this function from its main operations. Indeed, this project must be closely coordinated with scheduling the facilities for mainstream uses. The Win-Win Cleaning service is clearly a business activity outside the core competence of Viet-AID, a nonprofit in Boston whose purpose is to assist the local Vietnamese community with its social and economic needs. Although the venture offers employment and business experience to Viet-AID's target population, Win-Win is organized as a business cooperative with equity investments by Viet-AID and another equity capital group, and there is an explicit intention for these investors to make money.

The mission of the nonprofit Boomtown Café is to provide nutritious food in a safe environment for low-income and homeless people in Seattle. Its catering service started as a means to deliver meals to homeless shelters before the café opened. It has since branched out into the traditional catering market for weddings and other parties, explicitly for the purpose of generating a flow of income to support the café operation as a whole. The catering service is organized as a division of the café but is administered under the umbrella of another nonprofit that serves as fiscal agent and provides expertise and financial backup.

Well, that's all very interesting, the moderator observes. I'll bet things get even more complex when we look at social purpose projects. Maybe not, members of the group reply, and they come up with the following examples:

- Bookshare.org offers books in digital form to serve the visually handicapped in digital braille and talking-book formats. It is a program of Benetech, a nonprofit devoted to adapting technology to helping handicapped individuals.
- Greyston Bakery is a separately organized for-profit corporation belonging to the Greyston Foundation in Yonkers, New York. Its purpose is to employ ex-offenders and provide them with job experience and marketable skills.
- SmartWood is a timber certification program of the Rainforest Alliance, which promotes conservation and sustainable development. The service is offered to for-profit lumber companies to encourage healthy forest practices. While, in its development phase, SmartWood was originally organized as a partnership with local nonprofit environmental organizations, it has since been consolidated as a separate division within the Rainforest Alliance, which runs its business functions and works with its partners on educational and awareness programming.

Well, how about some examples of hybrid projects, the moderator asks. More examples flow from the group:

- Girl Scout cookies is a program of Girls Scouts USA that is intended both to raise net funds and to contribute to the character building of participating girls.
- Community Wealth Ventures is a for-profit subsidiary of Share Our Strength, a nonprofit devoted to addressing issues of hunger

and poverty. Community Wealth Ventures provides consultation on social enterprise to promote this concept in the nonprofit community while being intentionally profitable itself.

- The Vehicle Maintenance Service is a nonprofit subsidiary of DARTS, a nonprofit agency in Minneapolis–St. Paul that offers specialized transportation to senior and handicapped individuals. The subsidiary repairs and services vehicles used by DARTS and other social service organizations that have specialized vehicle transportation needs. The Vehicle Maintenance Service is intended to provide net profits to DARTS while maintaining a valued vehicle repair service to social service providers.

So how well do the identities fit the various organizational forms they have apparently taken? The group suggests once more that there are some natural fits and others that are more strained or risky. Maintaining intentionally for-profit ventures in-house may work if the core competencies required closely match those of the nonprofit's mainstream operations, but it risks a culture clash or mission drift if the for-profit mentality spills over into the general operation. On the other hand, failure to adopt a for-profit orientation for the venture dooms its success. For these reasons, the for-profit subsidiary often seems a better fit. The nonprofit subsidiary seems anomalous—it may make sense where the venture is outside the core competence of the parent organization but still requires a sensitivity to mission that might be lost if enshrined in a for-profit subsidiary.

Similarly, our detectives argue that a social purpose venture is best organized either in-house or, where core competencies do not match up, as a separate nonprofit subsidiary. A for-profit subsidiary in this case risks mission drift at the venture level and possible tension with the parent organization. Still, this option can make sense where the mission of the organization, such as helping certain groups to become employable or to learn business or entrepreneurial skills, requires a competitive market experience where the level of profit is a key indicator of success.

So, the moderator exclaims, I'll bet projects with a hybrid identity are as problematic as organizations with this identity. Well, maybe not—our detectives offer. The three alternatives seem to provide a good range of choices where the parent nonprofit wants to balance financial and mission goals. Greater emphasis on mission suggests an in-house choice, or perhaps a nonprofit subsidiary if core competency is an issue. More emphasis on financial returns suggests that a for-profit subsidiary might make the best choice. Certainly in all cases, projects will have to be carefully monitored to ensure that their direction remains consistent with the objectives of the parent organization and the place of the venture in the parent organization's overall strategy.

Well, what if the parent organization is a for-profit corporation interested in undertaking a social venture? Would the answers just be the mirror image of what you guys have just argued? Maybe so, say our detectives. We're really not interested here in for-profit ventures by for-profits; that's purely business. But social enterprise might consist of a social purpose venture or perhaps a hybrid venture undertaken by a for-profit corporation. Social purpose ventures might run up against tensions inside the corporation, but this would be ameliorated if it were clear to everyone how it ultimately contributed to the market success of the corporation. It wouldn't make much sense to set up a social purpose venture as a for-profit subsidiary unless the core competence required were very different from that of the parent company, but it might make a great deal of sense to set it up as a nonprofit subsidiary. That would avoid culture conflict and allow for differences in core competencies while permitting a close association between the corporation and the social purpose venture. This is the debate that takes place when a corporation considers whether its philanthropic program should be run in-house or established as a separate foundation.

That leaves hybrids again, says the moderator. Certainly the in-house alternative remains an option, the group agrees, but it would have to be carefully protected within the governance structure of the parent corporation to preserve the desired balance between profitability and social benefit. Otherwise, the dominant for-profit culture could squeeze out the social objective. Separate corporations have the advantage of creating new governance structures explicitly focused on the particular combination of objectives desired for the venture. If the balance is to be tilted toward profitability, then for-profit form may be the best choice. If the intent is to contribute more heavily to a social mission, the nonprofit form can be considered.

So where do we go from here, the moderator asks? Our discussion of alternative legal forms and arrangements certainly has shed some light on the nature of interactions between nonprofits and business as they relate to social enterprise. Are there other facets of social enterprise that help illuminate the interface between nonprofits and business? Yes, the management consultant suggests, there is a whole set of management practices undertaken by social enterprises that depend on the underlying identity of the organization or venture. Furthermore, the economist pipes in, the various identities for social enterprise have implications for what kinds of public policies should govern and regulate them. OK, says the moderator, it looks like we need two more conversations.

Business Practices

What sorts of management practices are we talking about? We've already considered outsourcing—what else? Well, the economist interjects, certainly the pricing of services and decisions on output and distribution, which will be influenced not only by identity (economists would say "objective functions") but the degree of competition in the marketplace. Social enterprises will also differ in their hiring practices, according to their intrinsic identities. Let me explain.

Social enterprise ventures with certain identities will want to set prices to maximize profits. This practice applies particularly to the profit-making venture designed to generate maximum net revenues for a parent organization. In such a case, a market clearing price and a level of sales will be sought, such that the marginal revenue on the last unit sold is just offset by the marginal cost of producing and selling that unit. Similarly, such a venture will want to hire the most productive workers and pay them competitive wages according to their productivity, so that the value of the marginal product of labor is equal to the value of the marginal product of any other input to the production of the venture's output. (See Young and Steinberg 1995.)

Wow, pretty technical, says the moderator. You mean that if a venture is really intended just to make profits, it will hire just the right number of the most productive workers at a competitive wage and it will sell its products at competitive prices to whoever will buy them? Essentially, says the economist. So now consider other social enterprise identities. A social purpose enterprise or project, or even hybrid enterprises or projects, will depart from these profit-maximizing practices. They may wish to sell at lower-than-market-clearing prices to increase output and consumption so that more people benefit from the service, if that fits the mission. For example, if the mission is to encourage reading or vaccinations against certain diseases, lower prices on such services will advance those missions. In some cases, sliding scales may be appropriate to subsidize some consumers at the expense of others willing to pay higher prices. For social purpose ventures or enterprises, a source of external subsidy may be required (e.g., grants). For hybrids, a compromise price structure might enable breaking even or achieving a modest profit while extending the social benefit beyond what it would be if the goal were solely profit maximizing.

Similarly, a social purpose or a hybrid venture or enterprise may have mission-related reasons to depart from competitive labor market practices by, for example, favoring certain target groups or hiring more workers than might be justified from a pure efficiency standpoint. For example, if the purpose of a restaurant is to develop marketable skills for ex-offenders, the restaurant will favor them in hiring, provide them with employment training as part of their work regimen, and hire them in greater numbers than an ordinary business would. Such practices will increase the costs of the venture or lower its productivity in producing meals and service of a given quality, but it will achieve more in intended social benefits.

Interestingly, these practices have important implications for the relationships between business and nonprofits. Unless the (social purpose or hybrid) nonprofit can choose a special niche for its venture where it can enjoy certain barriers to entry by potential competitors, such as a patent or copyright or a unique physical facility or expertise, it will face a competitive disadvantage vis-à-vis ordinary business. In such a case, it is likely to run at a loss, requiring some other source of subsidy, such as gifts and grants or a stream of investment income from endowment. We can expect, therefore, that most nonprofits will avoid highly competitive niches for their ventures and search close to home for social enterprise ventures. Those that do operate in such niches will necessarily have to pursue profit-making pricing and service policies to survive. Nonprofits in certain areas of service where for-profits have entered the market, such as hospitals and nursing homes, are often criticized for this.

Finally, says the economist, a note about the corporate philanthropy identity before I get off my soapbox. In this case, the organization (likely in the form of a for-profit but perhaps a nonprofit) sees its philanthropic work as an input to production, needed to maximize its profits. In its labor practices and pricing output decisions, however, profit-maximizing strategies will be pursued. In the case of a nonprofit, however, such as a large hospital or a university, policy constraints associated with the nonprofit form may require certain practices, such as discounts for lower-income clientele.

Public Policy

Well, says the moderator, that's interesting, and the detectives nod affirmatively. That seems to bring us directly to policy issues. What laws are needed to regulate and govern social enterprise, especially if some types seem to differ little from ordinary business?

It's an old issue, says the historian. Remember when New York University owned a spaghetti company? Yes, says the economist, but I'm not sure we've gotten things right yet. Obviously tax policy is important here. Currently we tax so-called unrelated business income for nonprofits and we tax for-profit businesses the same no matter what kinds of goods or services they provide. But if we consider the various identities that social enterprise can take, we face the question of whether this is a sensible way to proceed. For example, if a nonprofit is essentially a corporate philanthropy or a hybrid, shouldn't it be taxed like a business to a certain extent? And if a for-profit business is devoted to a social purpose, shouldn't it receive some tax consideration? And what about various limited profit forms such as cooperatives or regulated utilities, which presumably give explicit structural form to the concept of the hybrid social enterprise?

The unrelated business income tax is intended to address the first question by differentiating the purpose of the venture itself, and the non-distribution constraint on nonprofits is designed to avoid a corporate philanthropy or a hybrid in nonprofit form from blatantly distributing profits to owners. But as we know, these constraints can be subtly circumvented. Perhaps policy needs to be more finely tuned to distinguish identities and intentions within the nonprofit realm. I have some ideas on this, says the organization theorist, but let the economist go on for now.

Well, the economist continues, on social enterprise in for-profit form, some folks have proposed the so-called B corporation, a for-profit business eligible for tax exemption if it devotes all of its profits, after dividends are distributed to stockholders, to a charitable cause (Aspen 2005). Others have suggested that for-profit businesses in general should receive tax considerations for their social initiatives. All this seems fraught with difficulty, of course, especially when one tries to figure out how such arrangements can be protected from manipulation toward selfish ends.

Here's where my idea comes in, says the organization theorist. We really need to look at governance arrangements rather than alternative legal forms based on the degree of allowable profit making. Yes, says the international scholar. In Europe, the focus is on governance, with the balance between profit making and profit distribution versus social goals set by boards representative of the various constituencies important to the success of the enterprise—including target populations, government officials, workers, consumers, and investors.

So, says the moderator, to extend this idea, we would require any social enterprise to have proper representation on its governing board and certain boundaries within which it could balance profit distribution with social goal attainment? Well, says the management theorist, nonprofit boards and many corporate boards are pretty dysfunctional—I wouldn't want to complicate their operations even more. But perhaps a fresh look at their structure and operations—to include these ideas—would be helpful in the long run.

Conclusion

Overall, says the moderator, I think we've had an interesting, productive discussion. I'm not sure we've touched all parts of this elephant called social enterprise or that we've been able to put all the pieces together. But we seem to have decided that social enterprise comes in various forms, captured fairly well in the idea of alternative organizational identities. And from that framework, we've been able to see that different social enterprise identities can be expected to behave differently on pricing and output decisions and are best accommodated by different legal forms and practices for partnering and outsourcing. We've also noted that important policy issues arise as to how best to tax and regulate social enterprise, including some, shall I say, "radical" ideas for introducing new corporate forms and governing arrangements. Perhaps of most interest here, social enterprise illustrates how difficult it is to draw a line separating nonprofit organizations and business.

REFERENCES

Aspen Institute. 2005. *Enterprising Organizations: New Asset-Based and Other Innovative Approaches to Solving Social and Economic Problems.* Washington, DC: Aspen Institute. http://www.nonprofitresearch.org/usr_doc/EnterprisingOrgsBW.pdf.

Albert, Stuart, and David A. Whetten. 1985. "Organizational Identity." In *Research in Organizational Behavior* vol. 7, edited by L. L. Cummings and Barry M. Staw (263–95). Greenwich, CT: JAI Press.

Borzaga, Carlo, and Jacques Defourney. 2001. *The Emergence of Social Enterprise.* London: Routledge.

Burlingame, Dwight, and Dennis R. Young, eds. 1996. *Corporate Philanthropy at the Crossroads.* Bloomington: Indiana University Press.

Crimmins, James C., and Mary Keil. 1983. *Enterprise in the Nonprofit Sector.* New York: Rockefeller Brothers Fund.

James, Estelle. 1983. "How Nonprofits Grow: A Model." *Journal of Policy Analysis and Management* 2:350–66.

Kerlin, Janelle. 2005. "Social Enterprise in the United States and Europe: Understanding and Learning from our Differences." http://www.emes.net/fileadmin/emes/PDF_files/ISTR_EMES_Paris/PS_4/PS4_S2/PS4_S2d_ISTR-EMES_Kerlin.pdf.

Legoretta, Judith, and Dennis R. Young. 1986. "Why Organizations Turn Nonprofit: Case Studies." In The *Economics of Nonprofit Institutions,* edited by Susan Rose-Ackerman (196–204). New York: Oxford University Press.

Levy, Reynold. 1999. *Give and Take.* Boston: Harvard Business School Press.

McCarthy, Kathleen. 2003. *American Creed.* Chicago: University of Chicago Press.

McClelland, David C. 1973. "The Two Faces of Power." In *Human Motivation,* edited by David C. McClelland and Robert S. Steele (ch. 19). Morris, NJ: General Learning Press.

Olson, Mancur. 1965. *The Logic of Collective Action.* Cambridge, MA: Harvard University Press.

Oster, Sharon. 1995. *Strategic Management for Nonprofit Organizations.* New York: Oxford University Press.

Schumpeter, Joseph A. 1949. *The Theory of Economic Development.* Cambridge, MA: Harvard University Press.

Weisbrod, Burton A., ed. 1998. *To Profit or Not to Profit.* New York: Cambridge University Press.

Young, Dennis R. 1983. *If Not for Profit, for What?* Lexington, MA: Lexington Books.

Young, Dennis R., and Richard Steinberg. 1995. *Economics for Nonprofit Managers.* New York: The Foundation Center.

Zald, Meyer N., and J. D. McCarthy, eds. 1987. *Social Movements in an Organizational Society.* New Brunswick, NJ: Transaction Books.

3

The Changing Economy and the Scope of Nonprofit-Like Activities

Joseph J. Cordes and C. Eugene Steuerle

Traditionally, economists and legal scholars have argued that what differentiates nonprofit from for-profit organizations is a legal distinction sometimes called the "nondistribution constraint." Formally, because there are no owners of a nonprofit, the nonprofit managers and staff cannot directly appropriate any surplus (e.g., "profit") a nonprofit organization garners. In the past, the legal organizational boundary created by nonprofit status has been linked to other differentiations between for-profits and not-for-profits, including what goods and services are produced and how such goods and services are financed. For instance, pure charitable services that generate no revenue, if provided privately (rather than in the public sector), were traditionally seen as naturally falling in the domain of the nonprofit sector.

Though the nondistribution constraint that goes with nonprofit status is a meaningful one for the vast majority of nonprofit organizations, it has also always been somewhat arbitrary. For instance, although managers cannot directly appropriate profits, any surplus generated by providing nonprofit goods and services can be indirectly captured in wages. Indirectly, there may also be capital returns to nonprofit activities, as in the case of interest payments made to banks—payments that owners and depositors in the banks then earn.

Today, however, there is a growing sense that the boundary is becoming much more permeable. Nonprofits have found it increasingly advantageous to operate like businesses in some respects. Some for-profit businesses have adopted nonprofit attributes, and businesses and nonprofits have discovered mutual benefit from acting as partners, both in for-profit and in not-for-profit ventures.

The phenomenon of blending business ventures with charitable activities is not new, as evidenced by decades-old sheltered workshops that have created and operated businesses to provide employment opportunities for the disabled, and hospital and museum gift shops and restaurants. But many observers sense that something fundamental has changed. For instance, since 1980, "an entire specialty field of social entrepreneurship has emerged, complete with experts, publications, web sites, conferences, technical assistance organizations, and funders" (Cutler 2005, 1).

Is this merely a matter of charities or businesses pushing the edges of a legal boundary or anecdotal examples that are not indicative of a systematic change? We suggest and offer evidence here that the answer is a resounding "no," that the blurring of boundaries between organizational forms is a natural response to a number of changing social and market forces. Here we focus on how evolving economic factors have redefined the boundaries between for-profit and nonprofit organizational forms.

We proceed as follows. The next section identifies features of nonprofit and for-profit organizations widely believed to differentiate the two, but we then discuss why there is a continuum of organizational models for supporting the provision of charitable goods and services. We also present a typology of organizational forms. We then examine a range of economic factors likely to affect the choice of organizational form. We identify some of the relative economic advantages of nonprofit and for-profit organizational forms in financial markets, and in markets for goods and services, and discuss how changes in the economy at large, public policy, and organizational culture and norms can tilt the "economic balance," thereby affecting choice of organizational form.

Organizational Forms

The choice of nonprofit or for-profit form as a means of organizing the production and provision of a good or service is often perceived as a simple choice between two alternatives. The canonical nonprofit is widely seen as an entity that focuses on its mission of providing services or serving clients; has imposed on itself the nondistribution constraint, prohibiting the distribution of any economic surplus to its owners; relies primarily on contributions and grants for its revenue; and is accountable to multiple stakeholders, including its clients, donors, and the public. In contrast, the canonical for-profit enterprise is assumed to be an entity that focuses on profit, intends to distribute any economic surplus garnered to its owners, relies on sales of goods and services and access to private capital markets to finance its operations, and is accountable in the marketplace to its shareholders and creditors.

In practice, however, the reality is more complicated. It is widely documented that many nonprofit organizations rely as much or more on revenue from sales of goods and services as they do on contributions and grants; this is not a new development. What has changed, however, is that the concept of combining business and charitable activities has moved beyond a type of niche activity by a few types of nonprofits toward one undertaken by a wide range of traditional nonprofit organizations.

Thus, although one still finds many organizations conforming to the canonical ideal types of nonprofit versus for-profit organizations, among organizations classified as nonprofits, one is apt to find entities that combine tax-exempt status with commercial activities that, as Young notes in the previous chapter, "are seen either as a *strategic* means of generating income to support the mission, or as a *strategy* to carry out mission-related functions."

A set of case studies undertaken by Cordes, Poletz, and Steuerle provides some indication of the range of different organizational models. They undertook a detailed analysis of the organizational structure of 12 different nonprofits. These cases, which are presented in their entirety in the appendix to this chapter, represent four different examples of how entities with an avowed social purpose have embraced important features of businesses as elements of their core operating model.

Job Training

One model involves the operation of a commercial business as a direct means of fulfilling an organization's charitable mission. The most prevalent examples are found in the area of job training, where nonprofits create and operate businesses as means of providing training, rehabilitation, and employment to groups such as paroled criminals, drug addicts, and the disabled. In this case, there is a direct relation between mission and earned income. The businesses are run as training schools, and jobs are an integral part of the rehabilitation the nonprofit provides. Meeting market tests is regarded as enhancing the self-esteem of clients and providing them with marketable skills. A side financial benefit, which is increasingly recognized as important, is that if the business generates a steady and predictable flow of earnings, this revenue stream can be leveraged through outside investment.

Nonprofit Ventures and the Double Bottom Line

A more recent model is that of so-called double-bottom-line social ventures. In this case, unlike the job training model, where the for-profit business is an intermediate input in the production of the charitable activity, the charitable mission and earned income are directly related through the goods or services the nonprofit produces. The good or service has a commercial/private bottom line equal to the organization's profit (or loss) from sale of goods and services in the marketplace and a social bottom line equal to the social value of its activities that are not reflected in market sales. Sales of the good or service thus create a socially desirable outcome, although private returns based strictly on market sales are unlikely to pass a standard for-profit test. Together, the business and social bottom lines create a double bottom line that is the blended value of the nonprofit organization.[1]

Those familiar with the literature on public finance will immediately recognize this example as a private good that has external benefits. A traditional conceptual remedy for providing such a good would be to have a for-profit firm produce it, receiving a public subsidy in addition to revenues garnered from the market sales.

However, there is no reason why a good or service with positive externalities needs to be produced by a for-profit business or by government. It could just as well be produced by a nonprofit enterprise that combines revenues from market sales with revenues that reflect the social value of output not captured in the marketplace from sources such as private contributions or government grants.

Nonprofit Conglomerates

Some nonprofits have made a strategic decision to reduce their dependence on any single income source by diversifying. They have experimented with new program activities and taken advantage of considerable flexibility allowed by law (see chapter 4) to create complex structures involving nonprofit subsidiaries, for-profit subsidiaries, and partnerships with for-profit organizations. In addition to providing revenue diversification, such structures sometimes provide perfectly legal ways in which nonprofits can exploit their tax-exempt status by allocating costs and revenues among the various organizational entities in ways that minimize any taxes that might be owed on profitable earned-income opportunities.

Quid Pro Quo

Quid pro quo defines another type of relationship whereby nonprofits are able to exploit certain unique assets for financial gain in collaboration with for-profit businesses. Several analysts have noted that imposing the non-distribution constraint can be a means of signaling to potential customers that an organization can be trusted to produce goods of a certain quality. Such labeling can be of high value in situations where quality is both important and difficult to verify. In addition, because nonprofits are widely perceived as producing goods that benefit society, for-profit businesses have the opportunity to differentiate their brand through good corporate citizenship through partnerships with nonprofits.

For-Profit Socially Responsible Business

Each of the previous examples centers on nonprofits that operate like businesses in how they acquire resources or on nonprofits that avail themselves of opportunities for transforming mission-related assets and competencies into earned income that can then support the organization's core mission (Sagawa and Segal 2000). However, the blurring of organizational boundaries can also run in the opposite direction from for-profit businesses as a number of owners and managers of for-profit businesses see pursuing social purposes as good business strategy.

This recognition can take the more traditional form of for-profit firms donating funds to charity, although a new twist is that donated funds come not just from corporate foundations. A number of corporations have also committed publicly to donating a specific percentage of sales or profits to charities.

The implication of the examples is that between the organizational poles of the pure nonprofit and the pure for-profit, one finds a continuum of different hybrid organizational models (table 3.1).

Table 3.1. A Continuum of Organizational Forms

Organizational form	Examples/organizational features
A. Pure nonprofit	All receipts from contributions, not operations
B. Nonprofit operating business conducting charitable activities	Nonprofit health care and education
C. Nonprofit that operates businesses in areas related to its mission	University bookstores, hospital laundries and catering services, job training programs
D. Nonprofits in partnership with for-profit business	Cause-related marketing, corporate sponsorships
E. Nonprofits with active stakes in for-profit businesses	Nonprofits with substantial shares in for-profit affiliates
F. Not-for-profit firms	Organizations legally organized as private businesses or corporations but that distribute everything as wages
G. For-profit businesses contributing pre-announced shares of profits to charity	Ben and Jerry's, Target Stores, Newman's Own
H. For-profits in direct competition with nonprofits	Hospitals, for-profit education providers
I. Pure for-profit business	No outputs defined as education, health, or other product that could also be defined as charitable

Economic Factors Influencing Organizational Choice

An economic approach to studying organizations focuses less on classification of activity or legal form and more on identifying the comparative economic advantages and disadvantages of the different organizational forms. In the case of the nonprofit form, scholars have recognized that an organization accepting the nondistribution constraint provides valuable signals to two potential sources of finance: (1) potential donors and contributors, for whom imposing the constraint provides at least some assurance that contributions will finance public goods and (2) potential customers who seek important but hard-to-verify quality dimensions in certain types of goods and services (Bilodeau and Slavinski 1998; Glaeser and Schleifer 1998). The state attorneys general recognize the signaling role of the nondistribution constraint when, as a matter of consumer protection, they monitor the actions of nonprofits to ensure that there is truth in advertising behind the use of the nonprofit designation.

These advantages of the nonprofit form come at a price, however. Although the nondistribution constraint might make it easier to secure donations, grants, and contributions, it also limits access to capital markets in two ways. First, although some nonprofits can secure debt financing of their activities, nonprofits do not have access to equity capital. Second, when seeking debt financing, some nonprofits may encounter resistance from lenders wary of treating contributions, grants, and donations as bankable revenue. In addition, heavy reliance on contributions and grants can create dependency on these sources of finance among nonprofits.

Similarly, the for-profit organizational form has advantages that mirror the disadvantages of the nonprofit model. The acceptance of owners seeking profits for themselves limits access to contributions, donations, and grants but does provide access to capital markets and retained earnings. Potential customers of goods and services with important but hard-to-verify quality dimensions are also less likely to trust for-profit providers of such goods and services.

These differing features of organizational form suggest potential ways in which there are "gains from trade" by matching advantageous features of the for-profit form with the nonprofit form. We term such mixing and matching of organizational attributes "organizational arbitrage" because of its analogy to arbitrage in economics and finance, which involves taking advantage of price differentials between two markets. For nonprofits, pursuing organizational arbitrage provides opportunities to retain "trust" but gain access to capital markets, develop activities that are easier to collateralize, and reduce dependency on uncertain grants and contributions. Conversely, the potential benefits to for-profits of establishing business relationships with nonprofits are the ability to use the "trust attributes" of nonprofits to market commercial goods and services, and perhaps to move into markets where the ability to attract grants and contributions, when combined with revenue from business operations, may pose attractive financial opportunities.

Changes in Organizational Culture

Though incorporating business activities within nonprofit organizations is not new, there is evidence that the attitude has shifted from one of reluctant acceptance to one of need to supplement traditional revenue sources with income from commercial activities, to perhaps even one of actively embracing businesslike activities and organizational forms.

As some observers have noted, "nonprofits increasingly feel compelled to launch earned-income ventures, if only to appear more disciplined, innovative, and businesslike to their stakeholders" (Foster and Bradach 2005, 1). An important set of stakeholders in this respect are private foundations that have become more apt to treat grants as forms of seed capital rather than as operating revenue and strongly encourage nonprofits to develop sustainable and bankable sources of financial support (being able to serve as at least limited collateral for private-sector financing).

The Rise of Social Entrepreneurs

Estelle James (2003) notes that the desired mix of business elements in a nonprofit will depend both on the attitudes of nonprofit managers and on nonprofit entrepreneurs. Although the term *nonprofit entrepreneur* may appear an oxymoron, there is considerable evidence that the growth and evolution of the nonprofit sector is shaped by individuals who fit the definition of an entrepreneur as "someone who organizes, manages, and assumes the risks of a business or enterprise" (Cordes, Steuerle, and Twombly 2004, 115). James emphasizes that there is likely to be some self-selection into the roles of nonprofit manager and nonprofit entrepreneur. In the past, people selecting into these activities were more likely to have traditional notions of how nonprofits ought to be structured. Today the formal education that potential nonprofit managers are receiving makes them more open to identify potential opportunities for nonprofit–for-profit arbitrage. Additionally, as discussed more fully later, a changing economy presents potential entrepreneurs with a wider array of attractive opportunities for their talents in both sectors, often at the same time.

External Economic Factors

Perhaps the most wide-reaching factor that is creating a more porous border between nonprofit and profit-making organizations and activities is an economy-wide shift in consumer demand toward the kinds of goods and services that nonprofits provide, which leads profit-making organizations to compete more in these realms (Cordes et al. 2004). Thus, the current economy produces more products of the sorts associated with organizational models B and H in table 3.1—that is, entities that could but need not qualify as charitable under the United States Internal Revenue Code section 501(c)(3) definition.

A striking example is health care, which used to make up 1/30th of the economy and now is 1/6th. Similarly, the production of knowledge or information is a rapidly growing sector of the economy that, though often associated with the nonprofit sector, can be sold for profit or not. Perhaps just as important, as information-related goods have become more valuable, nonprofits also find themselves possessing potentially valuable assets that are produced jointly with their primary mission-related activities, and exploiting the revenue potential of such assets may require creating hybrid forms or partnerships with for-profits as in organizational models D, E, and F.

The data in tables 3.2, 3.3, and 3.4 provide statistical evidence of some of these trends. Table 3.2 shows that jobs in industries that produce "potentially charitable outputs"—which we define to be goods or services that traditional nonprofit organizations could provide—have grown much faster than industries in other sectors, and are projected to continue doing so. These trends are mirrored in table 3.3, which shows that occupations with significant nonprofit penetration have grown more rapidly than other occupations between 1983 and 1999, and table 3.4, which shows a 23.2 percent projected growth in jobs in nonprofit-oriented occupations between 2004 and 2014, compared with a 13 percent growth in jobs in all occupations over the same period.

As these inputs and outputs of production become more and more alike in both sectors, one should not be surprised to find more overlapping organizational structure through, for example, more subsidiaries (or related organizations) in one sector controlled by a member of the other sector, and more partnerships between nonprofits and for-profits producing related or complementary goods and services. At the individual level, workers in each sector would also be more apt to have easily transferable skills, permitting them to move back and forth between sectors not only at different points in their careers but also daily on the job.

This new economy is also likely to be more conducive to creating a pool of potential entrepreneurs whose skills could be used to found

text continues on page 64

Table 3.2. Relative Growth of Industries with Potentially Charitable Output

Industry title	NAICS	Jobs (1,000s)			Projected Change		Average Annual Growth Rate	Projected
		1994	2004	2014	1994–2004	2004–2014	1994–2004	2004–2014
Charitable Industries								
Computer systems design and related services	5415	531.4	1147.4	1600.3	616	452.9	8.0	3.4
Management, scientific, and technical consulting	5416	416.8	779	1,250	362.2	471.2	6.5	4.8
Social assistance	624	1,382	2,132	2,872	750.5	739.5	4.4	3.0
Internet and other information services	519	317.8	470	600	152.5	129.6	4.0	2.5
Museums, historical and similar institutions	712	81.8	117.1	140	35.3	22.9	3.7	1.8
Educational services	61	1,895	2,766	3,665	871.6	898.1	3.9	2.9
Ambulatory health services	621	3,579	4,946	7,031	1367.4	2085.1	3.3	3.6
Performing arts, spectator sports and related	711	296.1	364.8	443.2	68.7	78.4	2.1	2.0
Membership organizations	813	2,285	2,929	3,310	644.5	381.3	2.5	1.2
Scientific research and development	5417	475.8	547.6	612.9	71.8	65.3	1.4	1.1
Other professional scientific and professional	5419	367.8	503.4	646.1	135.6	142.7	3.2	2.5
Software publishers	5112	136.8	238.7	400	101.9	161.3	5.7	5.3
Legal services	5411	965.6	1161.8	1,340	196.2	178.1	1.9	1.4

				Other Industries			
Advertising	5418	375	425	520	49.9	95.2	1.3	2.0
Subtotal		13,105	18,529	24,431	5,424	5,902	3.5	2.8
Other services	Not included above	14,615	17,978	22,198	3,363	4,221	2.1	2.1
Utilities	22	689	570	562	−119	−8	−1.9	−0.1
Transportation and warehousing	493	3,701	4,250	4,756	548.9	505.9	1.4	1.1
Construction	23	5,095	6,965	7,757	1869.6	792.4	3.2	1.1
Retail trade	44,45,48,492	13,491	15,035	16,683	1543.4	1648.7	1.1	1.0
Wholesale trade	42	5,248	5,655	6,131	407.4	475.9	0.8	0.8
State and local government	N.A.	16,257	18,891	21,019	2634	2128.2	1.5	1.1
Federal government	N.A.	3,018	2,728	2,771	−290.5	43.4	−1.0	0.2
Finance, insurance, and real estate	52, 53	6,867	8,052	8,901	1185	849.4	1.6	1.0
Agriculture	11	2,891	2,140	1,910	−750.2	−229.9	−3.0	−1.1
Nonagricultural self-employed and unpaid family	N.A.	9,360	9,556	1,012	196.4	455.5	0.2	0.5
Goods producing	31,33	22,692	21,817	21,787	−874.3	−30	−0.4	0.0
Mining	21	576.5	523.2	477.4	−53.3	−45.8	−1.0	−0.9
Subtotal		104,500	114,159	115,965	9,660	10,807	0.9	0.2
TOTAL, nonagricultural wage and salary		114,984	132,192	150,877	17,208	18,685	1.4	1.3
GRAND TOTAL		129,246	145,612	160,795	16,366	15,183	1.2	1.2

Source: Adapted from Berman (2005).

Note: Subcategories of industries sum to grand total because of chain weighting. See Berman (2005).

Table 3.3. Change and Growth in Charitable and Noncharitable Occupations

Occupation	Category	1983 (1,000s)	1999 (1,000s)	Change, 1983–99 (1,000s)	Percent change, 1983–99
Occupations with significant nonprofit penetration					
Managers: medicine and health	Health	91	716	625	686.8
Computer scientists	Information/Technology	276	1,549	1,273	461.2
Teachers' aides and early childhood education	Education	348	1,198	850	244.3
Recreation and related workers	Social Service	131	270	139	106.1
Social workers	Social Service	407	813	406	99.8
Administrators: education and related fields	Education	415	821	406	97.8
Athletes	Entertainment	58	110	52	89.7
Child care workers	Social Service	408	764	356	87.3
Managers: marketing and public relations	Financial	396	739	343	86.6
Social scientists	Professional—other	261	460	199	76.2
Health assessment and treatment (therapists, pharmacists)	Health	528	891	363	68.8
Natural scientists	Science	357	578	221	61.9
Teachers: higher education	Education	606	978	372	61.4
Mathematics scientists (not computer)	Information/Technology	187	298	111	59.4
Writers, authors, and entertainers	Entertainment	1,486	2,344	858	57.7

Teachers: pre-K through 12	Education	3,365	5,277	1,912	56.8
Registered nurses	Health	1,372	2,128	756	55.1
Health technologies	Health	1,111	1,701	590	53.1
Lawyers and judges	Law	651	964	313	48.1
Protective services (police, fire)	Protective services (police, fire)	1,672	2,440	768	45.9
Health diagnosing occupations (physicians, dentists)	Health	735	1,071	336	45.7
Health services (not doctors or nurses)	Health	1,739	2,521	782	45.0
Librarians	Education	193	264	71	36.8
Welfare aids	Social Service	77	97	20	26.0
Clergy	Social Service	293	352	59	20.1
Education counselors	Education	213	247	34	16.0
Computer equipment operators	Administrative support	605	356	−249	−41.2
Subtotal		17,981	29,947	11,966	66.5
Other occupations					
Adjustors and investigators	Administrative support	675	1,802	1,127	167.0

(continued)

Table 3.3. (Continued)

Occupation	Category	1983 (1,000s)	1999 (1,000s)	Change, 1983–99	Percent change, 1983–99
Data entry	Administrative support	311	746	435	139.9
Financial managers	Financial	357	753	396	110.9
Architects	Professional—other	103	194	91	88.3
Information clerks, including receptionists	Administrative support	1,174	2,143	969	82.5
Executive, administrative and managerial (other)	Professional—other	8,408	14,897	6,489	77.2
Accountants and auditors	Financial	1,105	1,658	553	50.0
Sales—other including supervisors and proprietors	Sales	6,331	9,267	2,936	46.4
Other technicians (engineering, science)	Other	1,942	2,654	712	36.7
Construction	Production	4,289	5,801	1,512	35.3
Engineers	Professional—other	1,572	2,081	509	32.4
Transportation and material moving occupations	Operators, fabricators, and laborers	4,201	5,516	1,315	31.3
Other administrative support	Administrative support	1,642	2,087	445	27.1
Handlers and laborers	Operators, fabricators, and laborers	4,147	5,265	1,118	27.0
Material recording, scheduling (dispatchers)	Administrative support	1,562	1,959	397	25.4
Food workers	Personal services—other	4,860	6,091	1,231	25.3
Sales workers—retail and personal services	Sales	5,511	6,866	1,355	24.6
Mail and message distribution occupations	Administrative support	799	990	191	23.9
Records processing	Administrative support	866	1,047	181	20.9

Mechanics	Production	4,158	4,868	710	17.1
Cleaning services	Personal services—other	2,736	3,021	285	10.4
Other personal services	Personal services—other	1,793	1,936	143	8.0
Precision production occupations	Production	3,685	3,793	108	2.9
Supervisors—administrative support	Administrative support	676	675	−1	−0.1
Statistical clerks	Administrative support	96	94	−2	−2.1
Machine operators	Operators, fabricators, and laborers	7,744	7,386	−358	−4.6
Other private household care workers	Personal services—other	572	536	−36	−6.3
Mail clerks	Administrative support	68	63	−5	−7.4
Farming	Farming	3,700	3,426	−274	−7.4
Financial recording keeping (book keeping, record clerks)	Administrative support	2,457	2,181	−276	−11.2
Secretaries	Administrative support	4,861	3,457	−1,404	−28.9
Extractive occupations	Production	196	130	−66	−33.7
Communications operators (i.e., telephone operators)	Administrative support	256	158	−98	−38.3
Subtotal		82,853	103,541	20,688	25.0
Total		100,834	133,488	32,654	32.4

Sources:
1983 and 1993 figures adopted from "Statistical Abstract of the United States, 1994," Table 637
1999 figures adopted from "Statistical Abstract of the United States, 2000," Table 669

Table 3.4. Change and Growth in Charitable and Noncharitable Occupations: 2004–2014

Occupation	Category	2004 (1,000s)	2014 (1,000s)	Change, 2004–2014	Percent change, 2004–2014
Occupations with significant nonprofit penetration					
Managers: medicine and health	Health	248	305	57	22.8
Computer scientists	Information/Technology	3048	4,003	957	31.4
Teachers' aides and early childhood education	Education	601	782	181	30.1
Recreation and related workers	Social service	514	623	104	21.2
Social workers	Social service	562	686	124	22.0
Administrators: education and related fields	Education	442	515	73	16.6
Athletes	Entertainment	17	21	4	21.1
Child care workers	Social service	1280	1456	176	13.8
Managers: marketing and public relations	Financial	646	777	131	20.3
Social scientists	Professional—other	492	580	88	17.9
Health assessment and treatment (therapists, pharmacists)	Health	739	934	195	26.3
Natural scientists	Science	482	561	79	16.3
Teachers: higher education	Education	1628	2153	524	32.2

Mathematics scientists (not computer)	Information/Technology	107	117	10	9.7
Writers, authors and entertainers	Entertainment	142	187	25	17.7
Teachers: pre-k through 12	Education	4,270	5,051	781	18.3
Registered nurses	Health	2,394	3,096	703	29.4
Health technologies	Health	2,494	3,086	592	23.7
Lawyers and judges	Law	783	897	114	14.6
Protective services (police, fire)	Protective services (police, fire)	3,138	3,578	440	14.0
Health diagnosing occupations (physicians, dentists)	Health	717	873	156	21.7
Health services (not doctors or nurses)	Health	3,492	4,656	1164	33.3
Librarians	Education	159	167	8	4.4
Welfare aids	Social service	352	456	104	29.7
Clergy	Social service	422	474	52	21.4
Education counselors	Education	248	285	37	14.8
Computer equipment operators	Administrative support	149	101	-49	-32.6
Subtotal		29,566	36,420	6,854	23.2
All occupations		145,612	164,540	18928	13.0

Source: Hecker (2005).

either for-profit businesses or nonprofit organizations. Entrepreneurial skills are also portable between the nonprofit and for-profit sectors.

To offer a concrete illustration, compare a world where the typical industry is based in manufacturing, such as steel, to one where it is based on information goods, such as information technology and communication. In the former environment, the worker or manager of a steel company might live a divided life: making steel during the day and then going home and putting on his civic (i.e., nonprofit) hat. The inputs needed to make steel likely differ from those required to provide charitable services, as do the outputs of the two activities. In such a setting, a potential entrepreneur with a charitable impulse would be well advised to focus first on amassing wealth by engaging in the for-profit activity (steel manufacture) and then using such wealth to support charitable activities.

This situation may be contrasted with the case of a modern-day firm producing information goods and services. Because forms of intellectual capital figure heavily as both inputs and outputs for such enterprises, the inputs and outputs in the for-profit sector may be quite similar to those in the not-for-profit activity. Marketing and computer skills are also more likely to cut across sectors. Thus, changes in the economy create an environment in which it is only natural for nonprofit entrepreneurs to found for-profit ventures, for workers in profit-making firms to handle their nonprofit activities on the phone during the day, and for managers in both types of organizations to look to each other for ideas, sources of partnership and cooperation, and opportunities to compete.

Changes in Government Policy

Changes in government policy have in some cases reinforced these shifts in the economy. One is the move toward third-party government in which many public responsibilities are shared by government with a range of nongovernmental actors (Salamon 2002).

The third-party government model has increased opportunities for nonprofits and for-profits, acting jointly and separately, to provide government services. Government has influenced the business–nonprofit relationship through its increased tendency to contract out work. Steuerle and Hodgkinson (2006) document how the decline in government employment in recent decades is matched by an increase in nonprofit-sector employment. Because charitable contributions have not increased as a percentage of GDP during this time and government spending has not decreased, the nonprofit employment growth can be traced to government's increased tendency to contract out work.

The clearest case, of course, is health care. Medicare and Medicaid tend to contract with doctors and hospitals to provide services to patients. But government has also attempted more and more to contract out all sorts of activities ranging from social services to the running of prisons. This expansion of government activity often leads to expansions of nonprofit activity, which then can prompt entry and competition from for-profit firms. Such privatization also tends to create revenue streams for which some reporting on outputs and performance measurement is required, leading further to nonprofit organizations adopting businesslike attributes.

In addition, tax policy, which has traditionally served as the principal mechanism for defining the legal boundaries between nonprofit (tax-exempt) activity and for-profit (taxable) activity has shown itself to be quite flexible in permitting a wide variety of organizational arrangements involving traditional nonprofits and various profit-making ventures. These issues are taken up in more detail in chapter 4.

Issues Raised

As with any new development, exploitation of the organizational arbitrage possibilities at the boundaries is not without costs alongside the benefits. A major issue is the potential impact of organizational arbitrage on the credibility of the nondistribution constraint.

In many respects, it has been the presence of a credible nondistribution constraint that gives the nonprofit organizational form its distinctive economic character, which is the source of many of its advantages. Does the increased adoption of business practices and development of commercial activity reduce this advantage? It mainly depends upon the institutions and actors involved.

It has never been clear that the absence of a profit motive has prevented some people from exploiting charity for their own private gain. There have always been strong economic incentives for the stakeholders in nonprofits—such as wage earners, managers, and lenders—to seek to appropriate any surplus and, at times, convert charitable contributions into forms of private inurement. To the extent that businesslike practices become the norm rather than the exception among nonprofits, the scope of such self-interested behavior is likely to grow. But paradoxically, as this becomes known, the economic value of imposing the nondistribution constraint may also decline if people determine that a legal nonprofit is simply a for-profit in disguise (Weisbrod 1998). Attempts to wrestle with this issue have, for example, motivated the IRS to establish guidelines for determining the tax consequences for the nonprofit partner in a joint venture with a for-profit partner in the hospital sector. As Brody discusses in the next chapter, the guidance provided is that to preserve its status as a 501(c)(3) organization, the nonprofit participant must ensure that the joint venture (a) furthers the organization's charitable purpose, (b) permits the exempt organization to act exclusively in the pursuit of its charitable mission, and (c) is not primarily formed for the benefit of the for-profit partners. Such guidelines, while reasonable in principle, may be complex to administer and monitor in practice.

Future Trends and Policy Issues

There are several trends that favor further movement on the continuum away from pure nonprofit form. Among the economic factors that have been identified are the following:

- Shifting demand of society toward goods and services with attributes similar to charitable outputs
- Shifting of inputs and human skills toward activities that are valuable in either sector
- Changing attitudes about how nonprofits should behave
- Changing attitudes about how for-profits should behave

As with the mythical story of King Canute trying to turn back the ocean, it may make little sense for public policy to buck economic and social forces that are beyond government control. Rather, the task facing both tax and regulatory policy will be to monitor the performance of organizations, both individually and collectively, to achieve the best social outcome however hard that is to define. This task has become more challenging because it no longer reduces to a simple question of monitoring the behavior of a traditional nonprofit. It now includes mon-

itoring nonprofit–for-profit hybrid organizations, along with commercial activities within nonprofit organizations, to ensure a proper balance
between mission and pursuit of revenue to finance mission among entities that benefit from the use of the charitable or "501(c)(3)" brand.
Future challenges may arise as more for-profit enterprises become
involved in social goods.

Examples of Nonprofit– For-Profit Hybrid Business Models

Joseph J. Cordes, Zina Poletz, and C. Eugene Steuerle

Traditional Job Training Model

Job training programs for less-employable populations are among the oldest and most common types of social entrepreneurship organization. These nonprofit organizations set up and run for-profit businesses to provide the populations they serve with the opportunity to learn and practice marketable skills in a real-world setting. Revenues from the businesses are plowed back into the nonprofits, which generally also offer support services such as counseling, substance abuse treatment, and education to the clients/employees.

An example of a job-training nonprofit is the Delancey Street Foundation, a round-the-clock, long-term residential and work facility to rehabilitate former drug addicts and alcoholics. Founder Mimi Silbert began the organization in 1972 with the philosophy that antisocial behavior can only be changed in a mutually supportive, rigidly structured, totally self-sufficient environment in which individual responsibility is the paramount value.

While living in a "family" environment, clients are required to learn three marketable skills, earn a general equivalency diploma, and help other residents master life skills. Delancey Street's for-profit businesses are training schools for the clients to learn job skills. Clients work in the following businesses: moving company, restaurant and catering service, print and copy shop, Christmas tree sales and decorating, automotive service center, and retail or wholesale sales. Each company is managed as a subprogram of the organization's overall rehabilitation program. In 2000, revenues from the businesses accounted for 23 percent of total revenues. The organization records an additional 23 percent of revenue as the wages that workers would otherwise be paid; in the program, clients receive food, clothing, and shelter, but no wages. The remaining revenue comes from private contributions, government contributions, and interest.

Pioneer Human Services takes a slightly different approach. It was founded in 1962 by a disbarred lawyer upon his release from prison. It helps high-risk populations build a work history and realize personal, economic, and social development. Instead of an all-encompassing "family business," Pioneer reflects its white-collar roots with long-term corporate partnerships (especially Boeing and Starbucks), zero tolerance for drugs or alcohol, pay-for-performance compensation policies, and product quality. Pioneer's motto is "Chance for Change," and to offer its clients the best chance, the organization provides various support services such as substance abuse treatment, prison work release, youth and family counseling, and housing. Programs include support services and "enterprises," namely, the organization's businesses, in manufacturing, laser and water-jet cutting, aerospace machining, silk screening, food buying, subassembly, institutional catering, construction, and property management. Pioneer also owns and operates a café and deli at the Starbucks headquarters and the St. Regis Hotel in Seattle.

Pioneer receives 62 percent of its total revenues from sales of products and services, with another 29 percent coming from government contracts, such as prison work release. Less than 0.5 percent of total revenues are from contributions.

A third variant of the job-training program appears at Juma Ventures, a much newer organization, founded in 1993 in San Francisco to provide jobs and services to young people. Juma's businesses are Ben & Jerry's franchises—several stores in San Francisco, a Ben & Jerry's ice cream cart, and concessions at two sports arenas. The Ben & Jerry's businesses are program expenses of Juma Ventures. Juma also supplements the jobs with optional education programs, including financial management training, resume writing, college tours, and two collaborations with corporations. Collaboration with Citibank provides bank accounts and financial literacy for high school students, and a program with Merrill Lynch provides financial mentorship.

Juma Ventures' sales revenues are only 18.5 percent of total revenues, and contributions make up 68.8 percent of total revenues. The organization puts less emphasis on jobs and spends more on the additional programs, in part because it is competing with every other business that provides food service jobs for youths; the optional educational programs differentiate Juma jobs from just any job.

Relation of Mission and Income-Producing Activities

The many job-training programs in existence today speak to the underlying logic of organizing a nonprofit around business activities, as opposed to or in addition to receiving government grants or private contributions to teach classes in job skills to these populations. The programs emphasize the duality of the client worker's role, which is especially manifest in Delancey Street's motto, "each one teaches one." Pioneer and Minnesota Diversified Industries (a similarly organized manufacturing and packaging plant employing disabled and disadvantaged workers) both stress leadership training among their client workers, try to foster a sense of teamwork, and emphasize the quality of the products they create. Minnesota Diversified Industries boasts of its three plants' 99 percent efficiency rates and is ISO 9000 and 9001 certified. Clearly, an implicit part of the training is generated from the fact that the clients work in actual businesses with customers who have real expectations of quality. The assumption is that this situation provides clients with a more meaningful experience than training alone or a "workfare" program that requires some welfare recipients to work. These organizations' literature cites the attitude changes and self-esteem of clients as a function of their having a "real job."

Organizational Structure

The job-training programs described above have created affiliates or subsidiaries to increase the amount of mission-related work they can accomplish. Delancey Street's is the simplest. It has small affiliates in different geographic regions, one in New Mexico and one in North Carolina. These affiliates offer the exact same program and are set up the same way. The only difference is that they are able to reduce the cost of administration through centralization; each affiliate pays the main office an annual management fee for accounting and other administrative services.

Minnesota Diversified Industries follows a different model. Three related 501(c)(3) organizations each perform a specific function. Minnesota Diversified Industries is the administrative arm of the organization and provides all maintenance of equipment and facilities. MDI Commercial Services is a sheltered workshop for socially disadvantaged individuals that manufactures products and sells them to MDI Government, which employs 600–800 handicapped individuals who produce the products sold to the government.

Juma Ventures attempted to leverage the number of jobs it can provide youths by launching the Enterprise Center, a business incubator for socially responsible businesses. The idea was to help for-profit entrepreneurs get started in exchange for good jobs for youths down the road. Because operating franchises is a time-consuming process that requires a lot of for-profit management skills, Juma's management decided to expand its reach in this way. Two businesses have emerged from the Enterprise Center so far. One, Big Help, was an outsource provider of technical support. In addition to providing office space and utilities, Juma Ventures was also a first-round investor in Big Help. A second business was the Evergreen Lodge in Yosemite National Park. At-risk youths were recruited to stay and work in hospitality, recreation, or construction for a season. Juma discovered that relinquishing control over an enterprise also meant relinquishing control over risk. Big Help has already closed its doors. Evergreen Lodge is profitable, however, and continues to hire youths through Juma.

Pioneer Human Services also decided to leverage the number of jobs it could offer by investing in other businesses. It created a for-profit investment fund, Pioneer Social Ventures LLC, in 1999 to allow Pioneer access to private equity from investors interested in supporting the goals of community reinvestment while receiving a reasonable rate of return. Pioneer committed $1.5 million, or 35 percent, to the $4.4 million fund; other investors include banks, development corporations, and foundations. In return for the investment, Pioneer Social Ventures was to acquire businesses in which Pioneer Human Services would train and employ its clients. Pioneer Human Services would be the managing partner of this fund.

Nonprofit Ventures and Social Entrepreneurship

Some nonprofit ventures earn money while achieving their mission, which provides them with more revenue to make further progress on their mission.

Benetech was deliberately formed as a nonprofit venture under the social entrepreneurship model, on the proceeds of the sale of a previous nonprofit venture called Arkenstone. Arkenstone was a 501(c)(3) nonprofit and the world's leading maker for 10 years of reading machines for the blind. During this period, more than 99 percent of the organization's budget came from sales of its products—at a fair price—directly to blind people or to groups serving the visually impaired. Proceeds from Arkenstone's sale to a for-profit company were used to create a new organization, one that would expand on Arkenstone's mission beyond the disability field, to apply technology toward the solution of various social problems.

Benetech's business model was to be an incubator, providing project ideas with seed capital for market and technical feasibility studies, and the necessary infrastructure to bring the products to market. Benetech planned to replicate its success with Arkenstone by developing new technologies, building a market for them, and then selling the technologies to for-profit companies that can build and disseminate them efficiently and affordably. Often, research costs for technologies that serve a limited market prohibit private companies from getting involved in the development stage of a socially valuable product. Instead of grant proposals, Benetech leaders approached large donors with business plans with detailed budgets and quantifiable benchmarks. All of Benetech's projects emphasized a strong social, rather than financial, return on investment; however, they were meant to eventually reach a level of financial self-sustainability.

Some Benetech projects in development have included a subscription-based, online talking library, software for documenting and disseminating information on human rights abuses, a wireless handheld device that allows the visually impaired to use ATMs and vending machines, landmine detection technology, literacy tools for children with autism and Down syndrome, open-source desktop applications for people in developing countries too poor to buy software, and other innovative technological solutions.

The Green Institute, a neighborhood-based, entrepreneurial group focusing on greening projects, has also used technology in pursuit of its mission. Projects have included pollution prevention and sustainable transportation in the inner-city neighborhood where the Green Institute was founded in 1993 by local activists in response to the proposed construction of a solid waste transfer station.

The Green Institute's programs have provided a model for sustainable development activities nationwide. Its programs have included the following:

- Phillips Eco-Enterprise Center. A green commercial-industrial building located on the site originally intended for a garbage transfer station. The facility has health, energy, and material efficiency features, including 100 percent storm water retention and salvaged and recycled construction materials. Among the center's objectives has been to provide high-quality jobs for neighborhood residents.
- Green Resource Center. Housed in the Phillips building, the Green Resource Center has provided materials and design tools on green technologies and related practices in residential and commercial building.
- Re-Use Center. A 26,000-square-foot retail store selling salvaged building and construction materials so that hundreds of thousands of tons of reusable construction materials could be kept out of landfills.
- Deconstruction Services. Neighborhood workers dismantle buildings by hand to salvage materials. Deconstructed materials are then sold on site and at the Re-Use Center.

Relation of Mission and Revenue-Producing Activities

The two above-mentioned organizations are truly nonprofit businesses with a double bottom line. In both cases, the organizations provide socially valuable products and services at a market price, and achieving some measure of a financial return is a prerequisite for a continued social return. Benetech's business model relied almost exclusively on product sales, whereas the Green Institute received half its revenues from public support (mainly construction materials donated from dismantled buildings) and half from earned income. In each case, these organizations charged users for the cost of providing these services to remain viable. *However, these socially beneficial organizational models may not generate enough income to make sense as for-profit businesses.* Thus, the social and financial aspects of these two organizations support each other.

Organizational Structure

Benetech is the umbrella name for three organizations. Beneficent Inc. and Beneficent Technologies are 501(c)(3) public charities. There is also a wholly owned for-profit subsidiary, an engineering firm called Bengineering. The Green Institute consists of one 501(c)(3) public charity.

The two organizations have different missions but many underlying similarities. Both have been involved in the dissemination of technology. Both sell products and services that have legitimate monetary value to their users, who also have the means to pay for them. In both cases, the user's consumption of the product or service produced a socially desirable, mission-related outcome. Neither organization would have been likely to survive on contributions alone because of the nature of its mission. Their accomplishments are unlikely to tug at the heartstrings of most contributors. In the case of the Green Institute, there is a natural constituency of potential donors—neighborhood residents, who also happen to be the natural customer base for the Re-Use Center and Deconstruction Services. Benetech has not even accepted donations of less than $25,000 because it doesn't want the administrative burden of processing them. Most of its financial contributions have come from technology companies. Benetech does solicit contributions of time and expertise from technical specialists, entrepreneurs, and inventors.

Nonprofit Conglomerates

Other organizations are best described as nonprofit conglomerates. For example, New Community Corporation (NCC), a large community development corporation, claims to have held assets valued at more than $500 million and served 50,000 people in Newark's Central Ward every day. New Community offered a comprehensive array of services to its target population, including 3,000 housing units, commercial and residential real estate development, a homeless shelter, domestic violence shelter, charter schools and parochial schools, a credit union, a nursing home, medical centers, and counseling.

New Community also owned and managed a number of for-profit businesses in the Central Ward, including Priory Restaurant; a Pathmark supermarket; Dunkin' Donuts; NCC Neighborhood Shopping Center; The World of Foods food court, which housed Pizza Hut, Nathan's, Taco Bell, and NCC's Southern Kitchen; and the NCC Print & Copy Shop and Fashion Institute, which produces garments, upholstery, and uniforms. Not only did these businesses provide revenue for NCC's community-based programs, but they also benefited Central Ward residents by bringing valuable services and jobs into a depressed inner-city area. For example, the Pathmark supermarket returned 67 percent of its profits to NCC programs.

Another example examined here is Housing Works, which has provided housing, health care, advocacy, and social services to homeless New Yorkers living with HIV and AIDS. Its services include three clinics, four housing development funds, a thrift shop operation, and food services. Its Social Development Ventures Program housed all of the earned income strategies that Housing Works used. The ventures also provided the organization's clients with employment opportunities. Housing Works ran three thrift shops, a used book café, an institutional food service and catering business, and Gotham Assets property development and management company. In 2000, Housing Works received 34.1 percent of total revenue from earned income; its main source of revenue was Medicaid (47.8 percent).

Yet another example is the Manchester-Bidwell Corporation. Founder Bill Strickland was one of the first people in the country to identify himself as a social entrepreneur. In 1996, he received a genius grant from the MacArthur Foundation for his innovation. In 2001, Manchester-Bidwell ran two schools in Pittsburgh. Bidwell Training Center provided adult vocational training, and Manchester Craftsman's Guild offered a multicultural arts program for at-risk high-school students, a visual arts classes for adults, and a jazz concert series. Manchester-Bidwell programs have been quite entrepreneurial, with multiple sources of earned income. In 2001, ventures included cafeteria sales, program fees, jazz concert ticket sales, a jazz festival, CD sales from its own record label, and fees from classes and catering. Additionally, a subsidiary owned and managed an office building. In 2001, the corporation received 28.3 percent of total revenue from earned income. Its main source of revenue (63.5 percent) was from government grants.

Organizational Structure

Although the missions and activities of these three organizations are different, their underlying operating structures reveal many similarities. All three had relatively large holdings in real estate. All engaged in intercompany payables and receivables with numerous affiliates and subsidiaries, both for-profit and nonprofit. The organizations within the conglomerate shared board members. In each case, a parent organization provided administrative services to the subsidiaries, which performed separate program and management functions. The organizations actively tweaked their structures in response to changing conditions, adding new subsidiaries and shutting down ones that were no longer necessary.

In the case of New Community Corporation, NCC was the parent corporation, providing administrative services and coordinating the activities of 14 tax-exempt (nonprofit) affiliates and 33 nonexempt affiliates, all with interlocking ownership structures. Within this organizational structure, the nonprofits maintained partial or total ownership of the for-profit subsidiaries, invested in outside partnerships, and showed millions of dollars in intercompany receivables and payables on their balance sheets. Internally, New Community was organized into 13 programmatic and administrative departments. The subsidiaries and affiliates reported to the parent company along functional lines.

Housing Works was organized along the same lines as New Community, but on a smaller scale. The parent company provided management services to 11 nonprofit subsidiaries, organized by borough and programmatic function. In 2002, Housing Works started its first potential for-profit venture, an AIDS advocacy consulting firm. It was still considered an operating program of Housing Works, but there were plans to spin it off as a separate, but affiliated, entity.

Manchester-Bidwell Corporation was made up of a dynamic mix of nonprofit affiliates and for-profit subsidiaries.

- Bidwell Training Center and Manchester Craftsmen's Guild were the two affiliates that provided program services.
- Manchester-Bidwell Corporation provided Bidwell and Manchester with administrative services.
- Manchester-Bidwell Development Trust was organized to establish an endowment to sustain the programs of Bidwell and Manchester.
- Bidwell Industrial Development Corporation was merged into Manchester-Bidwell Corporation in 2001; its original function was to provide technical assistance to minority-owned enterprises in economically disadvantaged areas.
- Bidwell Food Services was a for-profit catering company that was liquidated in 2001.
- Harbor Gardens Park was a for-profit subsidiary of Bidwell Training Center, which owned and managed an office building.
- Denali Institute was founded in 2002 to develop the next generation of social entrepreneurs. Courses of study included a one-year executive education program and a three-year fellowship.

Relation of Mission and Revenue-Producing Activities

Each of these three entities engaged in a wide range of loosely related social services and for-profit ventures in pursuit of its mission. In the case of New Community, the for-profit ventures furthered the mission of community development by providing needed services and jobs in the neighborhood. Possibly, without NCC's involvement, business and franchise owners would not choose to locate in the Central Ward. On the other hand, Housing Works used its ventures primarily to increase its revenue stream, although the jobs created for HIV-positive adults also contributed to its mission. Finally, Manchester-Bidwell's entrepreneurial organizational culture reflected the thinking and optimism of its founder and the belief in unlimited opportunity that he sought to impart to his students.

There are other reasons, not necessarily related to mission, for an entity to organize itself into a conglomerate. It is a very fluid organizational structure, allowing resources to flow between affiliates. Creating separate affiliated entities gives an organization leeway to engage in activities that may be only peripherally related to its stated mission or to experiment with new program areas. Also, creating a for-profit subsidiary ensures that the organization will not lose tax-exempt status in case of substantial unrelated business income. At the same time, because the administration function remains fairly centralized, the loose program structure remains cost-effective.

Image management is another reason for a high-profit entity to construct a network of for-profit subsidiaries and obscurely named nonprofit affiliates. In the case of Manchester-Bidwell Corporation, the administrative costs displayed on the Forms 990 of Manchester Craftsmen's Guild and Bidwell Training School appeared as a very low percentage of total expenses (16.9 percent and 13.3 percent, respectively, in 2000). In fact, the separate Manchester-Bidwell Corporation existed to provide administrative services, and another organization was set up to raise money for the endowment, effectively transferring fundraising expenses for the organization as a whole into support program expenses.

High executive salaries can be divided among several organizations to make them seem more palatable. For example, Bill Strickland's salary was divided among three affiliates, with the bulk allocated to the low-profile Manchester-Bidwell Corporation. In the case of an entity with for-profit subsidiaries, executive salaries need not be reported on the returns of the affiliated nonprofits. None of the 501(c)(3) affiliates of New Community Corporation with Forms 990 available at GuideStar.org listed *any* executive salaries. Another well-publicized example of transferring executive compensation to wholly owned, for-profit subsidiaries took place in 1995 when a state legislator called on the Minnesota attorney general to investigate the salary of Minnesota Public Radio's president, Bill Kling. For a time, Kling refused to disclose his salary from that organization's for-profit affiliate.

Corporate Quid Pro Quo

The financial statements of a quid pro quo organization look identical to those of a traditional charity. A high percentage of revenue is reported as contributions, with little or no revenue from program services or sales. The similarity disappears, however, when one examines the activities used to generate those contributions. Quid pro quo organizations generate the majority of their revenue from cause-related marketing. In return for corporate contributions, these charities offer businesses marketing opportunities. It is a win-win situation; the charity is able to finance its mission-related activities with a relatively low investment of time and money spent on fundraising, while the corporation reaps the benefits of having its name linked to a worthy cause, creating a public perception of its civic-mindedness and a boost to employee morale.

First Book is a small organization with a big impact. In 2001, with a staff of only 14, First Book distributed 7 million new books to hundreds of thousands of low-income children nationwide by developing local advisory boards in each of the 700 participating communities to identify local literacy programs, distribute books, and hold special events. The organization also raised $34.7 million toward its mission while spending just over 1 percent of that amount on administration and fundraising through sponsorship and marketing agreements with corporations, nonprofits, and government entities.

First Book has worked closely with its partners to create memorable cause-based marketing campaigns that "drive traffic, increase sales, and build brand awareness for [the] . . . partners."[2] Often the campaigns involve the participation of several partners. For example, Universal Studios partnered with First Book for the release of its movie *How the Grinch Stole Christmas*.

One of the keys to First Book's success has been the close relationships it has developed with five major children's book publishers; their presidents serve on its board of directors, and the companies provide discounts on books, free shipping, and other goods for First Book recipient groups.

Whereas First Book had dozens of national and local partnerships, City Year has relied on a handful of major sponsors to support its work. City Year calls itself an action tank for national service, promoting the concept of national service by maintaining a year-long youth service corps in 13 cities nationwide, through large-scale community events, and by hosting an annual convention and policy forum on the power of national service.

City Year's largest source of revenue in 2001 was the federal government's Corporation for National Service, which provided 33 percent of City Year's total revenue through the AmeriCorps Program. Corporate contributions provided an additional 29.6 percent of total revenue. Four corporate sponsors each contributed at least $1 million in cash or in-kind contributions. For instance, the Timberland Company's support of City Year's programs included cash and in-kind donations and volunteering from the very highest levels down. Timberland's CEO served as City Year's board chair. Timberland's global headquarters housed the offices of City Year New Hampshire, and the company outfitted City Year corps members nationwide with uniforms, boots, and gear in addition to sponsoring various national service events and supporting City Year's international efforts in South Africa.

Timberland has received national recognition for its socially responsible corporate culture, which is a reputation that enhances its brand of outdoor gear. Another valuable benefit of its investment in the work of City Year has been high employee morale. Timberland has made clear that its culture includes a commitment to service and social justice. That commitment translates into employee involvement with City Year programs. All employees receive 40 hours of paid leave each year for community service. Timberland's CEO, Jeffrey Swartz, has emphasized that his company's service culture provides a differentiating advantage and improves the bottom line.

Organizational Structure

City Year and First Book were highly leveraged organizations that were very efficient at accomplishing mission-related work with a minimum of infrastructure and staff. They accomplished this by providing corporate sponsors with the opportunity to visibly associate with their popular, uplifting causes in exchange for resources. The volunteer time, expertise, products, and services that they received furthered the mission.

Although quid pro quo social entrepreneurs may look like the typical charitable nonprofit in their financial statements and in their simple organizational structure, they are markedly different in their staff composition. Instead of a large program staff with a small administrative department, these organizations' employees work primarily in marketing and outreach. For example, in 2001, First Book's staff of 14 included 6 positions in community development, 2 in corporate strategy, a senior vice president of national outreach, and a manager of national partnership initiatives. City Year had a larger program staff because it managed a far-flung operation of volunteer corps, but its staff also included such positions as director of national corporate partnerships.

Relation of Mission and Revenue-Producing Activities

Good corporate citizenship is a valuable differentiating factor for companies struggling to define and project their brand in a sophisticated, highly competitive marketplace. Brand is useful for attracting and retaining talented employees and loyal customers. During the economic boom of the late 1990s, companies realized that it was important to offer workers not only pay and benefits but also a positive feeling about their work. Companies that engaged in cause-related marketing were able to provide employees with opportunities to make a difference and volunteer for the company's chosen cause, thereby building morale.

Corporate quid pro quo social entrepreneurs have capitalized on the benefits that for-profits can gain by sponsoring nonprofit activities, thereby providing companies with a chance to be perceived as good corporate citizens. It is a classic example of gains from trade—each party benefits from the exchange, as do company employees and the beneficiaries of the mission-related work. These nonprofits act almost as administrative headquarters, delegating program operations to volunteers, while they focus on providing value to the sponsors in the form of marketing opportunities and publicity.

NOTES

1. BlendedValue.org, 2006. http://www.blendedvalue.org.
2. First Book Annual Report 2000–2001.

REFERENCES

Berman, Jay M. 2005. "Industry Output and Employment Projections to 2014." *Monthly Labor Review* (November): 45–69.

Bilodeau, Mark, and Al Slavinski. 1998. "Rational Nonprofit Entrepreneurship." *Journal of Economics and Management Strategy* 7(4): 551–71.

Cordes, Joseph, C. Eugene Steuerle, and Eric Twombly. 2004. "Dimensions of Nonprofit Entrepreneurship: An Exploratory Essay." In *Public Policy and the Economics of Entrepreneurship,* edited by Douglas Holtz-Eakin and Harvey Rosen. Cambridge, MA: MIT Press.

Cutler, Ira. 2005. *The Double Bottom Line: Lessons on Social Enterprise from Seedco's Nonprofit Venture Network 2001–2004.* New York: Seedco.

Foster, William, and Jeffrey Bradach. 2005. "Should Nonprofits Seek Profits?" *Harvard Business Review* 83(2): 92–100.

Glaeser, Edward, and Andre Schleifer. 1998. "Not for Profit Entrepreneurs." Working Paper 6810. Cambridge, MA: National Bureau of Economic Research.

Hecker, Daniel. 2005. "Occupational Employment Projections to 2014." *Monthly Labor Review* (November): 70–101.

James, Estelle. 2003. "Commercialism and the Mission of Nonprofits." *Society* 40(4): 29–35.

Sagawa, Shirley, and Elias Segal. 2000. "Common Interest, Common Good: Creating Value through Business and Social Sector Partnerships." *California Management Review* 42(2): 105–22.

Salamon, Lester. 2002. *The Tools of Government: A Guide to the New Governance.* Oxford: Oxford University Press.

Steuerle, C. Eugene, and Virginia A. Hodgkinson. 2006. "Meeting Social Needs: Comparing Independent Sector and Government Resources." In *Nonprofits and Government: Collaboration and Conflict,* edited by Elizabeth T. Boris and C. Eugene Steuerle (81–106). Washington, DC: Urban Institute Press.

Thomson, Allison. 1999. "Industry Output and Employment Projections to 2008." http://stats.bls.gov/opub/mlr/1999/11/art4full.pdf.

Tuckman, Howard, and Cyril Chang. 2006. "Commercial Activity: Technological Change and Nonprofit Mission." In *The Nonprofit Sector: A Research Handbook,* edited by Walter W. Powell and Richard Steinberg (629–45). New Haven, CT: Yale University Press.

Weisbrod, Burton A., ed. 1998. *To Profit or Not to Profit: The Commercial Transformation of the Nonprofit Sector.* New York: Cambridge University Press.

4

Business Activities of Nonprofit Organizations
Legal Boundary Problems

Evelyn Brody

U nderlying the title of this chapter is a core conundrum: "business" is not a useful term for distinguishing the legal regime that applies to nonprofit organizations from the legal regime that applies to for-profit entities. Nonprofit organizations have never been prohibited by law from engaging in commercial activities that further a nonprofit purpose. (Indeed, for this reason, some states designate these entities as "not-for-profit.") To many observers—and to for-profit competitors—nonprofit hospitals, day care centers, research facilities, multiunit housing, and theaters seem very much to be businesses. (See Brown and Slivinski 2006; Tuckman and Chang 2006.) As a separate matter, nonprofit organizations have dense ties with the business sector, not only as purchasers of goods and services, but also as joint venturers with and creators of for-profit affiliates. Add to this mix the extensive holdings in publicly traded corporations (and private equity capital) in university endowments and other nonprofit portfolios, and one can appreciate the complex role of nonprofits in the American economy.

For better or worse, the strongest legal constraints appear in the federal tax code. Indeed, the debate over how to treat business activities of nonprofit organizations is most clearly illustrated by the striking reversal in federal tax policy in 1950. Before Congress adopted the unrelated business income tax, profits produced by business activities of tax-exempt organizations could escape income tax under the "destination of income test"—that is, no tax applied to an income stream devoted to exempt purposes. The Revenue Act of 1950, however, instead focused on the type of commercial activity: Income from a business activity that is substantially related—aside from producing funds—to the exempt purposes of the organization is still tax exempt, but income from an unrelated trade or business is subject to normal corporate (or trust) tax. However, most forms of passive investment income, such as dividends, interest, rents, and royalties, remain exempt.

Overall, the legal framework for nonprofit business activity divides into three distinct (although sometimes conceptually overlapping) areas, which this chapter takes in order. First, the appropriate legal treatment for the business activities of a nonprofit organization often depends on the industry in which that nonprofit operates, and rarely does the law fence in or fence out nonprofits from particular industries. For example, the day-to-day operations of a nonprofit hospital are governed largely by laws that apply to health care organizations, both at the state and federal level, regardless of whether those hospitals are nonprofit, for-profit, or public. (Coverage of general law—such as contracts, employment, or tort law—and industry regulation, despite their importance, is beyond the scope of this chapter.[1])

Second, state laws define and regulate the formation and governance of nonprofit organizations, most commonly nonprofit corporations. As we will see, though, nonprofit corporation law has surprisingly little to say about business activity as such. (This chapter will not address fiduciary duties in detail, because they apply to all aspects of governing nonprofits.) Third, tax requirements—specifically, the federal and state rules for tax-exempt entities—provide the largest set of constraints on what nonprofits can and cannot do or, when they can do them, and whether the activities remain tax-exempt.

This chapter concludes by looking forward, considering the possible effects of piecemeal or fundamental substantive and tax legal reform. In recent years, proponents of social enterprise have asserted that business activity conducted by charities no longer meaningfully separates into mission related (such as education by a university or health care services by a hospital) and unrelated (such as university alumni travel tours).

Fundamentally, the law constitutes only a small portion of the powerful institutional forces that legitimate, and in many cases dictate and sanction (in both the sense of approving and disciplining), the behavior of nonprofit organizations and the people that deal with them. (See

Brody 1996b.) Indeed, constraints on behavior can result not from regulation or tax benefit but from agreement: a nonprofit—or a business corporation, for that matter—can limit the activities it engages in, either from commitment to a particular mission or by contract (such as the terms of government or foundation grants).

Organizational Form for Business Activity

Americans' propensity to form associations requires a great variety of transacting and formal organization. However, since early in American history, the law and social institutions did not distinguish between public and private entities, or even between nonprofit and proprietary ones (Hall 1992). Although each of the traditional three sectors undeniably stakes out discrete cores, there is no ideal sector for any particular collective activity (Brody 1996b). Many activities have, in various times and in various places, been produced in each sector, and often the same types of activities— although perhaps not identical—are produced simultaneously in more than one sphere.[2] Brown and Slivinski comment that "most studies find that organizations of different forms that operate in mixed industries behave differently in at least some (measured) dimensions" (2006, 154).

History admonishes us that it is futile to prevent proprietary businesses from entering traditionally nonprofit (or even public) areas, or to prevent the commercialization of nonprofit activity. Fee-generation has grown up, with its own scholarly rationales. James and Young (2006) describe how prices "efficiently allocate scarce goods and services to those who value them most"; "clients may take [services] more seriously if they have to pay, and staff may give their clients more serious attention if they know they are paying customers"; and "charging a nominal fee may help remove a stigma associated with 'charity.' " Howard Tuckman (chapter 5) observes that organizational form is a tool—for example, the nonprofit form might be driven by the choice of an activity that cannot support itself in the market, other than the market for donations.

Some governmental programs contain set-asides for nonprofit organizations (Smith 2006). However, the current scandal over credit-counseling agencies illustrates how legislatures can be tempted into mandating that certain activities with social value must be, and can only be, engaged in by entities organized as nonprofit organizations.[3] Some states require credit-counseling agencies to be nonprofit to protect consumers and then sue those that step over the line by overly enriching their founders. Similarly, in the view of the Internal Revenue Service (IRS), "some credit counseling organizations have moved from their original purposes, that is, to counsel and educate troubled debtors, to inappropriately enrolling debtors in proprietary debt-management plans and credit-repair schemes for a fee."[4] Despite this experience, under the 2005 federal bankruptcy law, a qualified credit-counseling agency must be nonprofit—although evidently not necessarily tax exempt—and in 2006, Congress tightened the requirements for exemption under Internal Revenue Code (IRC) section 501(c)(3) for credit counseling and debt management services.[5]

The two largest and most visible commercial subsectors are higher education and hospitals, but these industries also most clearly illustrate the blurred sectoral boundaries. With varying degrees of regret, modern university presidents predominantly see themselves as administrators rather than scholars. (See Selingo 2005, summarizing a survey revealing a focus on financial issues.) The "university–industrial complex" has replaced the "military–industrial complex" as the black-hole concentration of power in the political economy.

The evolution of the American hospital is even more striking. Modern nonprofit hospitals depend little on contributions: third-party reimbursements such as Medicare, Medicaid, and private insurance can make hospital operations self-sustaining. Similar economic forces (increasing costs and competition) cause nonprofit hospitals and for-profit hospitals to resemble each other. Most unsettling to the public—and to state and federal charity regulators—was the recent wave of sales of nonprofit hospitals to investor-owned chains. A majority of states adopted nonprofit hospital conversion statutes to prevent, among other adverse effects, improper financial benefit to private persons from the transaction. Complicating matters are the joint operating agreements sometimes found between a nonprofit hospital and a proprietary company. As discussed below, the IRS is struggling with the appropriate limits on "whole hospital joint ventures" and joint operating agreements between nonprofit hospitals and proprietary partners (including doctors).

Overall, dense financial ties among the sectors exist. The authority of corporations to engage in philanthropic activities is no longer debatable under corporate law, although the Internal Revenue Code limits the annual deduction for corporate philanthropy to 10 percent of income. Separately, businesses provide financing to nonprofit projects, such as loans and investments in tax credit partnerships, and businesses enter into a myriad of contracts with nonprofits. For example, while companies have run into difficulties obtaining contracts to run entire school districts, proprietary businesses fill niches in classroom teaching, provide tutoring and remedial education; supply computers and software; design curricula; and provide food services, transportation, maintenance, and security. Finally, charities might outsource administrative functions, such as asset management and online membership enrollment—and even donor solicitation (Ben-Ner 2004).

Nonprofit Corporation Codes

State "enabling" laws allow for the creation of nonprofit corporations (and less commonly, charitable trusts and unincorporated associations); nonprofit corporation law sets forth the legal framework for governing entities that, by definition, have no shareholders (Brody 2006). The term nonprofit is broader than "charity," although it is important to recognize the expansive definition of "charity" in Anglo-American common law: charities include not only alms-giving and disaster relief organizations, but churches, schools, hospitals, arts and cultural entities, and social service nonprofits. Economists and some state statutes instead use "public benefit" to distinguish the charitable and social welfare–serving nonprofits from the "mutual-benefit" organizations, such as labor unions, trade associations, and social clubs.

Indeed, a nonprofit corporation cannot always be distinguished from a for-profit corporation by the statement of purposes set forth in its articles of incorporation. Modern nonprofit laws typically permit nonprofits to be formed for any lawful purpose. As described below, however, a nonprofit typically adopts sufficiently tailored purposes to qualify for the appropriate federal tax-exemption classification under IRC section 501(c). The legal feature that distinguishes nonprofit corporations from for-profit corporations is the prohibition on shareholders—famously termed the nondistribution constraint by Henry Hansmann (1981).

Unfortunately, the nondistribution constraint alone cannot carry as much weight as some might want.[6] If the public simply looks to nonprofit status as a signal of trustworthiness, this legal form of organization bestows a halo on any nonprofit organization regardless of merit. After all, the nondistribution constraint is designed for enterprises in which the residual capital requirements are met by donations (including below-market loans and volunteer labor) (Steuerle 1998). In other words, the suppliers of equity do not demand (and legally cannot receive) an economic return on capital. This constraint does not bind, however, in an enterprise with low capital needs or where grants, contracts, borrowing, or retaining earnings can meet capital needs. In the service industries, which are labor-intensive, the supply-side stakeholders can draw out the "profit" through compensation. (See Twombly, chapter 8.) Under these circumstances, returns to capital can be fully satisfied, making these organizations indistinguishable from a "for-profit in disguise" (Weisbrod 1988, 12). By contrast, in the production of goods, there is less of an opportunity by the provider to capture the benefits of opportunistic behavior. (See Cordes and Steuerle, chapter 3.) Perhaps we see more nonprofit activity in the provision of services than of goods because manufacturing is more capital-intensive and presents less of an opportunity to siphon.

Moreover, just as it does for business corporations, the law grants plenary authority to the nonprofit board of directors to manage the affairs of a nonprofit corporation. Because of the presumed information asymmetry between the nonprofit and the patrons, however, the nondistribution constraint alone cannot assure the patron (Hansmann's term) that his or her donation (or fee) will achieve that patron's intent. If the public cannot tell what is happening inside the nonprofit, the patron cannot know if the nonprofit is using his or her money to maximize the quality of the charity's services, to reduce their cost to the public, to augment pecuniary and nonpecuniary compensation of the charity's workers, or even to save for the benefit of future patrons. Finally, even if the nondistribution constraint ensures that the sector as a whole is worthy, how does it help the public choose between competing nonprofits?

As described in the context of tax requirements, discussed below, resource-constrained nonprofits increasingly seek novel sources of revenue. Charitable conduct of business activities has exploded since President Reagan reduced government expenditures on social services. Much of the controversial activity involves the production of goods embodying no particular information asymmetry, such as museum gift shops selling reproductions. Economists assume that nonprofits engage in these activities (and indeed seek to maximize the profits from them) as a way to cross-subsidize their preferred nonprofit activities. Even where these commercial activities involve information asymmetry, however, "once we accept the fact that [nonprofit organizations] will find it in their utility-maximizing interest to cross-subsidize, and will engage in some activities simply to earn a profit (but won't tell you ahead of time which these are), the alleged superiority of [nonprofit organizations] under asymmetric information disappears" (James 1986, 155).

Affiliated Organizations and Effect on Charitable Purpose

A nonprofit organization might meet its capital needs by combining resources with other parties, including taxable investors (corporate or individual). If a corporate entity is the vehicle, the separate corporate existence of the investors and the subsidiaries will be respected if certain formalities are observed (Colombo 2002). In addition, nonprofit organizations have long pooled resources with other nonprofit or proprietary participants in various types of unincorporated pass-through entities— joint venture, general or limited partnership, or limited liability company (LLC). (See also the tax discussion to follow.)

One legal issue unique to nonprofit organizations results from their having to use membership in lieu of share ownership to create parent/ subsidiary structures for affiliated nonprofit corporations (which cannot issue stock). (In light of the rise of the limited liability company form, a charity might prefer to create a single-member LLC (SMLLC).[7]) The sole-member structure raises issues about the fiduciary duties of the board of the subsidiary and the difficulty of moving cash from the subsidiary to the parent in states that prohibit distributions to members. In the project on *Principles of the Law of Nonprofit Organizations* that I am drafting for the American Law Institute, I propose that if the purpose of a nonprofit affiliate includes the broader purpose of a member or group, then the board of the affiliate may properly take into account those larger interests in discharging the duty of loyalty. (See American Law Institute 2007b, Reporter's Notes to §210 [Charitable Purposes and Activities].)

Elsewhere in the project, I provide the following illustration:

B Community Health Center is a nonprofit corporation with two members, L Hospital and N Health Care System, both also nonprofit corporations. B Community Health Center's articles of incorporation provide that, unless designated by a unanimous resolution of its members, B will not retain revenues in excess of those required to meet the annual operating budget adopted by the board of directors for the fiscal year, but rather B will distribute excess revenues proportionately to its two members, L and N, based on their capital contributions "for the benefit of each member's mission to enhance health care services in the communities they serve." This declaration should be construed as part of B's charitable purposes. (American Law Institute 2007a, §310)

This illustration is based on an opinion of the Florida attorney general, except that the purposes clause appears in the articles of incorporation rather than in the bylaws and, with this change, reaches a contrary result.[8] The attorney general's opinion, applying current law, had rejected the argument "that it would be unreasonable and inconsistent to deny a family of nonprofit corporations the ability to transfer funds among themselves during their normal operations." In 2004, the Florida legislature amended the statute to permit a nonprofit corporation to make distributions to charities (or governmental entities) if the distributions do not inure to the benefit of any individual or for-profit entity. However, the governor vetoed the bill, expressing in part his concern that the bill was too broad: "Because it could fundamentally change the relationships between nonprofit organizations, the likelihood of unintended consequences appears high. Fraudulent activity at the expense of the public, negative tax consequences, and accounting and auditing problems might result. Although this bill is well intended, the potential for broad unintended consequences outweighs the narrowly aimed benefits."[9]

State and Federal Tax Exemption and Other Tax Benefits for Charities

Federal and state tax laws indirectly regulate the business activities of nonprofits (Brody and Cordes 2006). Tax requirements are independent of organizational law. Thus, an organization may be a nonprofit corporation yet be denied recognition of income- or property-tax exemption. On a case-by-case basis, the IRS has issued denials of exemption to nonprofit entities engaged in a variety of activities, including adoption, insurance, financial services, religious publishing, conference centers, low-income housing, and retreats for caretakers—generally on the basis of their resemblance to similar for-profit businesses.

Keep in mind, though, that the tax system's benefits are limited and, because favorable tax treatment is essentially elective, an organization may simply forgo tax-favored status if it wishes to avoid the strings that come attached. Thus, an activity operating at or below cost does not need income-tax exemption. An organization with revenues entirely from fees for services and investment income does not need to offer its donors deductibility for charitable contributions. An entity that will not access the bond market need not have the ability to issue tax-exempt 501(c)(3) bonds. Finally, an entity that does not own real estate does not need state and local property-tax exemption.

Although one might dismiss these examples as extreme, the reader should recognize that qualifying for tax exemption sometimes requires undesirable structures or limitations. Being able to engage in the business in the manner desired might outweigh loss of tax benefits.[10] Moreover, although the term tax exempt suggests that the nonprofit form uniquely enjoys state subsidy via the tax system, this has never been the case. No government can resist using tax abatements and other incentives to encourage certain activities. Since colonial times, the states have granted exemptions to infant business industries. This practice has been enjoying a resurgence, as states deliberately choose the tool of tax credits and property-tax abatements to entice business relocation. (See *Cuno v. Daimler Chrysler, Inc.*[11]) The federal income tax system also contains incentives, such as accelerated depreciation deductions, that are useful only to taxpaying entities (Brody and Cordes 2006).

Exemption from Property Taxes

State property tax exemption is generally available only for a nonprofit that qualifies as a charity (Brody 2007). Property tax exemption laws vary widely; many are less developed than the federal income tax regime, but some are extremely detailed. In some states, charities forfeit property tax exemption by using any of the property for an unrelated business, whereas in other states the exemption is apportioned. Cordes, Gantz, and Pollak (2002) produced a rough estimate of between $8 billion and $13 billion nationally for the annual value of property tax exemption.

State tax authorities are slowly awakening to the increasing sophistication of nonprofit organizations' use of property. For example, the South Carolina Department of Revenue recently issued guidance on a variety of properties commonly owned by nonprofit hospitals, applying the test of whether the property is "devoted to, and necessary for, the functional operation of the hospital."[12] Though facts and circumstances can change the result, generally property tax exemption is not available in South Carolina to a shopping center (received as a gift), a medical office

building (except for offices occupied by doctors who are employees), a
child care center for the convenience of employees, and a parking facility (but only to the extent used by or for unrelated businesses, including
nonemployee doctors).

In 1997, Pennsylvania adopted a unique statute that declares, in part,
"It is the policy of this act that institutions of purely public charity shall
not use their tax-exempt status to compete unfairly with small business."[13] The operative subsection provides, "An institution of purely
public charity may not fund, capitalize, guarantee the indebtedness of,
lease obligations of or subsidize a commercial business that is unrelated
to the institution's charitable purpose as stated in the institution's charter or governing legal documents."[14] A subsection, "Remedies," begins,
"The Department of State shall establish a system of mandatory arbitra-
tion for the purpose of receiving all complaints from aggrieved small
businesses relating to an institution of purely public charity's alleged vio-
lation of this section." (A "small business" is defined elsewhere in the
Pennsylvania statute as a taxable individual or firm with fewer than 101
full-time employees.)

Surprisingly little litigation has ensued under this Pennsylvania provision, and small business will not be encouraged by the results of that litigation. In *Selfspot, Inc. v. The Butler County Family YMCA*,[15] a for-profit
health club was unable to stop a nearby YMCA's "plans to build a new,
35,000-square-foot, full-service fitness center . . . , which will feature a
state-of-the-art health club and will operate as a tax-exempt charity."

Executive compensation is attracting greater attention, at both the
federal and state levels. The Pennsylvania Commonwealth Court denied
exemption to a nonprofit physicians clinic (federally exempt under section 501(c)(3)) that did not pay dividends to shareholders.[16] The court
ruled that because the clinic compensated physician employees on the
basis of productivity, the clinic did not prove that it operated free from
the profit motive. Compare a suit brought under Tennessee law by a
group of for-profit health club owners against the YMCA of Middle Tennessee. The Tennessee statute requires, among other things, that "directors and officers shall serve without compensation beyond reasonable
compensation." The appeals court rejected the plaintiff's claim that the
compensation paid to the YMCA's chief executive is "clearly excessive"
when "the record indicates that the YMCA has a $60 million operating
budget, it has hundreds of programs, which serve over 160,000 people,
and has approximately 2,900 employees and 3,100 volunteers."[17]

Federal Income Tax Exemption

Internal Revenue Code section 501(c)(3) extends tax exemption to an entity "organized and operated" for "religious, educational, or charitable" purposes. Most charities adopt limited-purpose language in their articles of incorporation to obtain federal (and state) tax exemption.

Under Treasury Department regulations, a charity may qualify for exemption under section 501(c)(3) "although it operates a trade or business as a substantial part of its activities, if the operation of such trade or business is in furtherance of the organization's exempt purpose or purposes and if the organization is not organized or operated for the primary purpose of carrying on an unrelated trade or business."[18] This requirement has become known as the "primary purpose" test. An entity is not entitled to exemption if its primary purpose is to benefit private interests. Moreover, the regulations add, "In determining the existence or nonexistence of such primary purpose, all the circumstances must be considered, including the size and extent of the trade or business and the size and extent of the activities which are in furtherance of one or more exempt purposes." A 1971 memorandum by the IRS office of General Counsel explained that the primary purpose test rejects objective tests such as "a comparison of the relative physical size and extent of organizational activities devoted to business endeavors and to charitable endeavors in which the ends to which the beneficial use of an organization's resources are applied."[19]

This 1971 legal memorandum observed, "In the years past, the Service sought by ruling and by litigation to deny the right of charities to engage in business, insisting that somewhere, somehow in the enactment of the exemption provisions Congress must have intended to limit the classification of exempt charities to those charities not engaging to any substantial extent in commercial endeavors." It is instead under separate provisions of the Internal Revenue Code that profits on an unrelated business are taxable. Moreover, a charity classified as a private foundation is subject to the "excess business holding" limits of IRC section 4943.

It can be difficult to parse the distinctions between purpose and activities, however, and case law tends to support the perhaps unfortunate result that nonprofits are often punished for efficient commercial operations.[20] Consider the extreme view of the law articulated by one federal appeals court in the case *Living Faith, Inc. v. Commissioner*: "The particular manner in which an organization's activities are conducted, the commercial hue of those activities, competition with commercial firms, and the existence and amount of annual or accumulated profits, are all relevant evidence in determining whether an organization has a substantial nonexempt purpose."[21] The court set forth at length factors showing that the organization's (Living Faith) operations resembled and competed with for-profit restaurants and health food stores, adding that Living Faith (modestly) paid employees rather than used volunteers, required management to have "business ability" and six months' training, and did not receive charitable contributions. The court downplayed Living Faith's exempt functions, such as Bible study classes and dissemination of religious literature. The court concluded,

> It is difficult to see how the experience of dining or shopping at Living Faith's restaurant and health food stores differs, if it does, from the same experience one might have while dining or shopping at other vegetarian restaurants and health food stores. Granting a tax exemption to Living Faith would necessarily disadvantage its for-profit competitors. . . . We do not doubt the sincerity of Living Faith's beliefs, and we recognize its good faith in asserting a religious purpose of health promotion. Based on the record before us, however, we must uphold the Tax Court's determination that Living Faith operates with a substantial commercial purpose as well, and is therefore not entitled to § 501(c)(3) tax-exempt status.[22]

Influential practitioner Bruce Hopkins (1992, 467) dubs the approach epitomized by *Living Faith* as the "commerciality doctrine" and harshly criticizes it:

> The commerciality doctrine was (1) conjured up by the courts, (2) never defined, but rather just asserted (as if everyone knew it was there all along), and (3) born out of the courts' concern over factors such as sizable net profits, accumulated funds, aggressive marketing, and competition between nonprofit and for-profit organizations. . . . The doctrine just evolved, growing from loose language in court opinions, which in turn seems to have reflected judges' personal views as to what the law ought to be (rather than what it is).

Nevertheless, the Service has increasingly invoked the commerciality doctrine, notably in a chief counsel advice cited with approval in the 2006 legislative tightening of exemption for credit counsel agencies (see CCA200431023, July 13, 2004). Recently, an IRS technical manager, reporting on exemption applications from organizations that purchase health insurance on behalf of the working poor at group rates and charge a fee for that service, commented: "We have been unable to find an alternative basis for exemption when the demo phase ends, because these programs are not limited to a charitable class and seem too commercial. . . .

We are taking a fairly hard-nosed line: approving the demonstration projects; but as soon as that ends, we view these as commercial-type products" (Stokeld and Young 2006). (See generally Colombo 2002, discussing the uneven application of the commerciality doctrine.)

In general, as discussed in more detail below, a nonprofit organization engaging in commercial activity must consider four sets of tax possibilities:

1. The direct conduct of commercial activity that is related to the charitable purpose forming the basis of the organization's tax exemption—for example, education delivered by a university—does not jeopardize the organization's tax exemption and is not taxed. However, application of the commerciality doctrine and the prohibition on private benefit could cause loss of exemption.

2. By contrast, the direct conduct of commercial activity that is unrelated to the organization's charitable purpose does not jeopardize overall exemption if the organization is not operated for the primary purpose of carrying on an unrelated business, but the income is subject to the unrelated business income tax.

3. If the nonprofit engages in a commercial activity indirectly through another corporation, the separate legal identities are respected, and that other corporation's income may independently qualify as exempt or taxable under the normal rules. If the other corporation is taxable, income received in the form of dividends by the nonprofit shareholder (and capital gains on the sale of the stock) is generally excluded from UBIT. As described below, however, special rules apply if the nonprofit owns more than 50 percent of the other corporation.

4. If the nonprofit engages in a commercial activity through a multi-owner pass-through entity—partnership, joint venture, or limited liability company—that entity is not itself eligible for tax exemption. The income that flows through to the nonprofit is taxable or exempt under the normal UBIT analysis. However, under recent case law and IRS guidance, the nonprofit participant might further jeopardize its overall exemption unless the activity is insubstantial or the nonprofit controls the charitable aspects of the pass-through venture in order to prevent private benefit. Leading practitioner Michael Sanders (2005) calls this the "UBIT plus control" test.

Brody and Cordes (2006) provide estimates of the potentially taxable income of nonprofit organizations—that is, the profit earned on unrelated activities undertaken with the specific intent of earning income to support its mission-related activities. (This assessment excludes donations and below-market fees received for providing mission-related services to clients.) Assuming a combined federal and state rate of 40 percent, tax exemption is estimated to increase the resources of nonprofit organizations annually by roughly $10 billion in the aggregate.

Unrelated Business Income Tax

A business activity that is unrelated to the organization's charitable purpose—aside from the production of income—is subject to UBIT if the activity is "regularly carried on." (Reporting occurs on Form 990-T.) Because the emphasis in UBIT is on "unrelated," a given activity is exempt or taxable depending on the purposes of the entity engaged in it: for example, science books sold by a science museum are not taxable, but science books sold by an art museum are.[23] The UBIT regime contains numerous carve-outs and allowances, leading one academic accountant to observe, "The commercial revenues that do slip through the exclusion webbing are not necessarily the most 'objectionable,' or even the most 'commercial,' but are quite possibly those for which either Congress did not think to exclude or those for which there was no political champion to promote a specific exclusion" (Yetman 2005, 17).

Notably, Congress provides exceptions from UBIT for businesses that are run entirely by volunteers, that sell donated goods, or that are conducted for the "convenience" of members, students, patients, or employees. Exceptions also extend to most forms of passive (portfolio) income, but not to investments that are debt financed (unless made by educational institutions) or to certain income from controlled subsidiaries. Additional special rules abound, most significantly for research and hospital medical services.

The tax applies only to unrelated business income net of connected expenses (and each organization may automatically claim a deduction of $1,000). In light of the overturning of the destination-of-income test, however, charitable contributions can be deducted only up to 10 percent of UBIT, the same percentage allowed to taxable corporations. Because many unrelated businesses make use of assets or employees already devoted to exempt activities, the allocation of a portion of dual-use expenses to the taxable activity can minimize net income; the IRS's own regulations limit its ability to reallocate claimed deductions.[24] Because it is easier to shift costs from tax-exempt activities to taxable activities when these activities are complements in production, nonprofit organizations appear to be selective in the types of unrelated business activities they undertake (Cordes and Weisbrod 1998; Hines 1999; Sansing 1998). Of course, errors in reporting and ignorance of the law can lead to under-reporting. Whatever the reason, most UBIT returns report net losses; Riley (2007) found that only 4 percent of the 263,353 charitable organizations filing Forms 990 or 990EZ also filed Form 990-T for 2003, and that the reported taxable unrelated business income from those 10,064 organizations came to only 1 percent of total revenue. Charities accounted for 37 percent of Forms 990-T filed that year but 46 percent of the approximately $220 million in total tax.

Following the creation of the unrelated business income tax in 1950, Treasury Department Regulations section 1.513-1(b) declared that the UBIT was adopted "to eliminate a source of unfair competition" between taxpaying entities and exempt organizations engaged in money-making activities. The 1950 tax writers also expressed revenue concerns—specifically, preservation of the corporate income tax base (Hansmann 1989). One congressman, referring to the infamous ownership of Mueller Macaroni by New York University Law School, had complained that without reform, "eventually all the noodles produced in this country will be produced by corporations held or created by universities . . . and there will be no revenue to the Federal Treasury from this industry."[25] Today, though, most courts do not require the identification of a specific injured competitor.

Henry Hansmann suggests that the income tax exemption might be designed to compensate nonprofits for their inability to access the capital markets by issuing stock (Hansmann 1981, 72–75; for other economic analyses, see Rose-Ackerman 1982; Rushton 2007; Steinberg 1991; and Yetman 2005). The UBIT does provide a one-level-of-tax result regardless of whether a charity conducts an unrelated business directly or invests in the stock of a taxable corporation (Hansmann 1989). Of course, the relative benefit of corporation tax exemption depends on the level of the corporate tax (and on the effective tax rate on capital income) and is otherwise sensitive to broader tax rules. In theory, the higher the corporate (and capital) tax burden, the higher the nonprofit's incentive to engage in (untaxed) related commercial ventures (and investment activities), and the lower its incentive to engage in unrelated business activity. (See Brody and Cordes 2006.) As discussed below, in some cases, nonprofits would find it more attractive financially to engage in nonexempt income-producing activities, which benefit from the investment tax incentives provided to for-profit businesses. Limiting the exemption to "related activities" probably reinforces internal incentives that nonprofits already have to limit their commercial pursuits to areas where excess returns are likely to exist—areas that exploit cost complementarities between the primary mission-related activity and secondary commercial activities (Cordes and Weisbrod 1998; James and Young 2006).

The UBIT exceptions for interest, dividends, capital gains, rents, and royalties are usually described as the exception for passive income, but this term is not in the statute. (See criticism in Stone 2005.[26]) The trickiest areas of dispute between the IRS and charities occur over the use of intangible assets, payment for which commonly takes the form of royalties, one of the excepted categories. An exempt organization might license its name, trademark, and other intangible assets for a fee, and the income will be excludible so long as the organization's contract rights do not rise to the level of performing services.[27] Notably, after a long and unsuccessful fight in the various federal circuits, the IRS has given up trying to tax an exempt organization's income from licensing its name for "affinity credit cards."[28] Royalties are a favorite way to transfer income back to an exempt organization in a form that is tax deductible to a subsidiary or affiliate.

It might be hard to see how gifts can be treated as unrelated business income, but again the question is whether the charity is performing services to a private party.[29] An enormous amount of corporate philanthropy is done out of self-interest, but the motive for giving does not generally alter the fundamental gratuitous nature of the transactions. Indeed, Congress has enacted (and is considering expanding) generous deductions for certain charitable contributions of inventory, which amount to billions of dollars of year (Stecklow 2005). Corporate sponsorship that simply acknowledges a donor by name does not convert the gift into service income to the charity, but the arrangement could rise to the level of providing advertising services, which would result in UBIT.[30] In reaction to the IRS's assertion that UBIT applies to the naming rights granted for the Mobil Cotton Bowl, Congress enacted an explicit exemption for qualified sponsorship payments. Qualified payments are those for which the organization provides only the use or acknowledgment of the sponsor's name or logo (or product lines), but not advertising messages, and whose amount is not contingent on the level of attendance, broadcast ratings, or similar factors. Of course, even if a product endorsement or logo licensing does not result in taxable income, it might still be unwise for a nonprofit to sell its name in a particular fashion. (See Andreasen, chapter 6; Galaskiewicz and Colman 2006; James and Young 2006; and New York Attorney General 1999.)

UBIT reform became an issue in the mid-1980s when small business lobbyists identified unfair competition by nonprofits as one of their top complaints (Brody 1998). The small business lobby found a sympathetic ear in Rep. J. J. Pickle (D-TX), chair of the House Committee on Ways and Means' Subcommittee on Oversight. At lengthy hearings in 1987 and 1988, witnesses debated issues ranging from whether existing rules were fully enforced to whether the "relatedness" test should be replaced with a "commerciality" test. The oversight subcommittee, with the assistance of the Treasury Department, drafted an extensive set of recommendations that included detailed narrow rules targeted at health and fitness facilities, the royalty exclusion, dual-use facilities (property used for both exempt and unrelated activities), and income from a controlled subsidiary (U.S. Congress, House Committee on Ways and Means 1988a).

Both the small business and the nonprofit sectors generated letter-writing campaigns that filled a 950-page volume (U.S. Congress, House Committee on Ways and Means 1988b). Congress faced a difficult choice between two important constituencies, each wearing a white hat. At the same time, small business's complaint that tax exemptions allow the non-profit to lower the price of the goods or services charged to customers sounded disingenuous. Either nonprofits underprice proprietary firms or they don't. If they do, isn't that what they're supposed to do? How can business be heard to complain if charities offer their exempt-purpose goods and services at as close to cost as possible? Moreover, for unrelated business activities, no theory or evidence would suggest that nonprofits find it in their interest to earn a lower return on their investment capital than the market will bear. Of course, the more entrants in an industry, the more prices will be driven down. In the end, it appears that to small business, any competition is by definition unfair.

In their written testimony, charities compellingly cited increased pressure to seek new sources of revenue, and most suggested that taxes on profits from certain activities constitute punishment (U.S. Congress, House Committee on Ways and Means 1988b). The charities often were as, if not more, concerned about a consequent loss of state or local tax exemption. Some charities recognized the specific benefits of continued federal tax exemption, including the ability to attract donations and to issue section 501(c)(3) bonds. Others were unable to view tax subsidies as equivalent to government funds. In sum, exempt organizations criticized these proposals on the grounds that rather than creating parity between exempt and taxable entities, the proposals would overtax exempt entities and that existing rules of reallocation between related parties under an arm's-length standard could adequately police abuses.

In the end, the small business lobby proved no match for the charity lobby, and the law remained unchanged (Brody 1998). The debate did stimulate public awareness of the existing rules, and UBIT collections subsequently skyrocketed—although, as mentioned above, sophisticated tax planning has since minimized UBIT liability, and the ratio of tax dollars paid to the total revenue of the sector is still small.

Preventing Undue Benefit to Private Persons

Charitable purposes must be viewed in the context of the prohibition on private benefit. Commentary to the *Restatement (Third) of Trusts* recognizes that the "common element of charitable purposes is that they are designed to accomplish objects that are beneficial to the community— i.e., to the public or indefinite members thereof—without also serving what amount to private trust purposes" (American Law Institute 2003, § 28, general comment *a*). The federal tax requirements develop a similar theme: "it is necessary for an organization to establish that it is not organized or operated for the benefit of private interests such as designated individuals, the creator or his family, shareholders of the organization, or persons controlled, directly or indirectly, by such private interests."[31]

The Internal Revenue Service perpetually worries that nonprofit organizations are being created or used to transfer tax benefits to businesses and other private persons.[32] One area of concern is preventing excess compensation or other excess benefits to charity insiders (the prohibition on "private inurement"). A separate area of concern is preventing the charity from subordinating its charitable focus to the private interests of outsiders (the prohibition on "private benefit"). These prohibitions are not the same. Properly applying the prohibition on private benefit can be particularly challenging, if not intractable, because by definition private parties—employees and those who contract with the entity as much as beneficiaries—benefit from the operations of nonprofit organizations. For criticism of the IRS's shifting and expanding application of the private benefit doctrine, see Colombo (2006).

Consider *United Cancer Council v. Commissioner,*[33] in which Judge Posner rejected the IRS's assertion that a proprietary fundraiser unrelated to the charity became an insider for purposes of the prohibition on private inurement by negotiating a one-sided contract with a charity desperate to survive. Apparently, the Internal Revenue Service was concerned that the tail had begun to wag the dog—that the taxable fundraiser, W&H, was the real party in interest, and the exempt UCC was essentially an accommodation party. But Judge Posner was unsympathetic to the IRS's assertion of private inurement:

> The Service and the Tax Court are using "control" in a special sense not used elsewhere, so far as we can determine, in the law, including federal tax law. It is a sense which . . . threatens to unsettle the charitable sector by empowering the IRS to yank a charity's tax exemption simply because the Service thinks its contract with its major fundraiser too one-sided in favor of the fundraiser, even though the charity has not been found to have violated any duty of faithful and careful management that the law of nonprofit corporations may have laid upon it.[34]

Instead, the court remanded the case to see whether the contract resulted in so much private benefit that the charity no longer operated for an exempt purpose. However, the parties settled before the Tax Court could rule on the issue.

As Judge Posner's discussion suggests, the federal tax rules, like state nonprofit law, better address problems of self-dealing (private inurement) than weak management. Since 1969, the tax code has contained outright prohibitions on self-dealing transactions (except for payment of reasonable compensation) between private foundations and its insiders. For non-private foundations, in 1996, Congress adopted "intermediate sanctions" that impose a penalty tax rather than (automatic) loss of exemption in cases of isolated private inurement.[35]

Under these excess-benefit rules, if a "disqualified person"—defined as anyone in a position to exercise substantial influence over the affairs of the charity (or a related person)—receives a financial benefit from the charity greater than the value of goods or services he or she provided, then the benefited insider must pay a tax equal to 25 percent of this excess. (A second-tier, confiscatory tax of 200 percent of the amount of the excess benefit applies if wrongdoing is not corrected by making the charity whole.) A separate tax (whose cap was doubled in 2006 to $20,000 per transaction) applies to charity trustees and directors who knowingly approved the transaction, unless the participation was not willful and is due to reasonable cause. For this purpose, a disqualified person includes those who served within five years of the transaction. The Internal Revenue Service may abate these taxes when appropriate.

The existence of intermediate sanctions on excess benefits does not displace the general authority of the Internal Revenue Service to revoke an organization's tax exemption under section 501(c)(3) in appropriate cases of private inurement or private benefit. See recently finalized regulations that set forth for the first time illustrations of the prohibition on private benefit.[36]

In contrast to the excise tax regime imposed on private foundations,[37] the excess-benefits tax regime does not reach other breaches of fiduciary duty. Thus, in the absence of private benefit, the IRS has no explicit authority to address such inadequacies of governance as running an ineffective charitable program, accumulating excess income, or paying insufficient attention to investment returns. As a practical matter, though, the IRS has been able to negotiate sometimes fundamental management reforms as part of the exemption application process or in an audit. For example, the IRS can threaten revocation of recognition of exemption to bring the charity to the bargaining table, and then settle for a "closing agreement" that spells out detailed governance changes. (See Brody 1999a.)

Incidentally, a key reason for the lack of data on the commercial activities of charities is that Forms 990 and 990-PF must be publicly disclosed, but business tax returns, including the Form 990-T, are not public documents. This will change somewhat with the 2006 adoption of the requirement that Forms 990-T filed by 501(c)(3) organizations must generally be available for inspection; however, tax returns business corporations file remain confidential, giving charities one more reason to spin off unrelated business into for-profit corporations (compare JCT 2007 with JCT 2000).

Use of Limited Liability Companies and Joint Ventures with Private Parties

We described above the use of a variety of unincorporated legal forms for pooling resources with other investors. (See generally Sanders 2002.) Under the Treasury Department Regulations, the default classification regime for an unincorporated entity is a partnership if there are one or more owners, and a "disregarded entity" if there is only one owner. Thus, if the sole member of an LLC is itself an exempt organization, the single-member LLC (SMLLC) is viewed for tax-exemption purposes as a division or branch of that member. In either case, the profits are taxed (at most) only once, because the income flows through and is reported instead by the partners or members. Alternatively, the regulations permit an unincorporated entity to elect to be treated as an association taxable as a corporation. Accordingly, a partnership or LLC of charities—including a SMLLC—that "checks the box" to be treated as a corporation may apply for separate exemption. (See generally Treas. Reg. § 301.7701-3.)

An entity treated as a partnership for tax purposes is not eligible for separate recognition of federal tax exemption under IRC section 501(c)(3).[38] Under IRC section 512(c), a nonprofit partner's share of income is treated as exempt or unrelated business income depending on what the tax result would be if the partner earned the income directly. Accordingly, if the only partners are themselves charities and the enterprise is engaged in charitable activities, the partners' exemptions are not in jeopardy, and the income will not be taxable. Special rules apply if exempt organizations enter into partnerships with taxable participants; these rules reduce the tax benefits of making certain disproportionate allocations of income to the exempt partners and of deductions to the taxable partners.[39]

In Revenue Ruling 98-15, the Internal Revenue Service ruled on the tax consequences of a "whole hospital" joint venture with a nonexempt participant.[40] Somewhat unhelpfully, the ruling provided two extreme fact-dependent examples, which have come to be known as the "good" and the "bad" joint ventures. Under this ruling, a section 501(c)(3) organization may form and participate in a partnership and meet the operational test if participation in the partnership furthers a charitable purpose, and if the partnership arrangement permits the exempt organization to act exclusively in furtherance of its exempt purpose and only incidentally for the benefit of the for-profit partners. The IRS's position was essentially confirmed in *Redlands Surgical Services v. Commissioner* (ceding "effective control" of partnership activities impermissibly serves private interests).[41]

Revenue Ruling 2004-51 (I.R.B. 2004-22, 974) deals with what is known as an ancillary joint venture, in which a section 501(c)(3) organization forms a limited liability company with a for-profit corporation and contributes only a portion of its assets to and conducts an insubstantial portion of its activities through the LLC. In the ruling, a university joined with a business to develop a distance-learning venture. Each party made equal capital contributions, owned 50 percent of the LLC, could appoint three members to the governing board, and would receive equal allocations of income and distributions. All decisions require mutual agreement, except that the university has "the exclusive right to approve the curriculum, training materials, and instructors, and to determine the standards for successful completion of the seminars"; and the business has "the exclusive right to select the locations where participants can receive a video link to the seminars and to approve other personnel (such as camera operators) necessary to conduct the video teacher training seminars." The ruling addresses issues of both the university's continued qualification for exemption and whether the organization's share of the LLC's income is subject to UBIT. Of course, the LLC itself is not entitled to tax exemption. However, because participation in the LLC is an insubstantial part of the university's activities, it will not jeopardize the university's exemption. Moreover, under the ruling, because the facts establish that the LLC's activities are substantially related to the exercise and performance of the exempt organization, the exempt organization is not subject to UBIT.

The IRS recently announced that it will no longer issue private letter rulings on whether a joint venture with a for-profit organization will result in unrelated business income or adversely affect an organization's tax-exempt status, other than as part of an application for recognition of exempt status.[42] The position of the IRS and the courts on exempt-organization joint venture activities with taxable participants is still developing. Simon, Dale, and Chisolm (2006) suggest further inquiry into the border patrol measures the tax system applies. Specifically, they ask, "In the interest of protecting the third sector from distortion of purpose or from public distrust, should legislative and administrative policymakers build less permeable fences between the nonprofit and the for-profit territories? Or will such barriers have perverse effects on both of these sectors? And, in any event . . . , are either of these questions properly addressed by the tax system?"

Aggregation and Controlled Subsidiaries

One significant provision in the 1969 Tax Reform Act obligates private foundations to divest stock in controlled businesses; echoing the fears that prompted the initial enactment of the UBIT, Congress sought to prevent foundation donors or managers from pursuing private business interests through the foundation. As the Treasury Department explained, "where a foundation becomes heavily involved in business activities, the charitable pursuits which constitute the real reason for its existence may be submerged by the pressures and demands of the commercial enterprise. . . . Business may become the end of the organization; charity, an insufficiently considered and mechanically accomplished afterthought" (U.S. Treasury Department 1965, 35). Today, a private foundation may own no more than 20 percent of an unrelated business, reduced by the percentage owned by "disqualified persons" (they together may hold 35 percent if a third party has effective control).

As charities in the 1980s adapted to the wrenching financial forces that pushed them into more and more fee-generating activities, the IRS affirmatively encouraged charities to transfer unrelated business activities into separate, for-profit subsidiaries. Such a mechanism provides a clean structure for separating nontaxable (related and investment) activities from taxable activities. However, some of the resulting complex holding-company organizational charts resonated of big business, and invited unwanted attention, catching the attention of a skeptical oversight subcommittee of the House Ways and Means Committee, which worried that "the managers of the parent could devote their attention to maximizing business profits, rather than their exempt missions" (U.S. Congress, House Committee on Ways and Means 1998a, part VI.G).

This fear of "empire building" inspired the subcommittee to embrace an aggregation proposal that deprives a charity of its exemption if the activities of for-profit affiliates outweigh its charitable activities. The subcommittee's aggregation proposal required the Committee on Ways and Means, in consultation with the Treasury Department, to develop objective tests to ascertain when the activities of the charity's subsidiaries should be reviewed in applying the primary purpose test to the charity (U.S. Congress, House Committee on Ways and Means 1988a, Part VI.G).

The aggregation proposal must be read against the backdrop of the IRS's frustrating litigation experience in trying to revoke the exemption of charities that engage in "too much" business activity. (See Eliasberg 1965.) As described above, the primary purpose test under section 501(c)(3) requires determining the charity's purposes for engaging in the business activity; in effect, the "destination of income test" survives in testing the entity's basic entitlement to exemption, even if particular activities wind up being subject to tax (Aprill 1989, 1107). "The fact is," the IRS office of Chief Counsel earlier acknowledged, "that business purpose and the devotion of charity property to business use to produce income in the administration of charity properties can be perfectly compatible with and fully in furtherance of exclusively charitable purpose in the administration of such properties."[43]

Indeed, that 1971 general counsel memorandum acknowledged the obligation of charity managers to make investment assets productive. In light of the IRS's encouragement to separate taxable activities into subsidiaries, aggregating the activities of all affiliates in testing the (c)(3) status of the parent struck the charitable sector as "gotcha" legislation.[44]

The problem for proponents of the aggregation test is one of line drawing. Given the desirability of an objective standard, should excess business be defined by ownership percentages, such as those in the private foundation prohibition? The oversight subcommittee's recommendation applied aggregation only to high-percentage investments (using an 80 percent ownership threshold). In addition, the subcommittee enumerated five factors that should be taken into account in developing objective tests: (1) the time, attention, and importance given by the parent organization's board of directors to tax-exempt activities as compared with unrelated business activities; (2) the organization's expenditures for exempt activities as compared with expenditures for unrelated business activities; (3) income derived from the different activities; (4) reasonable expectation of earning a profit; and (5) staff time spent on different activities. The oversight subcommittee's report, though, did not specify the degree to which satisfying one or more of the criteria would tip the balance. More fundamental, however, was the issue of why aggregation is a federal tax concern if all the proper tax is collected under the existing regime.

The aggregation proposal died, along with the rest of the UBIT proposals, in 1991. However, another one of the 1988 recommendations reappeared in the Taxpayer Relief Act of 1997. Under section 512(b)(13) as enacted in 1969, UBIT applies to an exempt organization that receives income in the form of interest, royalties, rents, and annuities from a "controlled" corporation or partnership. Congress feared that controlled subsidiaries could reduce or eliminate taxable income by making inflated payments of these deductible items, while the exempt parent would claim the corresponding UBIT exclusions for such classically passive items. (By contrast, dividends are not deductible by the paying corporation.) The definition of "control" had long required at least 80 percent ownership (and no attribution rules applied to reach stock owned indirectly). It was assumed that an outsider who owned more than 20 percent of the enterprise would police the fairness of these payments. However, such a loose definition of control easily permitted exempt organizations to avoid section 512(b)(13) by, for example, issuing multiple classes of stock or dropping the business into a second-tier subsidiary. One of the 1988 UBIT reforms would have amended section 512(b)(13) by reducing the control requirement to more than 50 percent of vote or value and by including attribution of ownership.

The years after the death of UBIT reform highlighted the weaknesses of section 512(b)(13), particularly when the IRS ruled that a second-tier subsidiary of the National Geographic Society would not be a controlled subsidiary. Apparently out of the blue, Congress reformed section 512(b)(13) in the Taxpayer Relief Act of 1997 in the manner suggested in the earlier UBIT reform attempt. In testing the effects of the reduction of control from 80 percent to more than 50 percent, Yetman found that "beginning in 1999 and continuing the average profitability of the taxable subsidiaries sharply rises [from the pre-1998 average of 6 percent], consistent with charities stripping less income out due to the new threshold rule." Moreover, "charities with taxable subsidiaries earn significantly higher amounts of rent and royalty income, consistent with setting up those subsidiaries so as to avoid taxes" (Yetman 2005, 21). Nevertheless, in yet another startling reversal, the Pension Protection Act of 2006 replaces this automatic-UBIT regime with one that includes interest, rent, and royalties from controlled subsidiaries in unrelated business income only to the extent that those amounts exceed the sum that would be paid in an arm's-length transaction—but only for payments made under a binding written contract in effect on August 17, 2006, and only for payments received or accrued between January 1, 2006, and December 31, 2007. Separately, the statute requires a report from the Treasury on the effectiveness of the IRS in administering the provision and on the extent to which payments by controlled entities to the controlling exempt organization meet the required arm's-length standard (see JCT 2007, 571–72).

The proper resolution of this issue is not obvious. Under current law, a stream of income bears tax that would not bear tax if paid from an uncontrolled entity to the exempt organization. If, indeed, the payments of interest, rent, or royalties represent fair value for the use of the exempt organization's assets, then Congress is overtaxing the arrangement. On the other hand, an arm's-length rule allows a deduction for a payment that could not be claimed if the charity conducted the unrelated business activity directly. To create parity, we would need to exempt an amount of directly conducted unrelated business income equal to an interest-like return—but this would be a radical cutback of the UBIT regime (Halperin 2005).

Indirect Value of Other Tax Preferences

Of growing importance to charities is the indirect benefit from a host of tax preferences that, deliberately or incidentally, stimulate demand for the services that charities provide (Brody and Cordes 2006). The exclusion from workers' income for employer-provided health insurance has long been one of the largest tax expenditures; while doctors and other proprietary firms benefit, so do the hospitals, dominated by nonprofits. The education tax credits, designed to keep college affordable for the middle class, immediately made the list of top tax expenditures; many education experts believe that colleges and universities capture the credits' value through higher tuition or lower internal aid. Nonprofit day care providers benefit from the dependent-care credit. Nonprofit housing developers benefit from the low-income housing tax credit. Although the nonprofits' share of these subsidies cannot be quantified, for 2006–2010 the Joint Committee on Taxation's estimates by "budget function" peg the cost of tax expenditures—aside from the charitable-contribution deduction—at $6 billion for education, $9.5 billion for social services (ignoring $23 billion for the child credit), and a staggering $671.5 billion for health (mostly for exclusion or deduction of health insurance) (JCT 2006, table 1).

When Nonprofits Forgo Nonprofit Status

An Emerging Issues in Philanthropy seminar, sponsored jointly by the Urban Institute's Center on Nonprofits and Philanthropy and by Harvard University's Hauser Center for Nonprofit Organizations, identified a strikingly long list of reasons why nonprofits might prefer to use for-profit affiliates to carry out charitable activities for which tax exemption would be available. Steuerle (2001), in summarizing the discussion at the seminar, lists the following advantages of the for-profit form:

- *Raising financial capital or gaining access to human capital.* For-profit investors might prefer to contribute capital to a for-profit entity to "increase the likelihood that management of the activity will be directed toward maximizing profit."
- *Cashing in on and selling a new venture.* Start-up and growth businesses often have negative or low income "and require minimal to no income tax payments." The later sale of stock in the enterprise

will usually not be subject to UBIT. As described above, royalty payments will generally be deductible by the enterprise and excluded from the exempt recipient's unrelated business income, subject to the special rule for controlled subsidiaries. ("Thus, economically equivalent transactions can produce different tax results. For example, to exclude royalties from licensing arrangements, the nonprofit must take a passive role and let the for-profit partner regulate the activity. By contrast, to exclude income from a joint venture with a taxable partner, the nonprofit must retain control over the [charitable] activity.")

- *Separating certain activities.* Using taxable affiliates can simplify accounting procedures and steer clear of UBIT requirements, sometimes with favorable expense-allocation consequences— although the IRS can challenge the allocation of expenses for dual-use assets.

- *Paying property tax.* Nonprofits may forgo exemption on some portion of their rental real estate and pay property tax, but depreciation and interest expenses often will minimize or even eliminate taxable income.

- *Gaining some flexibility in compensation.* "Particular nonprofits may have explicit or implicit caps on employees' salaries to reflect the culture of the organization or to keep salaries from discouraging outside contributions. . . . A for-profit can also offer additional types of compensation, such as deferred compensation and equity-based compensation (e.g., participating stock, deeply discounted stock, stock appreciation rights, and options of all kinds) to potential leaders of the enterprise."[45] However, using a taxable affiliate reduces transparency, because the for-profit affiliate's return is not public. Moreover, "compensation packages offered in the for-profit subsidiary can cause dissension in the ranks." (See also Abelson 1998.)

Reform Proposals

The public often reacts negatively to the operational ways in which nonprofits have come to resemble for-profits. Such behavior as high salaries, fierce competition, and bottom line–oriented management brings calls for legal reform. Most reform proposals fail to address the real concerns.

For example, endowing the public with standing rights to bring suit for breach of fiduciary duty (see SFC 2004) does not disturb the charity manager's strongest defense, the business judgment rule. Worries about misleading fundraising by charities can lead to greater required disclosure, but charities would be wise to do more, by better informing the public about their financial needs.

Reform proposals are not all alike, and the wrong kind of laws can make things worse. Why should states want to say to any enterprise, "Thou shalt be owned" or "Thou shalt not be owned"? Proposals limiting the scope of the nonprofit sector to specified "worthy" enterprises require that we agree on how the intersectoral debate should be resolved, but, as described in the introduction above, no resolution is possible. Often the best law is no law, so that activities can be conducted by the most efficient and responsive firms, regardless of organizational form; any necessary regulation can focus on the aspects of firm activity or specific industries.

Alternatively, policymakers might decide to withhold or tailor a government subsidy, such as favorable tax treatment. Of course, subsidies induce investment in particular activities and overregulation discourages investment. As we have seen, subsidies are just one of the fluid characteristics of our mixed economy, and it might even make sense for a particular enterprise to forgo tax-exempt (or even nonprofit) status.

Reforming Tax Exemption

The existence of robust "mixed" industries leads to calls for targeted repeal of exemption. The House Committee on Ways and Means held a hearing in April 2005 examining the underlying rationale for the federal tax exemption of nonprofit organizations operating in various industries, including hospitals, elder-care facilities, credit counseling organizations, low-income housing, and college athletics (JCT 2005). More narrowly, in October 2005, the IRS announced that one of its compliance initiatives includes hospitals, "to determine how hospitals determine and pay executive compensation as well as how they meet the community benefit standards for purposes of section 501(c)(3)" (Internal Revenue Service 2005, 12). By letter to the American Hospital Association, in addition to asking about discounts to the uninsured and developing a standardized accounting of charity care, Senate Finance Committee Chairman Chuck Grassley identified other areas of "serious concern": "investments in joint ventures, taxable subsidiaries, venture-capital funds and other financial arrangements, contracts for health care, management and administrative services, executive compensation, travel and expense reimbursement, billing and debt collection practices, use of tax-exempt bond proceeds, conflicts of interest and other governance issues, and accounting, reporting, public disclosure, and general transparency issues" (Grassley 2006, 2). As described above, in 2006 Congress adopted new requirements for granting exemption for credit counseling and debt management (JCT 2007, 607–19).

Congress has from time to time repealed exemption for organizations in identified industries that no longer warrant subsidy. The list of previously tax-exempt organizations includes building and loan associations, commercial-type insurance such as Blue Cross/Blue Shield, and TIAA-CREF. In 1991, the Committee on Ways and Means held hearings on whether nonprofit hospitals should be required, as a condition of their tax-exempt status, to provide specified levels of care to indigents, but the proposals died. With further change to the character of nonprofit hospitals in recent years, evidence suggests that nonprofit hospitals provide a level of charity care comparable to that of for-profit hospitals (Government Accountability Office 2005; but see the nuanced analysis of over 200 empirical studies comparing performance of for-profit and nonprofit hospitals, nursing homes, and managed care organizations in Schlesinger and Gray 2006). As the IRS continues to struggle with the private-benefit implications of whole hospital joint ventures and joint operating agreements with proprietary partners, Congress could decide simply to revoke the hospital exemption. Moreover, as a strategic matter, the charitable sector might consider supporting such a move to protect the rest of the sector from health care's pervasive and highly visible commercial taint.

Higher education would then be the next most vulnerable subsector. As the Congressional Budget Office (2005, 4) reports, "two business activities of nonprofit colleges and universities have received considerable attention: research in areas that may have substantial opportunities for licensing and patenting (rather than basic research whose results are available to everyone without compensation), and sports teams that compete with professional teams for the dollars of advertisers and sports fans." (See also Grassley 2007, requesting CBO analysis of commercialization in higher education, especially college athletics.) The Congressional Budget Office then added in a footnote, "Some people argue that even the basic 'mission' of higher education—offering courses—represents the sale of a private good that benefits the student making the investment. Some 40 for-profit accredited institutions of higher education that grant degrees were listed on U.S. stock exchanges in 1999."

However, the Congressional Budget Office cautions that simply taxing the "untaxed business sector" might not produce the results proponents want: "For-profit firms that favor taxing untaxed entities as a way to level the competitive playing field might find that their competitors' prices were reduced even further. . . . People who favor taxation as a way to reduce waste might find some entities avoiding the tax by passing on more of their surplus in the form of above-market compensation or other expenses" (2005, iii). The Congressional Budget Office concludes,

> A lesson from CBO's analysis is that the market presence and impact of the untaxed business sector do not result solely from the sector's exemption from income taxes—they also derive from the organizational structure of entities in the sector, especially the absence of shareholders who demand that any surplus be distributed as dividends or retained as earnings. And an entity's choice of organizational structure is made within a welter of state laws and regulations that are beyond the control of the federal government. (Congressional Budget Office 2005, iii)

Alternatively, Congress could replace or supplement the indirect subsidies of the tax system with the direct subsidy of activities with social value, regardless of the organizational form of the provider (nonprofit or for-profit—or governmental, for that matter). Recent years have brought a revolution in the types and extent of commercial activities undertaken by nonprofits, as well as an influx of proprietary enterprises into traditionally nonprofit fields, such as hospital care and higher education. As Russell Hardin observed, "technically speaking, there may be no good of any political or economic significance that is inherently subject to non-exclusion. Indeed, the technology of exclusion is a growth industry with frequent innovation" (1997, 27–28). (See generally Tuckman and Chang 2006.) As described above, the recent shift to demand-side tax subsidies (such as the education credits) and vouchers (such as Medicare and Medicaid) have this effect, so long as the provider is not required to be a nonprofit organization. (See generally Brody 1999b.)

Reforming the UBIT

As described above, both the IRS and nonprofits devote significant resources to a UBIT regime that produces comparatively little tax, and arguably not on the right activities. UBIT might usefully be repealed on the grounds that forces other than the tax laws more appropriately govern nonprofits' commercial behavior. (See Yetman 2005, proposing repealing the UBIT but requiring exempt organizations to drop business activities into for-profit subsidiaries.) However, the appearance of a check on unrelated business activity has at least symbolic value to policymakers and the public. Should it prove too hard to define taxable income for nonprofits, Congress could instead simply impose a (probably low-level) tax on investment income, making all nonprofit organizations potentially taxable (Brody and Cordes 2006).

The oversight subcommittee's detailed 1988 recommendations might form the basis for renewed reform discussion of the unrelated business income tax. Indeed, the Treasury subsequently issued rules on travel and tour services, and Congress revised the treatment of controlled subsidiaries and adopted legislation on corporate sponsorship. (See also Colombo [2002, 495]: "if we are not prepared to adopt a radical restructuring of the tests for exemption (the best solution to the commerciality issue), then we should seriously consider the second path of expanding the UBIT to cover all commercial activities as an alternative way to address the policy issues raised".) Admittedly, though, no wholesale UBIT reform appears to be on the horizon. Indeed, as described above, even the relaxed rules on controlled subsidiaries are temporary.

Pressures on Property-Tax Exemption

Recently, lawsuits and proposed legislation asserting tighter state and local definitions for exemption reflect a growing divergence of federal and state policies on tax exemption and a burgeoning view of a quid-pro-quo rationale, notably for health care organizations.[46] At the state level perhaps more than at the federal level, the special claims of nonprofit hospitals fade in the sunshine of data showing their resemblance to the operations of for-profit hospitals, particularly in the level of charity care and billing practices for uninsured patients (but see Schlesinger and Gray 2006). Illinois hospitals have been shaken by the 2006 ruling of the state Department of Revenue that Provena Covenant Medical Center, a nonprofit hospital in Urbana, should lose its $1 million a year exemption because it spent less than 1 percent of revenue on charity care. (The hospital won in the trial court in July 2007, but the Department is appealing.) This ruling came on the heels of an unnerving legislative proposal by Illinois attorney general Lisa Madigan that would condition property-tax exemption for a hospital on its spending at least 8 percent of operating costs on charity care. This proposal was quickly tabled but is scheduled to return in some form. Separately, in February 2007, the Revenue Department revoked the exemptions of Carle Hospital and Richland Memorial Hospital—even though, in the case of the latter, the town had no objection to exemption.

By contrast, the Michigan supreme court found that no particular monetary level of charity care is required by the state statute (*Wexford Medical Group v. City of Cadillac*).[47] In that case, the total amount of pure charity care in one year was $2,400 (out of a total budget of $10 million). The court described the difficulty of determining what forgone revenue to count as charity care, concluding: "Clearly, courts are unequipped to handle these and many other unanswered questions. Simply put, these are matters for the legislature."

Broader Measures of Social Benefit

Other chapters in this book describe the socioeconomic approach called social return on investment—also called blended value capital and double bottom line—which combines traditional stock reporting with an assessment of social costs and benefits (Smith 2006).[48] For example, the Roberts Enterprise Development Fund (REDF) has examined specific nonprofit social enterprise organizations, such as thrift stores, bakeries, and bicycle repair shops.[49]

Consider *Aid to Artisans, Inc. v. Commissioner*,[50] upholding the tax exemption of an organization whose primary activities were the purchase, import, and sale of handicrafts produced by disadvantaged artisans in the United States and in developing countries. These activities, the court ruled, furthered charitable and educational purposes: the economic stabilization in disadvantaged communities where handicrafts are central to the economy, and the education of the American public in the artistry, history, and cultural significance of these handicrafts. Although the organization's activities were commercial, they were undertaken to accomplish exempt purposes (Lasprogata and Cotten 2003, 80).

A nonprofit organization whose purpose is not recognized as tax-exempt, however, is taxed as an ordinary business corporation. As such, it can reduce taxable income by charitable contributions, but not in excess of 10 percent of taxable income in a given year (IRC § 170[b][2]). Moreover, it is unlikely that under section 162, a nonexempt enterprise could deduct "business expenses" motivated by reasons other than the production of profit.[51]

Interesting developments are also occurring in the private foundation subsector, which is starting to rebel against the traditional distinction between investments and program-related activities. The fundamental constraint arises under IRC section 4942's requirement that a private foundation must annually distribute for charitable purposes at least 5 percent of the value of its investment assets. Clearly an outright grant to a charity counts toward the payout requirement, but so does a grant to a non-charity, so long as it is consistent with the foundation's charitable purpose and, for grants made to those other than public charities, the foundation exercises "expenditure responsibility" over the recipient's use of the grant. Moreover, a "program-related investment" also counts toward the minimum payout requirement. For an investment to qualify as program-related, however, the foundation must not have the primary intent to earn income. That is, a market-rate loan is simply a redeployment of investment assets, whereas the entire principal amount of a significantly below-market-rate loan to a proper object of the foundation's charitable purpose counts toward the current payout—even though the amount will, hopefully, be repaid in a later year.

Private foundations seeking to fund socially worthwhile activities by private businesses, either as grants or as program-related investments, can take some (but not precedential) comfort in Private Letter Ruling 2006-03-031 (Oct. 25, 2005), in which the IRS blessed a private foundation's proposed program to make "grants, contracts, or program-related investments with private industry" for the purpose of spurring pharmaceutical and biotechnology companies "to discover, develop, and deploy solutions addressing the diseases that disproportionately impact the developing world." See generally the systematic "Corporate Involvement Initiative" of the Ford Foundation (2005), describing a role for foundations in providing research and development funding for new business strategies and credit enhancement for new financial models that enable businesses to better serve low-income populations and to develop a new field of practice.

Some foundations do not see a clear line between their investment activities and their charitable activities. For example, as the "blue moon fund" declares on its web site,[52] "Over the long term, the fund hopes to create an integrated investment strategy that breaks down the distinctions between the program portfolio and the investment portfolio such that they are mutually supportive and fully consistent with the fund's philosophy." Mission-related investments, as opposed to program-related investments, however, would not satisfy the payout requirement. The Annie E. Casey Foundation, for example, is not committed to exist in perpetuity; with its high payout rate, it does not need to count its mission-related investment to satisfy the 5 percent requirement (see Sonenstein and Velasquez, chapter 7).

As part of the Companies Act of 2004, England enabled a new type of legal entity, the "community interest company" (CIC).[53] The CIC's assets are subject to an "asset lock"—meaning that they are permanently dedicated to charitable or community purposes—but the CIC may pay dividends (up to a cap) to its shareholders. The CIC's income is taxable, and investors cannot deduct any contributions they make to the CIC. To some reformers in the United States, the CIC provides a model (albeit an imperfect one) for encouraging greater use of social enterprise organizations.[54] Under current U.S. law that compartmentalizes commercial activities, besides the inability to zero out income through charitable contributions, specific barriers arise from (1) the ability of a nonprofit to borrow (and pay interest) but not to issue stock (and pay dividends); (2) the ability of a charity (but not a non-(c)(3) or taxable enterprise) to attract tax-deductible charitable contributions; (3) the uncertain ability of private foundations to make grants to businesses; and (4) the ability to design appropriate governance, investment-return, and compensation structures. The theoretical and practical considerations of recognizing a hybrid "social-purpose business" in the United States are only beginning to be explored by legal practitioners and academics.[55]

Conclusion

Because there is no single right way to allocate business activity among the public and private sectors, we do the least harm if we limit legal solutions to legal problems. Successful reforms are likely to be narrowly targeted. For example, if society does not want to subsidize certain types of nonprofits, it can remove those subsidies, such as by revoking tax exemption for nonprofit hospitals that fail to provide free charity care. As a result of the limits of the law, nonprofit entities, like other organizations, will continue to be governed primarily by other social institutions. Social institutions can still—though not ideally—work their will within a laissez-faire legal framework.

NOTES

1. Moreover, antitrust laws, which bar restraints on trade and attempts to monopolize a product in a market, apply not only to such mutual-benefit nonprofits as labor unions, trade associations, amateur athletic associations, and professional regulatory associations, but also to commercial charities (notably nonprofit hospitals) and universities. (See *California Dental Association v. Federal Trade Commission*, 526 U.S. 756 [1999] [trade association].) In addition, labor and employment issues abound. Universities face union-organizing lawsuits from graduate students in their roles as teaching assistants. Thwarted unions seeking to organize hospital workers are taking their unhappiness to state legislatures, which are considering imposing certain levels of charity care as a condition of property-tax exemption. Intellectual-property rules might be changing in the academy, with distance-learning and patent ownership rights at issue.

2. Sometimes the for-profit activity differs in focus from the nonprofit activity—consider commercial trade schools. Sometimes, however, for-profit businesses seek to provide competing services, not always with success. See, for example, the action by the New York State Board of Regents to impose a moratorium on new for-profit colleges and other state initiatives, as discussed in Arenson (2006).

3. The Credit Repair Organizations Act, 15 U.S.C. § 1679 et seq., effective April 1, 1997, imposes restrictions on credit repair organizations but excludes § 501(c)(3) organizations. In eight states, only nonprofit credit counseling agencies can operate. (See Mayer 2006.)

4. IRS Commissioner Mark Everson, testimony before the Senate Finance Committee, April 2005. http://www.senate.gov/~finance/hearings/testimony/2005test/metest040505.pdf.

5. The Pension Protection Act of 2006 amended IRC section 501 by adding a new subsection (q) that sets forth detailed rules for credit counseling agencies seeking exemption.

6. Ironically, though, the situation is little better on the proprietary side. The "separation of ownership and control" in large business corporations leads to their own "principal–agent problem"—how the shareholders (the principals) can ensure that the board members (the agents) act in their interests. Granted, business boards are subject to additional disciplines, such as stock markets that continuously value corporate performance. Nevertheless, the striking legal difference between the for-profit model and the nonprofit model would be more apparent than real if, in practicality, the nonprofits' untethered, self-perpetuating board structure were not unique to the nonprofit sector. In reality, because shareholders usually elect directors from a slate nominated by the current directors, the board of a publicly held corporation faces much the same replication imperative as a self-perpetuating nonprofit board. (See Brody 1996a.)

7. The LLC has been embraced as the ideal form of pass-through entity because it allows for active participation of all of the members without exposing any of them to personal liability. However, as described in a 1999 announcement by the Internal Revenue Service (IRS Ann. 99-102, 1999-43 I.R.B. 545), "Some state limited liability statutes—notably those of California, New York, and Texas—appear to require that an LLC be formed for a business purpose. However, no case law has decided this issue. . . . The IRS requires the satisfaction of 12 conditions, one of which is the LLC represent that state law permits its charitable status." See also McCray and Thomas (2001).

8. Op. Fla. Atty Gen., No. 99-23, 1999 Fla. AG LEXIS 23, April 30, 1999.

9. For an example of a state statute explicitly providing for distributions to members that are nonprofit corporations, see the 1997 Wisconsin Nonstock Corporation Act, § 181.1302(3).

10. Fremont-Smith (1991, 29) found that current law does not prevent a charity from relinquishing tax exemption "so long as the charitable organization's fiduciaries can demonstrate that they made a good faith determination that loss of exemption was in the best interests of the organization."

11. *Cuno v. Daimler Chrysler, Inc.* 386 F.3d 738 (6th Cir. 2004), vacated and remanded for lack of standing, 126 S.Ct. 1854 (2006).

12. S.C. Revenue Ruling 05-18, Dec. 13, 2005, available at http://www.sctax.org/NR/rdonlyres/52FC5E2A-82A8-4153-9806-CFB6DC1025F4/0/RR0518.pdf.

13. Pennsylvania Act 1997-55, at 10 Pennsylvania Statutes § 378(a) (2005).

14. Pennsylvania Act 1997-55, at 10 Pennsylvania Statutes § 378(b) (2005). Existing commercial activities are grandfathered (unless expanded), and exceptions are provided to a charity for "commercial business . . . intended only for the use of its employees, staff, alumni, faculty, members, students, clients, volunteers, patients or residents"; "commercial business [that] results in sales to the general public that are incidental or periodic rather than permanent and ongoing"; and "investment in publicly traded stocks and bonds; real estate, whether directly or indirectly."

15. *Selfspot, Inc. v. The Butler County Family YMCA,* 818 A.2d 587 (Pa. Commw. 2003).

16. *Guthrie Clinic, Ltd. v. Sullivan County Board of Assessment Appeals,* 898 A.2d 1194 (Pa. Commw. 2006).

17. *Club Systems of Tennessee, Inc. v. YMCA of Middle Tennessee,* 2005 STT 248-26 (Tenn. App. Dec. 19, 2005).

18. Treas. Reg. § 1.501(c)(3)–1(e)(1). See, for example, *Airlie Foundation v. Internal Revenue Service,* 283 F. Supp. 2d 58 (D.D.C. 2003); *Redlands Surgical Services, Inc. v. Commissioner,* 113 T.C. 47 (1999), *affirmed,* 242 F.3d 904 (9th Cir. 2001); *Housing Pioneers, Inc. v. Commissioner,* 58 F.3d 401 (9th Cir. 1995); *American Campaign Academy v. Commissioner,* 92 T.C. 1053 (1989); *B.S.W. Group, Inc. v. Commissioner,* 70 T.C. 352 (1978); *Church by Mail, Inc. v. Commissioner,* 765 F.2d 1387 (9th Cir. 1985); *Plumstead Theatre Society, Inc. v. Commissioner,* 675 F.2d 244 (9th Cir. 1982); *est of Hawaii v. Commissioner,* 71 T.C. 1067 (1979), *affirmed without published opinion,* 647 F.2d 170 (9th Cir. 1981); *Goldsboro Art League, Inc. v. Commissioner,* 75 T.C. 337 (1980); *Aid to Artisans, Inc. v. Commissioner,* 71 T.C. 202 (1978); *Harding Hospital, Inc. v. United States,* 505 F.2d 1068 (6th Cir. 1974).

For similar, but not identical language, see the Treasury Regulations for requirements of exemption under other IRC sections. For example, Treas. Reg. §1.501(c)(4)–1(a)(2)(i) provide "an organization is operated exclusively for the promotion of social welfare if it is primarily engaged in promoting in some way the common good and general welfare of the people of the community . . ." Services to members only do not qualify. Subsection (ii) further provides that an organization is not "operated primarily for the promotion of social welfare if its primary activity is . . . carrying on a business with the general public in a manner similar to organizations which are operated for profit." See, for example, *Vision Service Plan v. United States,* 96 A.F.T.R.2d 2005-7440 (E.D. Cal. 2005), *affirmed* 101 A.F.T.R. 2nd 656 (9th Cir. 2008) (unpublished) (exemption under § 501(c)(4) denied for private benefit).

19. IRS General Counsel Memo 34682, November 17, 1971.

20. Compare similar thinking under state property-tax exemption law. But see the criticism of the Minnesota Supreme Court in a case involving an assisted living center:

> The tax court's failure to consider whether Croixdale's services were below "cost" penalizes Croixdale for becoming more professional and fiscally responsible. If, to be exempt, a charity must be fiscally irresponsible, not use best management practices, and depend on operating donations to constantly bridge the shortfall in its cash needs, then most exempt charities will not survive because they cannot realistically depend on perpetual operating contributions. The whole purpose of the charitable exemption, to encourage and support the societal contributions of true charities, would be defeated by requiring that they be casually managed. More specifically, a charity that improves its infrastructure and establishes break-even budgets will be one that can stabilize and maximize the care that it can provide to the residents in need. These enhancements should be seen as being supportive of, not contradictory to, the charitable mission. (*Croixdale Inc. v. County of Washington*, 726 N.W.2d 483, 489 [Minn. 2007])

In *Croixdale*, however, the court held that the center failed to meet its burden of proof.

21. *Living Faith, Inc. v. Commissioner*, 950 F.2d 365, 371 (7th Cir. 1991). But see *Presbyterian Reformed Publishing v. Commissioner*, 70 T.C., 1070, reversed, 743 F.2d 148 (3rd Cir. 1982).

22. *Living Faith*, 375–76.

23. Under the "fragmentation rule" of Code § 513(c), "an activity does not lose identity as trade or business merely because it is carried on within a larger aggregate of similar activities or within a larger complex of other endeavors which may, or may not, be related to the exempt purposes of the organization." The classic examples are museum shops, in which taxability is determined item by item, and paid advertising in an exempt organization's educational magazine. Similarly, if the organization conducts an activity "on a larger scale than is reasonably necessary for performance" of the charitable purpose, the excess income will be subject to UBIT. Treas. Reg. § 1.501(c)(3)-1(d)(3). See, for example, Revenue Ruling 73-127, 1973-1 C.B. 221, involving an organization that operated a retail grocery store in a high-poverty area. While operating in a manner similar to profit-making businesses in the area, the store sold groceries at substantially lower prices than its competitors. The organization allocated 4 percent of its earning for a training program for the chronically unemployed, providing training in the various jobs in a retail food store (along with a small salary). Denying exemption under § 501(c)(3), the ruling held that although the purpose of providing job training for the unemployed is charitable and educational, operating a low-cost grocery store is an independent objective. Moreover, the grocery store operation was conducted on a scale larger than was reasonably necessary for the organization's job training program and was not intended to nor did it serve solely as a vehicle for carrying out the training program.

24. The IRS lost an attempt to allow the university deductions only for the marginal costs of renting out a hockey stadium. *Rensselaer Polytechnic Inst. v. Commissioner*, 732 F.2d 1058 (2d Cir. 1984). The Treasury regulations permit an allocation of dual-use expenses on "a reasonable basis" [Treas. Reg. § 1.512(a)-1(c)].

25. Kaplan (1980, 1433 and n. 17), quoting Revenue Revision of 1950: Hearings Before the House Comm. on Ways and Means, 81st Cong., 2d Sess. 580 (1950) (remarks of Rep. Dingell).

26. The debate leading up to the 1969 act, which, among other changes, imposes limits on business holdings of private foundations, in part reflected Congress's concern that foundation managers paid too much attention to maintaining and improving business interests to the detriment of their focus on charity. But to the extent Congress was motivated by the " 'diversion' of the foundation managers' attention to business affairs, 'away from their charitable duties,' " John G. Simon (1973) observed that "the diversified portfolio of a non-corporate-controlling foundation may require just as much financial attention as the single predominant investment of a corporate-controlling foundation."

27. See Revenue Ruling 81-178, 1981-2 C.B. 135, which contrasted two situations. In the first, the fact that the agreements granted the exempt organization the right to approve the quality and style of the licensed products did not alter the character of the income as royalties. However, the second organization would be compensated for endorsement of products and services, including personal appearances and interviews by its members, thus taking the income out of the royalty exclusion.

28. See *Sierra Club v. Commissioner*, 86 F.3d 1526 (9th Cir. 1996) (permitting the Sierra Club to approve the bank's promotional material, provide some telephone responses to members having problems with the program, and devote about 50 hours of mostly secretarial and clerical work over two years); *Oregon State University Alumni Association v. Commissioner*, 193 F. 3d 1098 (9th Cir. 1999) (holding that the compensation was for the use of the property rights, not for the minimal services).

29. As a separate matter, in 2004, Congress cracked down on the rules for claiming deductions for charitable donations of patents or other intellectual property (other than certain copyrights or inventory). The initial charitable deduction is the donor's basis or, if less, the fair market value of the property. The donor may then deduct certain additional amounts in the years the charity earns income from the donated property; the additional deductions are a specified percentage of the charity's net income that properly is allocable to the intellectual property itself (as opposed to the activity in which the intellectual property is used).

30. Compare "cause-related marketing," in which an amount will be donated to the charity based on the sales of a company's products or use of its services. See Galaskiewicz and Colman (2006), citing New York Attorney General (1999, 1): "the advertiser seldom mentions in the ad that it paid the nonprofit for the use of its name and logo and that the nonprofit has agreed not to enter into a similar agreement with a competitor."

31. Treas. Reg. § 1.501(c)(3)-1(d)(1)(ii).

32. Similar rules apply to other categories of exempt organizations. Particularly difficult can be determining when an activity of § 501(c)(6) trade association is exempt (because it advances a line of business) or taxable (because it provides services to members rather than the public). Consider two revenue rulings issued by the IRS. *Revenue Ruling 67-182*, 1967-1 C.B. 141, holds that an organization whose only activity is providing a reference library of "electric logs," maps, and information services used solely by its members in their oil exploration businesses is not exempt under § 501(c)(6). Because membership is limited and the facilities of the organization are available only to participating members, the organization's activities are not aimed at the improvement of business conditions in the industry as a whole. By contrast, *Revenue Ruling 67-296*, 1967-2 C.B. 212, holds that when a § 501(c)(6) professional association conducts classes to qualify persons for a specific status within the profession, no UBIT results.

33. *United Cancer Council v. Commissioner,* 165 F.3d 1173 (7th Cir. 1999).

34. *United Cancer Council v. Commissioner.*

35. See Brauer and Henzke (2004). See *Caracci v. Commissioner,* 118 T.C. 379 (2002). See also TAM 200435020 (May 5, 2004) (excise taxes asserted against church founder for excess benefit transactions); TAM 200435021 (May 3, 2004) (same, as against founder's spouse); TAM 200435019 (May 5, 2004) (same, as against founder's son); TAM 200435022 (May 5, 2004) (same); TAM 200435018 (May 5, 2004) (same, as against founder's son-in-law). It is unclear why the church in these rulings did not lose its tax exemption.

36. See Treas. Reg. § 1.501(c)(3)-1(d) and (f) (as amended in 2008).

37. For private foundations, Congress enacted specific penalty taxes not just for self-dealing, but also for failure to distribute a minimum payout for charitable purposes, maintenance of excess business holdings, and jeopardizing investments.

38. A section 501(c)(3) organization obtained a ruling from the IRS that its SMLLC would be disregarded even though the majority of the governing board of the SMLLC would be appointed by another entity—specifically, a local educational or civic organization that has similar charitable purposes and a strong, established presence in the region to be served. ("Under your state law, this will not make [the local organization] a member of [the SMLLC].") The organization seeking the ruling "believes this new structure will encourage and foster local community involvement while maintaining and institutionalizing [its] traditional standards of excellence." *Private Letter Ruling 2005-51-023* (September 28, 2005) (released December 23, 2005).

39. See Code § 514(c)(9) for debt-financed real estate investments by education institutions and Code § 168(h) for depreciation of "tax-exempt-use property."

40. *Revenue Ruling 98-15,* 1998-1 C.B. 718.

41. *Redlands Surgical Services v. Commissioner,* 242 F.3d 904 (9th Cir. 2001). Similarly, under *St. David's Health Care System v. United States,* 349 F.3d 232, 236-237 (5th Cir. 2003), it is not enough for the charitable participant to keep its exemption that "the partnership provides some (or even an extensive amount of) charitable services." Rather, the nonprofit partner must also have the "capacity to ensure that the partnership's operations further charitable purposes" (*id.* at 243). "The nonprofit should lose its tax-exempt status if it cedes control to the for-profit entity" (*id.* at 239). See also Colombo (2001); Jones (2005); Korman and Balsam (2000); Salins, Kindell, and Friedlander (1998, 13). For discussion of the IRS's view of revenue sharing arrangements, see Jones (2000, 633 n.178).

42. Revenue Procedure 2006-4, 2006-1 IRB 132, § 6.12.

43. IRS General Counsel Memo 34682, November 17, 1971.

44. The oversight subcommittee acknowledged this history and suggested, "Inasmuch as some exempt organizations have stated that the IRS, in reviewing the structure of their operations, did not object to proposals to spin off substantial unrelated activities into controlled subsidiaries as a means of not jeopardizing their exempt status, the Subcommittee recommended in particular that the Committee develop phase-in rules or other appropriate provisions to accommodate such existing arrangements" (U.S. Congress, Committee on Ways and Means 1988, VI.G).

45. But see Rev. Rul. 97-21, 1997-1 C.B. 121 (permitting tax-exempt hospitals to provide certain types of financial recruitment incentives to potential physicians) and, for

example, the incentive bonus program approved in Private Letter Ruling 2006-01-030 (Oct. 12, 2005) (but this private ruling explicitly did not address whether overall compensation was reasonable).

46. At the federal level, see the testimony presented at the April 20, 2005, hearing "Overview of the Tax-Exempt Sector," of the Committee on Ways and Means, available at http://waysandmeans.house.gov/hearings.asp?formmode=detail&hearing=400. See generally JCT (2005).

47. *Wexford Medical Group v. City of Cadillac,* 713 N.W.2d 734 [Mich. 2006].

48. Separately, a debate is occurring over the usefulness of "outcomes measurement" for charitable programs, but there is some interest in at least requiring charities to report their outcomes on the Form 990. See SFC (2004).

49. REDF's web site (http://redf.org) asserts, "The true impact of the collective work taking place in the nonprofit sector is undervalued by those both within and outside the sector due to an absence of appropriate metrics by which value creation may be tracked, calculated, and attributed to the philanthropic and public 'investments' financing those impacts. . . . As the nonprofit sector continues to compete for limited charitable dollars it becomes increasingly important that we be able to understand not simply that a program is a 'good cause,' but rather that its social returns argue for increasing our investments in their work." See generally the links on the web site of the Social Enterprise Reporter at http://www.sereporter.com/resources.php.

50. *Aid to Artisans, Inc. v. Commissioner,* 71 T.C. 202, 209-10 (1978).

51. Cf. *South End Italian Independent Club, Inc. v. Commissioner,* 87 T.C. 168 (1986), *acq. in result only* 1987-2 C.B. 1; *Women of the Motion Picture Industry v. Commissioner,* 74 T.C.M. 1217 (1997); and Technical Advice Memo. 1999-41-043 (June 28, 1999). Under applicable state law in these cases, only a licensed nonprofit organization could lawfully engage in these gambling activities. These authorities allowed section 162 business deductions for the full amount of bingo proceeds required by state law to be expended for charitable purposes (the deduction is allowed in the year distributed to or spent on charity).

52. http://www.bluemoonfund.org/grants/.

53. For more information on the law and regulations, go to http://www.cicregulator. gov.uk.

54. On April 30, 3008, Vermont became the first state to enact legislation allowing the creation of "low-profit limited liability companies" (L3Cs) (http://www.sec.state. vt.us/corps/dobiz/llc/llc_l3c.htm).

55. See Allen Bromberger's postings at http://www.socialedge.org, under "Nonprofit vs. For-Profit" (Aug. 19, 2005), and under "Creating a Hybrid For-Profit/Non-Profit Social Enterprise Structure" (June 6, 2005); see also Daniel Alcott's posting (June 6, 2005) (suggesting that if "there were a legal form recognized under tax code section 501 that was perhaps partially income tax exempt, could receive tax deductible contributions, but which was also permitted to generate income and reward shareholders for risking their capital in order to enable these companies to grow and flourish, these 'for benefit' companies could spend less time concerning themselves about legal structures and more time making a difference in their communities and society at large"). (Note that nonprofits are not eligible for Small Business Research grants.) More recently, see Wexler (2006) and Malani and Posner (2007).

REFERENCES

Abelson, Reed. 1998. "Charities Use For-Profit Units to Avoid Disclosing Finances." *New York Times,* February 9, A1.

American Law Institute. 2003. *Restatement (Third) of Trust.* Philadelphia: American Law Institute.

———. 2007a. *Principles of the Law of Nonprofit Organizations, Tentative Draft No. 1.* Philadelphia: American Law Institute.

———. 2007b. *Principles of the Law of Nonprofit Organizations, Council Draft No. 5.* Philadelphia: American Law Institute.

Aprill, Ellen P. 1989. "Lessons from the UBIT Debate." *Tax Notes* 45:1105–12.

Arenson, Karen W. 2006. "Regents Impose Limit on Colleges That Seek Profit." *New York Times,* January 21, A1.

Ben-Ner, Avner. 2004. "Outsourcing by Nonprofit Organizations." In *Effective Economic Decision Making by Nonprofit Organizations,* edited by Dennis Young (67–83). New York: The Foundation Center.

Brauer, Lawrence M., and Leonard J. Henzke Jr. 2004. " 'Automatic' Excess Benefit Transactions Under IRC 4958." In *IRS Exempt Organizations' Continuing Professional Education Technical Instruction Program for Fiscal Year 2004.* http://www.irs.gov/pub/irs-tege/eotopice04.pdf.

Brody, Evelyn. 1996a. "Agents Without Principals." *New York Law School Law Review* 40(3): 457–536.

———. 1996b. "Institutional Dissonance in the Nonprofit Sector." *Villanova Law Review* 41(2): 433–504.

———. 1998. "Of Sovereignty and Subsidy: Conceptualizing the Charity Tax Exemption." *Journal of Corporation Law* 23(4): 585–629.

———. 1999a. "A Taxing Time for the Bishop Estate: What Is the IRS Role in Charity Governance?" *University of Hawaii Law Review* 21(2): 537–91.

———. 1999b. "Charities in Tax Reform: Threats to Subsidies Overt and Covert." *Tennessee Law Review* 66(3): 687–763.

———, ed. 2002. *Property-Tax Exemption for Charities: Mapping the Battlefield.* Washington, DC: Urban Institute Press.

———. 2006. "The Legal Framework for Nonprofit Organizations." In *The Nonprofit Sector: A Research Handbook,* 2nd ed., edited by Walter W. Powell and Richard Steinberg (243–66). New Haven, CT: Yale University Press.

———. 2007. "The States' Growing Use of a Quid-Pro-Quo Rationale for the Charity Property Tax Exemption." *Exempt Organization Tax Review* 56(June): 269–88.

Brody, Evelyn, and Joseph J. Cordes. 2006. "Tax Treatment of Nonprofit Organizations: A Two-Edged Sword?" In *Nonprofits and Government: Collaboration and Conflict,* 2nd ed., edited by Elizabeth T. Boris and C. Eugene Steuerle (141–80). Washington, DC: Urban Institute Press.

Brown, Eleanor, and Al Slivinski. 2006. "Nonprofit Organizations and the Market." In *The Nonprofit Sector: A Research Handbook,* 2nd ed., edited by Walter W. Powell and Richard Steinberg (140–58). New Haven, CT: Yale University Press.

Colombo, John D. 2001. "A Framework for Analyzing Exemption and UBIT Effects of Joint Ventures." *Exempt Organization Tax Review* 34:187–96.

———. 2002. "Commercial Activity and Charitable Tax Exemption." *William and Mary Law Review* 44:487–567.

———. 2006. "In Search of Private Benefit." *Florida Law Review* 58:1063–1105.

Congressional Budget Office. 2005. *Taxing the Untaxed Business Sector*. http://www.cbo.gov/ftpdocs/65xx/doc6567/07-21-UntaxedBus.pdf.

Cordes, Joseph J., and Burton A. Weisbrod. 1998. "Differential Taxation of Nonprofits and the Commercialization of Nonprofit Revenues." In *To Profit or Not to Profit: The Commercial Transformation of the Nonprofit Sector,* edited by Burton A. Weisbrod (83–105). Cambridge: Cambridge University Press.

Cordes, Joseph J., Marie Gantz, and Thomas Pollak. 2002. "What Is the Property-Tax Exemption Worth?" In *Property-Tax Exemption for Charities: Mapping the Battlefield,* edited by Evelyn Brody (81–112). Washington, DC: Urban Institute Press.

Eliasberg, Kenneth C. 1965. "Charity and Commerce: Section 501(c)(3)—How Much Business Activity?" *Tax Law Review* 21:79–93.

Ford Foundation. 2005. "Part of the Solution: Leveraging Business and Markets for Low-Income People." http://www.fordfound.org/pdfs/impacts/part_of_the_solution.pdf.

Fremont-Smith, Marion R. 1991. "Relinquishing Tax Exemption: State and Federal Constraints." Paper presented at the Nonprofit Forum, New York City, October 16.

Galaskiewicz, Joseph, and Michelle Sinclair Colman. 2006. "Collaboration between Corporations and Nonprofit Organizations." In *The Nonprofit Sector: A Research Handbook,* 2nd ed., edited by Walter W. Powell and Richard Steinberg (180–204). New Haven, CT: Yale University Press.

Government Accountability Office. 2005. *Nonprofit, For-Profit, and Government Hospitals: Uncompensated Care and Other Community Benefits.* http://www.gao.gov/new.items/d05743t.pdf.

Grassley, Charles. 2006. Letter to Richard J. Davidson, president of the American Hospital Association. http://hospitalpricing.com/SenatorGrassleyLetterToAHA.pdf.

———. 2007. "Grassley Seeks CBO Analysis of Certain Aspects of College Athletics' Tax Exemption, Universities' Tax Exempt Financing." Press release, April 4. http://finance.senate.gov/press/Gpress/2007/prg040407.pdf.

Hall, Peter Dobkin. 1992. *Inventing the Nonprofit Sector.* Baltimore: Johns Hopkins University Press.

Halperin, Daniel. 2005. "The Unrelated Business Income Tax and Payments from Controlled Entities." *Tax Notes* 109(December 12): 1443–49.

Hansmann, Henry. 1981. "The Rationale for Exempting Nonprofit Organizations from Corporate Income Taxation." *Yale Law Journal* 91(1): 54–100.

———. 1989. "Unfair Competition and the Unrelated Business Income Tax." *Virginia Law Review* 75:605–35.

Hardin, Russell. 1997. "Economic Theories of the State." In *Perspectives on Public Choice,* edited by Dennis C. Mueller (21–34). New York: Cambridge University Press.

Hines, James R. 1999. "Nonprofit Business Activity and the Unrelated Business Income Tax." In *Tax Policy and the Economy,* vol. 13, edited by James M. Poterba (57–84). Cambridge, MA: MIT Press.

Hopkins, Bruce R. 1992. "The Most Important Concept in the Law of Tax Exempt Organizations Today: The Commerciality Doctrine." *Exempt Organization Tax Review* 5(March): 459–67.

Internal Revenue Service. 2005. *FY 2006 Exempt Organizations (EO) Implementing Guidelines.* http://www.irs.gov/pub/irs-tege/fy_2006_implementing_guidelines.pdf.

James, Estelle. 1986. "Comments." In *The Economics of Nonprofit Institutions: Studies in Structure and Policy,* edited by Susan Rose-Ackerman (152–58). New York: Oxford University Press.

James, Estelle, and Dennis R. Young. 2006. "Fee Income and Commercial Ventures." In *Financing Nonprofits: Bridging Theory and Practice,* edited by Dennis R. Young (93–121). Latham, MD: AltaMira Press.

JCT. See U.S. Congress, Joint Committee on Taxation.

Jones, Darryll K. 2000. "The Scintilla of Individual Profit: In Search of Private Inurement and Excess Benefit." *Virginia Tax Review* 19:575–681.

———. 2005. "Special Allocations and Preferential Distributions in Joint Ventures Involving Taxable and Tax Exempt Entities." *Ohio Northern University Law Review* 31:13–39.

Kaplan, Richard L. 1980. "Intercollegiate Athletics and the Unrelated Business Income Tax." *Columbia Law Review* 80:1430–73.

Korman, Rochelle, and Dahlia Balsam. 2000. "Joint Ventures with For-Profits after Rev. Rul. 98-15." *Exempt Organization Tax Review* 27:441–50.

Lasprogata, Gail, and Marya N. Cotten. 2003. "Contemplating 'Enterprise': The Business and Legal Challenges of Social Entrepreneurship." *American Business Law Journal* 41:67–112.

Malani, Anup, and Eric Posner. 2007. "The Case for For-Profit Charities." *Virginia Law Review* 93:2017–64.

Mayer, Caroline E. 2006. "IRS Revoking Exemptions of Credit Counselors." *Washington Post,* January 13, D1.

McCray, Richard A., and Ward L. Thomas. 2001. "Limited Liability Companies as Exempt Organizations—Update." http://www.irs.gov/pub/irs-tege/eotopicb01.pdf.

New York Attorney General. 1999. *What's In a Name? Public Trust, Profit, and the Potential for Deception.* http://www.oag.state.ny.us/press/reports/nonprofit/full_text.pdf.

Oversight Subcommittee. See U.S. Congress, House Committee on Ways and Means, Subcommittee on Oversight.

Riley, Margaret. 2007. "Unrelated Business Income Tax Returns, 2003: Financial Highlights and a Special Analysis of Nonprofit Charitable Organizations' Revenue and Taxable Income." *Statistics of Income Bulletin* (Winter) no. 26: 88–115. Washington, DC: Internal Revenue Service. http://www.irs.gov/pub/irs-soi/03eounrel.pdf.

Rose-Ackerman, Susan. 1982. "Unfair Competition and Corporate Income Taxation." *Stanford Law Review* 34:1017.

Rushton, Michael. 2007. "Why Are Nonprofits Exempt from the Corporate Income Tax?" *Nonprofit and Voluntary Sector Quarterly* 36(4): 662–75.

Salins, Mary Jo, Judy Kindell, and Marvin Friedlander. 1998. "Whole Hospital Joint Ventures." http://www.irs.gov/pub/irs-tege/eotopica99.pdf.

Sanders, Michael I. 2002. *Joint Ventures Involving Tax-Exempt Organizations,* 2nd ed. New York: Wiley.

———. 2005. "The Push and Pull of Tax Exemption Law on the Organization and Delivery of Health Care Services: Health Care Joint Ventures Between Tax-Exempt Organizations and For-Profit Entities." *Health Matrix* 15(1): 83–123.

Sansing, Richard. 1998. "The Unrelated Business Income Tax, Cost Allocation, and Productive Efficiency." *National Tax Journal* 51(2): 291–302.

Schlesinger, Mark, and Bradford Gray. 2006. "Nonprofit Organizations and Health Care: Some Paradoxes of Persistent Scrutiny." In *The Nonprofit Sector: A Research Handbook,* 2nd ed., edited by Walter W. Powell and Richard Steinberg (378–414). New Haven: Yale University Press.

Selingo, Jeffrey. 2005. "Leaders' Views About Higher Education, Their Jobs, and Their Lives." *Chronicle of Higher Education,* November 4, A26.

SFC. See U.S. Congress, Senate Finance Committee.

Simon, John G. 1973. "On the Role of Foundations Today and the Effect of the Tax Reform Act of 1969 upon Foundations." Statement submitted to the Subcommittee on Foundations, Committee on Finance, U.S. Senate (October 2), 93rd Cong., 1st sess. 175, 185, n.2.

Simon, John G., Harvey Dale, and Laura B. Chisolm. 2006. "The Tax Treatment of Nonprofit Organizations: A Review of Federal and State Policies." In *The Nonprofit Sector: A Research Handbook,* 2nd ed., edited by Walter W. Powell and Richard Steinberg. New Haven, CT: Yale University Press.

Smith, Stephen Rathgeb. 2006. "Government Financing of Nonprofit Activity." In *Nonprofits and Government: Collaboration and Conflict,* 2nd ed., edited by Elizabeth T. Boris and C. Eugene Steuerle (219–56). Washington, DC: Urban Institute Press.

Stecklow, Steve. 2005. "How Companies Help Charities and Cut Inventory." *Wall Street Journal,* December 10, A1.

Steinberg, Richard. 1991. " 'Unfair' Competition by Nonprofits and Tax Policy." *National Tax Journal* 44:351–58.

Steuerle, C. Eugene. 1998. *Just What Do Nonprofits Provide?* Washington, DC: The Urban Institute.

———. 2001. "When Nonprofits Conduct Exempt Activities as Taxable Enterprises." *Emerging Issues in Philanthropy* Brief No. 4. http://www.urban.org/url.cfm?ID=310254.

Stokeld, Fred, and Sam Young. 2006. "IRS Pursuing Excess Benefit Transactions Involving EOs." *Tax Notes* 1117(October 31).

Stone, Ethan G. 2005. "Adhering to the Old Line: Uncovering the History and Political Function of the Unrelated Business Income Tax." *Emory Law Journal* 54:1475–1556.

Tuckman, Howard P., and Cyril F. Chang. 2006. "Commercial Activity, Technological Change, and Nonprofit Mission." In *The Nonprofit Sector: A Research Handbook,*

2nd ed., edited by Walter W. Powell and Richard Steinberg (629–45). New Haven, CT: Yale University Press.

U.S. Congress, Joint Committee on Taxation. 2000. *Study of Present-Law Taxpayer Confidentiality and Disclosure Provisions as Required by Section 3802 of the Internal Revenue Service Restructuring and Reform Act of 1998, Volume II: Study of Disclosure Provisions Relating to Exempt Organizations.* JCS-1-00. Washington, DC: U.S. Congress, Joint Committee on Taxation. http://www.house.gov/jct/s-1-00vol2.pdf.

———. 2005. *Historical Development and Present Law of the Federal Tax Exemption for Charities and Other Tax-Exempt Organizations.* JCX-29-05. Washington, DC: U.S. Congress, Joint Committee on Taxation. http://www.house.gov/jct/x-29-05.pdf.

———. 2006. "Estimates of Federal Tax Expenditures for Fiscal Years 2006–2010." JCS 2-06. Washington, DC: U.S. Congress, Joint Committee on Taxation. http://www.house.gov/jct/s-2-06.pdf.

———. 2007. "General Explanation of Tax Legislation Enacted in the 109th Congress." JCS-1-07. Washington, DC: U.S. Congress, Joint Committee on Taxation. http://www.house.gov/jct/s-1-07.pdf.

U.S. Congress, House Committee on Ways and Means, Subcommittee on Oversight. 1988a. "UBIT Recommendations." LEXIS, Fedtax Library, Tax Notes Today File, June 24, 88 TNT 132-5.

———. 1988b. "Written Comments on Discussion Options Relating to the Unrelated Business Income Tax." WMCP 100-30. Washington, DC: Government Printing Office.

U.S. Congress, Senate Finance Committee. 2004. "Senate Finance Committee Staff Discussion Draft, Tax Exempt Governance Proposals, June 22, 2004." http://www.finance.senate.gov/hearings/testimony/2004test/062204stfdis.pdf.

U.S. Treasury Department. 1965. *Treasury Department Report on Private Foundations.* Printed for the use of the Committee on Ways and Means, 89th Cong., 1st sess. Washington, DC: Government Printing Office.

Weisbrod, Burton A. 1988. *The Nonprofit Economy.* Cambridge, MA: Harvard University Press.

Wexler, Robert A. 2006. "Social Enterprise: A Legal Context." *Exempt Organization Tax Review* 54:233–44.

Yetman, Robert J. 2005. "Causes and Consequences of the Unrelated Business Income Tax." Presented at National Tax Association meeting, Miami, December.

5

The Strategic and Economic Value of Hybrid Nonprofit Structures

Howard P. Tuckman

Weisbrod (1998a) argues that since institutions are the fundamental arrangements through which societies seek to deal with social and economic problems, it is important to understand the effectiveness of the alternative forms that they take. Proper design of a nonprofit can play an important role in helping it to achieve its goals. Structure affects ability to acquire resources, how services are organized and delivered, how effectively risk is managed, legal standing, and how an organization is perceived. It can also affect the environment in which the business of the organization is conducted and its culture. For these reasons, it behooves a nonprofit to treat its structure as strategic and to incorporate explicit discussions of the value of different organizational mixes into its planning process.[1]

We use the term structure in this chapter to refer to the legal form(s) nonprofits choose for conducting their business, to the number of entities that make up the organization, and to the relationships among these entities. A simple structure consists of one nonprofit delivering its services to a target clientele in one location, whereas a hybrid structure (a structure consisting of at least one for-profit or equivalent and one nonprofit) involves a holding company with one or more nonprofit and for-profit entities. The use of for-profits by nonprofits arises out of the fact that, in an era of increasing financial pressure, increased donations are not probable for most nonprofits; hence, interest has grown in increasing commercial revenues (Weisbrod 1998b). Which structure is best for an organization depends on its goals and circumstances and on the constraints placed on it by the legal, political, and operating environment.[2]

The chapter focuses on a particular form of hybrid involving a for-profit subsidiary controlled by a nonprofit. The decision to form such a hybrid may initially be prompted by potential economic benefits from modifying the operations of a nonprofit. However, for such a change to succeed, there must be a match between the strategic reasons for creating the hybrid and the structure of such an entity. To examine this issue, I first discuss the relationship between strategy and structure generally and then consider specific strategies, their relation to the creation of a hybrid structure, and issues that arise in operating a hybrid structure and when structure and strategy are not aligned. I also present evidence on the prevalence of hybrid structures among operating nonprofits and an example of a hybrid structure.

Strategy and Structure

Key to organizational success—along with an environment of quality leadership, a supportive culture, and an aligned rewards system—is a structure matched to strategy (Pearce and Robinson 1991). The principle of matching the two can be applied either within the context of a single firm or as a factor in the design of a hybrid structure. A nonprofit must be appropriately organized if it is to act efficiently; well-developed goals, objectives, strategies, and policies will not be sufficient to ensure success unless structure facilitates the carrying out of these elements of strategy. A poorly designed structure can impede action, create perverse incentives, slow service delivery, or lead to serious miscommunication. It can also cause an entity to have lower revenues or higher expenditures than it might have under a more optimal arrangement.

Chandler's (1962) classic study of 20 large corporations over a long period found a four-part pattern in organizational adaptation: choice of a strategy, administrative problems that develop and result in performance decline, adoption of a new structure in closer alignment with strategic needs, and improved profitability and execution. When structure failed to change to reflect strategic needs, organizational performance became inefficient because of a mismatch between the way activities are carried out and what is required.

Changes in strategy are not the only basis for structural change; non-profits face constraints that affect their strategies, and changes in these can cause a need to restructure. Consider, for example, the situation of an advocacy organization lobbying for action to reduce global warming. A single 501(c)(3) nonprofit faces legal constraints on how much of its revenues can be spent on lobbying. It can create a separate entity as a 501(c)(4) organization and collect revenues for lobbying, but the donors that contributed to the organization cannot deduct these for tax purposes. It then uses the 501(c)(3) to engage in educational activities, thus increasing its total activity in support of its mission. In this case, the nonprofit changes its structure to take advantage of both the tax benefits and an entity that facilitates lobbying.

Likewise, consider a nonprofit symphony orchestra that is poorly endowed but has the potential to claim income from the sale of music videos for its performance. It can earn revenues from this source without changing its structure as a single nonprofit, but limits exist on the amount of commercial revenue it can receive without loss of its tax-exempt status. If the videos are judged to be an unrelated business activity then the limit will apply. Creation of a for-profit to produce, own, and sell the videos avoids the chance that the nonprofit will have its tax exemption challenged, but the for-profit must pay taxes on its earnings and it cannot be the parent of the nonprofit.

Economic Motivations to Create Multiple Structures

Since the structure of a nonprofit is explicitly chosen to support its strategies and to help it overcome environmental constraints, identifying the most common strategic needs of nonprofits and the types of constraints that affect them is useful. Three broad economic strategies may be identified that can potentially be facilitated by creating a hybrid structure.

Supply/Cost

This category of economic strategies focuses on costs and how they affect production. In the case of a single nonprofit, the issue is whether creating multiple subsidiaries can reduce costs, either by increasing access to the consumer of the product or by reducing operating, tax, or other costs. The decision to create a hybrid usually involves identifying the lower costs or improved product that will result by establishing a for-profit subsidiary. This is especially the case when a nonprofit decides to undertake a new commercial activity and must consider whether the new business will perform better under a hybrid structure with a central entity rather than as a stand-alone business. The nonprofit must also decide whether to start a new business, acquire an existing one, or form a joint venture.

Economic strategies also involve taking advantage of the presence of economies of scale and scope. Economies of scale (obtaining lower average costs by increasing the volume of production of the service) are a factor in the decision to add a new entity to the structure; two or more businesses can lower their production costs by increasing their joint volume, usually by sharing activities. In contrast, economies of scope strategies are based on the ability of two or more businesses to produce a range of cost savings because multiple products can share part of the cost structure, thus lowering the costs of production. An example is when a for-profit subsidiary that produces, uses, rents, and sells scenery attains economies of scale because the same sets are used over multiple productions, reducing the average cost of staging each production. A health care company can attain economies of scope if it does marketing, accounting, legal work, and hiring out of the corporate parent and provides these services to multiple subsidiaries. However, as the complexity of the structure rises, the potential for diseconomies of scale and scope rises as well. Moreover, creation of a separate subsidiary, particularly a hybrid, may result in higher costs if the original consumers of the nonprofit's services are split across more companies, making it more expensive to provide the same total level of services.

A major source of economies of scale is when the parent provides accounting, advertising, financing, human resource, and problem-solving services. The savings under these circumstances can be considerable, but recent developments enabling nonprofits to outsource many of these functions have reduced the advantages to centralizing these functions.

Demand/Revenue

The strategies that fall into this category involve ways to use demand for one service to build demand for another (complements), augment demand through the use of substitute services, use the array of services and products to create a one-stop shopping advantage, use differentiation strategies that emerge from the creation of the hybrid, or use unrelated business-acquisition strategies to balance fluctuations in demand. Health care chains build demand for their products both through offering complementary services (e.g., diagnostic testing and physician services) and providing substitutes designed to capture a different market segment (e.g., the offering of "wellness services"). Nonprofit universities offer one-stop shopping by providing housing, food, housecleaning, formal degrees, and certificate programs as a package or in pieces. Product differentiation, designed to enable the charging of premium prices, is achievable by using a famous name, such as the Museum of Modern Art, to augment the sale of objects ranging from wristwatches and scarves to reproductions of statues and pieces of furniture. The effectiveness of the hybrid structure in delivering goods and services determines (in part) the effectiveness of these strategies.

Portfolio balance becomes important here, but in a different sense than the one described earlier. The parent can implement financial strategies to offset downturns in one revenue source by creating an offsetting revenue source, thus at least partially hedging against downturns. Although this type of activity involves substantial funding and strong investment skills, it poses unique opportunities for some nonprofits. For example, given substantial size and resources, the parent of a large theater-based hybrid may be able to offset small audiences from inclement weather by purchasing financial contracts that pay off when bad weather occurs. Alternatively, a research hospital may be able to offset a decline in government research monies with revenues from clinical trials, and advocacy groups can add political action committees to their portfolios to mitigate the effects of congressional limits on 501(c)(3) activities. The goal of these and similar portfolio balance strategies is to take advantage of the hybrid structures to reduce business risk.

Strategies involving diversification into businesses with little, if any, relation to the mission of the parent also can have a positive effect on stabilizing revenues. The goal may be to build significant financial resources for the parent, and to do this, the new business should be acquired on attractive financial terms. An issue arises as to whether a nonprofit parent has the expertise to make better acquisitions than its for-profit competitors since operating an unrelated business involves hiring knowledgeable managers and learning a new industry. Such strategies require careful thought and an awareness of what is feasible. For example, the Museum of Modern Art may find it more attractive to use its gift shops to sell fine jewelry created by others than to buy the jewelry company.

Strategies That Respond to Competition

Tuckman (1998) explores differences in the competitive strategies of nonprofits in markets where they compete with other nonprofits and in those where they compete with for-profits. After providing examples of the differences in strategy, I argue that nonprofits competing in mixed-mode product markets employ several different strategies to improve their revenues and that they adjust both their organizational forms and their product content in response to competitive pressures.

A hybrid structure potentially offers several competitive advantages, including greater organizational diversification, a larger product line, more resources for potential use, a broader and more diverse array of talents available within the organization, and economies of scale and scope. A key question for senior management is whether the assembled structure has achieved strategic fit; realization of this goal can produce lower costs or transfer of key skills, expertise, and managerial solutions. A related question is whether the actions of the parent recognize the competitive advantages the structure itself offers or whether they focus on taking advantage of individual parts. It takes time and a willingness to adapt behavior to take advantage of the benefits of the hybrid structure, and it may also involve a change in the thinking of the nonprofit parent's senior management.

Organizational Benefits of Creating For-Profit Subsidiaries

Creation of a hybrid with a for-profit subsidiary offers additional organizational advantages that complement the economic advantages described above. First, many nonprofits need to protect their assets, especially when undertaking unrelated business-income-generating activities. For example, a nonprofit theater selling parking spaces incurs the risk that someone will be injured on the lot and sue for damages, an attempt that, if successful, could reduce the nonprofit's assets. To protect against this risk, a for-profit enterprise is formed to operate the parking lot as a separate corporation, which legally isolates the financial risk of the for-profit entity from the nonprofit. This protection is especially important for nonprofits with a weak asset base (Anheier and Toepler 1998).[3]

Second, segregation of assets may be helpful in attracting donors who would otherwise be concerned that their gifts would be used in unacceptable ways (e.g., dissipated on operations or spent on purposes other than the donor intended). For example, a nonprofit serving the homeless has weak finances and is subject to constant cash flow problems. It identifies a potential donor who has a strong desire to see the nonprofit feed the homeless but who is concerned about the reliability of the homeless nonprofit. The nonprofit establishes a separate and new nonprofit subsidiary with the mission of feeding the homeless and appoints a subsidiary board of directors to oversee preservation of the donor's endowment. The donation is secured because the subsidiary can provide assurance that the endowment to feed the hungry will not be used to meet the cash flow problems of housing the needy. Similarly, creation of a separate foundation may also provide assurance to the donor that trustees with a particular interest will pursue it apart from the day-to-day operations of an entity running programs or delivering services.

Third, subsidiaries may be useful in targeting assets to specific groups. For example, a hospital may set up a separate subsidiary to provide hospice services. By operating it with a different name and a separate identity, it becomes feasible to find a donor who has no interest in the hospital but a strong concern with improving the care of those who are dying. The subsidiary also has strategic value if it attracts patients who believe they will receive better treatment from the hospice than they would if they remained in the hospital, or if it can treat dying patients more cost-effectively than the hospital (Sloan 1998).

Fourth, we have noted that too much commercial activity in a nonprofit may endanger its tax status. The unrelated business income tax falls on commercial activity that is a trade or business, is regularly carried on, and is not substantially related to the tax-exempt mission of the organization. A nonprofit with such activity is potentially in danger of losing its status if the IRS determines it is no longer operated exclusively for its exempt purpose (see Brody's chapter 4), but there are no explicit guidelines as to how much unrelated business is too much. Some nonprofits set up a for-profit entity for peace of mind, to not have to worry about unexpected growth in income, and others do it because they have or expect substantial sources of revenues.

Fifth, multiple subsidiaries create the opportunity to share the salaries of senior management across multiple entities. This has the advantage of enabling the nonprofit to account for the time spent on each entity more accurately than if all the salary were allocated to one activity. For example, the president of a health care delivery system may spend considerable time on the nonprofit hospital subsidiary, the nonprofit hospice subsidiary, and the nonprofit educational program subsidiary. Apportionment of his salary across these activities has value from a budgeting, planning, and strategy perspective. However, this practice can also obscure the earnings of senior management from the public view.[4]

It is less clear if salaries can be allocated to for-profit entities because, under some state laws, the law limits the ability of nonprofit administrators to receive payment from their for-profit subsidiaries. Moreover, the IRS has launched a comprehensive enforcement project to address the practices used to set tax-exempt organization compensation, to report it, to define the form it takes, and to oversee it (Everson 2004).

Sixth, hybrid structures enable the nonprofit to separate employees with different talents, skills, and career goals. Young (1981) has argued that managers attracted to the nonprofit sector differ from those who enter the for-profit sector, and some individuals may do very well in dispensing services but are not skilled in business practices. Given the differences, it may make sense to establish different environments for those engaged in commercial activity. Creation of a separate for-profit enables management to use different incentive structures, to create synergies by grouping people with similar skills, and to establish appropriate policies as to how work is carried out and evaluated. For example, the employees of a public television station may focus on high standards of artistic creativity, long and precise research, and provision of programs that educate the public. These individuals may find it difficult to engage in commercial activities such as making commercials that emphasize quick creation of videos, limited research, and production values that meet the expectations of their sponsors and the general public. Creation of a for-profit joint venture enables the station to hire employees who meet these commercial needs while preserving the appropriate environment for those on the public television side of the business.

Finally, a hybrid structure may be desirable if it creates greater flexibility for a nonprofit to work with a for-profit partner. If a public television station wishes to earn revenue by making commercials, it is easier to accomplish this goal through a for-profit entity that operates with dif-

ferent operational and financial rules than the nonprofit station normally uses. The new entity may allow joint ownership of the equipment
and intellectual property, making it easier to pay high salaries to celebri-
ties and to provide co-branding of the product. Implementation of the
hybrid strategy creates an ability for organizations with different legal
structures to collaborate (LaMay and Weisbrod 1998).

An Example of a Hybrid Structure

This section examines a specific example of why and how nonprofit and
for-profit entities created a hybrid organizational structure. The case
involves a nationally known nonprofit testing agency that created a for-
profit subsidiary and another involves a for-profit used car company that
opened a nonprofit company to provide automobiles to low-income
people. The purpose is to shed light on the reasons for creating a hybrid
and to briefly examine its structure.

A Simple Hybrid: Vehicles for Change/Freedom Wheels

A for-profit entity, Precision CertiPro Warehouse, was an aftermarket
auto parts distributor located in College Park, Maryland, until it went
out of business in 1966 or 1967 because of mismanagement. The president and general manager of Precision conceived the idea of creating a
501(c)(3) nonprofit that would provide cars to needy individuals at low
prices in communities where CertiPro did business. With a $10,000
interest-free loan from Precision and a grant of $20,000 from the presi-
dent and general manager, the nonprofit Vehicles for Change (VFC) was
founded "to assist less fortunate families who are ready, willing, and able
to advance themselves to become financially secure and help others"
(http://www.vehiclesforchange.org). Essentially, the nonprofit selected
families that met its criteria and sold them reliable automobiles at low
prices and helped them pay for auto insurance, title, tags, and taxes. The
nonprofit's intention was to assist those who wanted to work to become
self-sufficient by addressing their need for transportation, thereby increasing their sense of independence, self-confidence, and self-esteem.

Precision had a different mission as a for-profit. It was not formally
part of the hybrid structure, but it supplied donated or reduced-cost parts
for auto repair; assisted VFC to gain funding from corporate partners

such as Marriott, BB&T Bank, and Giant Food; and encouraged its senior management to serve on the VFC nonprofit board. Volunteers from Precision were also involved in soliciting car donations, seeking out garages willing to perform repairs at a discount, doing volunteer work, and attracting donations from new and used car dealers.

The nonprofit subsidiary was created for the tax benefits it provided. These included the tax advantage to those who donated a used auto to VFC and the deductions for donations of repair work and parts. The nonprofit created a more complex structure by collaborating with local social service agencies and other government entities able to identify individuals who qualify for assistance and, in 2005, VFC was awarded a $365,000 contract to bring its programs into eight new counties in the state. In addition, new contracts were awarded to expand the program in several regions where the program has operated for the past several years. The new regions include the cities of Lynchburg and Fredericksburg, and Amherst, Bedford, Campbell, Caroline, King George, Spotsylvania, and Stafford counties, Virginia.

VFC created a for-profit subsidiary, Freedom Wheels, to assist with purchase of automobiles in the marketplace after it found that donated automobiles were not sufficient to meet the demand. It used the new entity to buy used autos in the marketplace. This created a hybrid structure with a nonprofit parent, a for-profit subsidiary, and collaborative and contractual relationships with state and county entities.

The Three Dimensions of Structure

Several structural features of a hybrid nonprofit are likely to play an important role in how such an entity functions, and indeed, in whether moving to a more complex organizational form is advantageous to the nonprofit. There are at least three ways to describe the structure of a hybrid nonprofit: by how operational and fiscal control is exercised among its component parts, by the legal forms of the entities composing the structure, and by its complexity.[5] These are not mutually exclusive.

Control

At the most basic level, there are several reasons why when the setting is one in which (a) the commercial venture to be exploited arises as a joint product of the core activities of a nonprofit, and (b) a nonprofit seeks to exploit these opportunities to generate income to support its core mission, that a hybrid structure involving a nonprofit parent which exercises control over a for-subsidiary may be appropriate. Since the driving strategy for creating the hybrid in the first place is to enable the nonprofit to better fulfill its nonprofit mission, the nonprofit parent should be at the center of the structure with considerable say in the activities of the for-profit subsidiary. For its part, the for-profit subsidiary is able to undertake activities, including issuing stock, not permitted to the nonprofit parent. Based on this logic, a hybrid entity will have a nonprofit parent that gains the benefits of its charitable status and one or more for-profits that follow a strategy of earning revenue with the goal of using some portion of this to finance the strategic initiatives of the parent; these subsidiaries exist to facilitate its operation and enhance its fiscal position (Oleck 1988; Weisbrod 1998a).

Operational control involves the extent to which a parent controls the implementation of the policies, strategies, and actions of its subsidiaries. A strategic planning process with input from each of the entities of the structure will best determine the strategies. In the case of affiliations, alliances, and joint ventures, strategies are likely to be jointly determined, and the role of each party will likely be specified in the documents creating the arrangement; the parent may be a new entity created to represent the parties to the venture. In most cases the strategies the hybrid follows will usually reflect the priorities of the parent, but there are cases where legal separation of the entities is necessary to establish the subsidiary's independence. For example, section 509(a)(3) organizations are intended to be public charities that, in carrying out their missions, support another exempt organization (e.g., support agencies that provide key services for hospitals). The Internal Revenue Service (IRS) argues that an abuse that can result in the loss of tax-exempt status occurs if, almost immediately after a charitable donation is made to the 509(a)(3) organization, it makes an unsecured loan of all or a significant proportion of the funds back to the donor (Everson 2004).

A multitude of different execution arrangements can exist across hybrid organizations, ranging from purely independent to strongly monitored oversight of the process by the parent. To some degree, the selected organizational form reflects this range of options—for example, loose affiliation of entities, membership organizations, associations, alliances, joint ventures or partnerships, corporations, outsourcing to entities outside the structure to entities tightly controlled by the parent through legal agreement, use of overlapping corporate officers on the parent and subsidiary board, and informal understandings between senior management teams.[6]

The need for elaborate control mechanisms is somewhat less important when a subsidiary produces services that have little impact on the main mission of the parent or its reputation. For example, a subsidiary of a hospital that provides catering services will likely operate largely autonomously, as might a subsidiary performing diagnostic testing. In these types of operations, it can be easier to set a dollar target for a commercial nonprofit subsidiary and leave it free to operate without parental constraints. However, situations exist where the parent's needs require some degree of control. For example, a for-profit subsidiary monitoring clinical trials for a hospital can have substantial effect on its reputation and hence require monitoring. Similarly, a joint venture between a university and a pharmaceutical company may necessitate more oversight than a venture between a housing developer and the same university because of the problems in drug development. Who exercises the control, and how, is also important in determining the tax status of the parent.[7]

A second dimension of control involves how much parental control exists over the fiscal affairs of its subsidiaries. Since an important reason a parent creates a hybrid structure is to implement a strategy of revenue augmentation, it may expect some control over the returns of its subsidiaries. Control can be specific targets set centrally with no input from the subsidiary, targets jointly determined, or targets set by the individual subsidiaries and provided to the parent. Most likely is a joint agreement between parent and subsidiary on the basis of a realistic forecast of revenues and expenditures of the business and of the needs of the parent. In a mixed hybrid structure (namely, multiple nonprofits and for-profits) this type of agreement will exist for both types of entities because both have the potential to produce revenues for the parent. The requirement that nonprofit subsidiaries return revenues to the parents means that the latter gets to reinvest earnings across entities in a way that implements the strategic goals of the organization.

Indeed, a further aspect of fiscal control involves the parent's role as portfolio manager (Thompson and Strickland 1993). Not only can a parent set targets for each subsidiary to earn, it can also determine how earned income will be distributed and used. Consider, for example, the case of a parent with a portfolio of two nonprofit and two for-profit subsidiaries. If the parent operates efficiently, it will return some earnings to the for-profits to reinvest, following a strategy of increasing the capacity of its subsidiaries to earn revenues. It will also decide how much it will invest in each of the nonprofits, either by allowing them to accumulate their revenues or by using for-profit subsidiary earnings to subsidize their operations. Finally, it will allocate a portion of the earnings to itself, to grow its operations, to diversify its activities, or to set funds aside for future use. This type of allocation process is similar to that of diversified global companies, but the difference is that the ultimate goal of the parent should be the successful realization of its nonprofit mission. Hence, the parent may not use the same criteria to deploy its resources across its subsidiaries as does a diversified for-profit corporation.

Legal Form

A parent can construct a hybrid structure that consists of entities with a variety of legal forms; the issue arises as to which to choose. The decision can be separated into three parts: arriving at the conclusion that another entity is needed to accomplish the parent's mission, the choice of the nonprofit or for-profit form, and, within each of the latter categories, which legal form will best accomplish its objectives.

Consider, for example, a nonprofit theater company that makes scenery and sells it to the public. It decides that it can enhance its scenery sales by assigning this task to a new entity on the basis of a variety of factors, including the concern that too much unrelated business income may trigger IRS scrutiny of its tax status, a desire to gain access to more capital, and a wish to operate more efficiently. It chooses the for-profit form for the new company because it offers greater access to bank loans and private investors and because it expects the growth of the for-profit business to augment the parent's revenue, leading to the potential threat that the IRS would rule the nonprofit activity as not sufficiently mission-related to justify retention of its tax-exempt status. A for-profit subsidiary is set up as a corporation because it offers the most flexibility to the hybrid.

Suppose that the theater company subsequently decides it can take advantage of an adjacent parking lot to earn revenue. Its strategy calls for buying the lot from a private owner and lodging it in a separate, for-profit entity. The specific form of this entity is chosen on the basis of which form best facilitates the implementation of the strategy. This strategy leads to a new hybrid structure consisting of a parent nonprofit and two for-profit corporate subsidiaries; one with the purpose of earning revenue from the sale of scenery and the other of earning revenue from the sale of parking spaces. The new structure facilitates a strategy of diversifying revenue sources and of tapping new sources of revenue to augment donations and earnings from ticket sales.

For the for-profit sector, the legal entities take such forms as limited liability corporations, regular corporations, joint ventures, general partnerships, and limited partnerships. Similarly, nonprofits can be formed as charitable corporations, nonprofit corporations (with or without members), and in some cases limited liability corporations. A variety of affiliations are available and have been created as solutions to various problems that organizations face; they are best chosen in conjunction with knowledgeable attorneys. The guiding principle is that legal form follows need and is based on strategy.

Complexity

Various factors determine the complexity of an organization's structure, including the organization of the relationship between the parent and its subsidiaries, the number and various types of entities in the structure, the interactions within and among the entities, and the nature and kinds of goods and services produced. Oleck (1988, 38) argues that mixing profit-seeking activities with "ultimate nonprofit purposes" is both acceptable and necessary for some nonprofits, but these hybrid structures tend to introduce complexity for a variety of reasons, such as tax considerations and the fact that administrators of nonprofits may have different values and goals than those at for-profits, making communication and goal setting difficult between the two groups.

Generally speaking, complexity increases as hybrids expand to encompass more business lines, to vertically integrate, or to expand geographically. These sources of expansion are similar to what is found among large corporations (Thompson and Strickland 1993).

Concerns with the Hybrid Structure

Although creating a hybrid structure offers a number of benefits to nonprofits seeking to broaden sources of revenue, there are potential downsides. One important issue involves how the complexity of a hybrid structure affects the time that its senior management must spend on activities unrelated to the mission. This is probably not a major problem for a small hybrid consisting of a nonprofit orchestra and its for-profit parking subsidiary, but it is almost certainly an issue for a health care system with a nonprofit parent and 15 or 20 different subsidiaries. In the latter case, individual heads of businesses may run the subsidiary, but the president, CFO, and other senior managers probably spend large amounts of time on planning, budgeting, and operational issues that relate to both the nonprofit and for-profit elements of the business. There is no simple measure of how much time is needed for the nonprofit end of the business, nor is it clear whether senior management needs to spend most of its time on this if strong leadership is available in the nonprofit entities. The issue that warrants study is how much time the head of a hybrid should devote to for-profit, as opposed to nonprofit, activities.

A related question arises as to whether a senior management team that spends its time ensuring the effective operation of the hybrid structure is so focused on running a commercial business that it loses its ability to give priority to the nonprofit mission for which the structure was established, especially if the team is paid by, or provides governance to, both enterprises. While it may be true that running a large and complex business, nonprofit or for-profit, requires business skills, the fact remains that many nonprofits have boards made up of business leaders who have learned how to balance their business approach with an appreciation of the charitable good works that their nonprofits perform. We simply do not know how the hybrid structure affects service delivery, but it seems likely that great care is needed to keep senior management focused on its primary nonprofit mission.

Hybrids also face important governance issues that have largely gone unrecognized in the literature. Control of a hybrid structure may be lodged in a single governance board or spread out across several governance entities within the structure. It can involve centralized decisionmaking at the parental level, governance via a board made up of representatives of the subsidiaries, or decentralized decisionmaking, which relies on yearly targets and central oversight to ensure effective operation. An interesting issue that emerges is what the governance structure of the parent should represent. If its primary goal is to ensure the success of the nonprofit mission, then representatives from the for-profit subsidiaries should have minimum representation. But if the concern is with ensuring that the for-profit businesses provide the most revenue to the parent, then significant nonprofit representation is important.

Good articulation and integration of the goals of the parent with those of the subsidiary is critical if the structure is to operate effectively. The parent should have a mission that can act as an umbrella for all the subsidiaries, and that initial mission must be broad enough to encompass the role of the multiple entities within the structure. Who should be a member of the parent board and how much overlap there should be between the central board and subsidiary boards are important issues influenced by the Sarbanes Oxley Act's emphasis on independent directors, some of whom have strong financial skills, serving on key committees. The initial understanding as to why the subsidiaries formed and when they will be terminated is important. To the extent that the hybrid grows gradually from initial nonprofit to a multiple hybrid structure, a system structure may emerge by default rather than strategic intent. If the structure is to be effective, there must be a basis for reviewing the contribution of each subsidiary and for rewarding those that contribute to the growth of the hybrid while providing for the exit of inefficient entities. Although this review involves a cost for providing evaluation of and feedback to the entity, it is essential for ensuring that structure matches strategy.

Public and donor perceptions of the structure are important for determining how the hybrid is perceived. At present, the public is largely unaware of the internal structures of the nonprofits it patronizes. For the theater patron who parks adjacent to the nonprofit theater, it may not be clear whether this is a payment to the theater for leased or owned space or to a separate commercial entity. Some donors are reluctant to provide funding to a nonprofit that engages in unrelated commercial activity. In part, their concern is that philanthropic motivations may be undermined in a culture that focuses on the bottom line. Or there is concern over the use of partnerships and subchapter S corporations to facilitate transactions that obscure detection. For example, income can be shifted from an individual shareholder of an S corporation to an unrelated tax-exempt accommodation party. Indeed, the IRS reports that it has identified dozens of S corporation transactions involving hundreds of millions of dollars (Everson 2004).

Evidence on the Prevalence of Hybrid Structures

Remarkably little information is available on either the prevalence of different hybrid structures, the most common structures, or the control and complexity of these organizations. The logical place to get such information is from the IRS Form 990. However, the IRS 990 asks nonprofits only to list for-profit subsidiaries in which the nonprofit has an owner-ship stake of 50 percent or greater, providing space for four entities with a request to report additional subsidiaries on separate pages. The num-bers reported are self-reported and there is no audit of the reliability of these self-reports.

Notwithstanding these data limitations, the data reported on the IRS 990 provide at least suggestive information on how often nonprofits avail themselves of hybrid structures, as well as some clues about economic fac-tors that seem conducive to using this particular hybrid form. Responses to questions on the IRS 990 about holdings of for-profit subsidiaries are made available on the annual sample of nonprofit organizations con-ducted by the Statistics of Income Division (hereafter the SOI sample). The SOI sample includes 100 percent of the 990s filed by the largest nonprof-its in a given year, and samples of the IRS 990 filed by smaller nonprofits. In 2002, the year of the SOI sample used in this analysis, sampling rates ranged from 1.03 percent for $501(c)(3)$ organizations with assets of less than \$500,000 to 100 percent for organizations with assets of \$30 mil-lion or more. A total of 17,569 returns were sampled, yielding a total of 16.923 usable observations for purposes of this analysis.[8]

The first use of the data is to examine the frequency with which non-profits in the SOI sample report holding a significant ownership stake (50 percent or more) in a for-profit subsidiary. Table 5.1 shows the num-ber of nonprofits with and without a hybrid structure (nonprofits that consist of at least one nonprofit and one for-profit), in five asset group-ings. Each row shows the number of organizations in each asset size class and in the entire SOI sample with and without a hybrid structure, and the percentage that such hybrids represent for each asset interval.

While table 5.1 provides a reliable indication of the percentage of non-profits in different size classes that reported holdings in at least one tax-able subsidiary, the numbers provide an inflated sense of how often such structures are likely to be found in the nonprofit sector as a whole because large nonprofits, which are the most likely to have hybrid struc-tures, are "overrepresented" in the raw data. To gain a better sense of the overall importance of hybrid structures in the nonprofit sector, we there-fore apply the sampling weights for the different asset size classes to pro-duce the estimates shown in table 5.2.

Both tables 5.1 and 5.2 paint a similar picture about one fact about the creation and use of hybrid structures among nonprofits. Namely, while such structures appear with considerable frequency among the largest

Table 5.1. Number and Distribution of Taxable Subsidiaries by Asset Size (Unweighted), 2002

Total assets of organization	No hybrids (%)	One or more hybrid (%)	Total organizations
<$1 million	1,678 (99.7)	5 (0.3)	1,683
$1 million to $5 million	3,209 (97.7)	74 (2.3)	3,283
$5 million to $10 million	1,813 (95.7)	81 (4.3)	1,894
$10 million to $30 million	3,037 (92.2)	256 (7.8)	3,293
≥$30 million	5,074 (74.9)	1,696 (25.1)	6,770
Total	14,811 (87.5)	2,112 (12.5)	16,923

Source: Internal Revenue Service, Statistics of Income Division (2005). Sample of IRS 990 Returns filed by Nonprofit Organizations. http://nccsdataweb.urban.org/NCCS/Private/index.php?page=CHome&server=localhost

nonprofits (e.g., those with assets of $30 million or more), the frequency declines with asset size. Because of the prevalence of relatively small organizations within the nonprofit sector, the overall weighted percentage of nonprofits with hybrid structures is less than 2 percent. Nonprofits reporting at least one hybrid entity, however, account for 39 percent of all nonprofit expenditures in the weighted tabulations both among health-related nonprofits and in other sectors.

While size plays an important role in a nonprofit's decision to create and participate in a hybrid structure, most studies show that the mission

Table 5.2. Number and Distribution of Taxable Subsidiaries by Asset Size (Adjusted by SOI Sampling Weights), 2002

Total assets of organization	No hybrids (%)	One or more hybrid (%)	Total organizations
<$1 million	137,270 (99.7)	339 (0.3)	137,609
$1 million to $5 million	63,479 (98.7)	828 (1.3)	64,307
$5 million to $10 million	9,053 (95.8)	401 (4.2)	9,454
$10 million to $30 million	6,090 (92.2)	513 (7.8)	6,603
≥$30 million	5,082 (74.7)	1,697 (25.3)	6,779
Total	220,974 (98.7)	3,778 (1.3)	224,752

Source: See table 5.1.

of the nonprofit plays an important role in how it is structured and its ability to earn unrelated business income (Tuckman 1998; Weisbrod 1998b). Hence, examining how hybrid structures vary by mission category is useful. Tables 5.3 and 5.4 provide unweighted tabulations, controlling for asset size, of the frequency with which hybrid structures are used in different NCEE mission categories.[9] These categories were created by the National Center for Charitable Statistics and roughly correspond to the missions that nonprofits perform. Each table shows the number and percentage of nonprofits with no hybrids, and the number and percentage with one or more hybrids.

Several patterns are evident in tables 5.3 and 5.4. One is that among the largest nonprofits, hybrid structures are found with some frequency in a number of different NCEE categories. Among nonprofits with assets of $30 million or more, mission categories (with at least 40 organizations in a cell) in which hybrid structures were reported by at least 10 percent of all entities include arts and culture (14.8 percent); education excluding higher education (10.5 percent); higher education (15.6 percent); environment (11.9 percent); health excluding hospitals (23.9 percent); hospitals (48.4 percent); diseases, medical disorders, and medical disciplines (18.6 percent); medical research (18.1 percent); housing and shelter (24 percent); human services (11.1 percent); community improvement (22.6 percent); science and technology (30.3 percent); and religion-related (23.8 percent). Tables 5.3–5.4 also indicate that mission matters. For example, hybrids seem most likely to be found in health-related activities. A plausible conjecture is that nonprofits with health-related missions have greater opportunities for exploiting commercial ventures that lend themselves to formation of nonprofit subsidiaries.

Several inferences can be drawn from the data. First, that the propensity of nonprofits to have significant ownership stakes in for-profit subsidiaries varies with the mission of the nonprofit parent indicates that economic strategy matters in the decision to create a hybrid structure. Hybrid structures are more likely found in NCEE groups within the nonprofit sector, such as health, education, housing, and science and technology, where creating for-profit subsidiaries is also more likely to have clear economic payoffs to the nonprofit parent. Second, the fact that large nonprofits are more likely to have for-profit subsidiaries is consistent with the view that complex organizational forms are likely to make more sense for larger nonprofits. Third, the fact that hybrid entities are found within many different NCEE groups suggests that while the potential benefits

Table 5.3. Distribution of Hybrids by Mission Category (Asset Size $30 Million or Greater), 2002 Reporting Year

National Taxonomy of Exempt Entities (NTEE) Classification	No hybrids (%)	One or more hybrids (%)	Total organizations
Arts and culture	305 (85.2)	50 (14.8)	355
Education (not higher)	739 (89.5)	97 (10.5)	826
Higher education	773 (84.4)	143 (15.6)	916
Environment	59 (88.1)	9 (11.9)	67
Animal related	48	3 (5.9)	51
Health (not hospitals)	471	143 (23.9)	614
Hospitals	1,037 (51.4)	972 (48.4)	2,009
Mental health/crisis intervention	30 (72.9)	9 (23.1)	39
Diseases, disorder, medical disciplines	57 (71.4)	13 (18.6)	70
Medical research	59 (81.9)	13 (18.1)	72
Crime and legal related	10 (90.9)	1 (9.1)	11
Employment	18 (81.8)	4 (18.2)	22
Food, agriculture, nutrition	4 (100)	0 (0.0)	4
Housing and shelter	149 (76.0)	47 (24.0)	196
Public safety	4 (100.0)	0 (0.0)	4
Recreation/sports	32 (88.9)	4 (11.1)	36
Youth development	22 (95.6)	1 (4.4)	23
Human services	553 (88.9)	69 (11.1)	622
International affairs	50 (81.6)	12 (19.4)	62
Civil rights, social action advocacy	8 (100.0)	0 (0.0)	8
Community improvement capacity building	72 (77.4)	21 (22.6)	93
Philanthropy, voluntarism, grant foundations	395 (90.2)	43 (9.8)	438
Science/technology	46 (69.7)	20 (30.3)	
Social science	16 (80.0)	4 (20.0)	20
Public and societal	26 (74.3)	9 (25.7)	35
Religion related	48 (76.2)	15 (23.8)	63
Mutual and membership	38 (95.0)	2 (5.0)	40
Unknown	5 (62.5)	3 (37.5)	8
Total	5,074 (74.9)	1,695 (25.1)	6,770

Source: See table 5.1

Table 5.4. Distribution of Hybrids by Mission Category
(Asset Size $10 Million to $30 Million), 2002 Reporting Year

National Taxonomy of Exempt Entities (NTEE) Classification	No hybrids (%)	One or more hybrids (%)	Total organizations
Arts and culture	197 (95.6)	9 (4.4)	206
Education (not higher)	444 (97.6)	11 (2.4)	455
Higher education	102 (96.2)	4 (3.8)	106
Environment	57 (93.4)	4 (6.6)	61
Animal related	26 (96.3)	1 (3.7)	27
Health (not hospitals)	366 (89.9)	45 (10.1)	411
Hospitals	245 (83.0)	50 (17.0)	295
Mental health/crisis intervention	76 (86.4)	12 (13.6)	88
Diseases, disorder, medical disciplines	53 (89.8)	6 (10.2)	59
Medical research	48 (96.0)	2 (4.0)	50
Crime and legal related	13 (92.9)	1 (7.1)	14
Employment	38 (97.4)	1 (2.6)	39
Food, agriculture, nutrition	17 (85.0)	3 (15.0)	20
Housing and shelter	219 (86.2)	35 (13.8)	254
Public safety	6 (100.0)	0 (0.0)	6
Recreation/sports	36 (94.7)	2 (5.3)	38
Youth development	55 (96.5)	2 (3.5)	57
Human services	531 (96.2)	21 (3.8)	552
International affairs	18 (90.0)	2 (10.0)	20
Civil rights, social action advocacy	7 (100.0)	0 (0.0)	7
Community improvement capacity building	79 (79.4)	21 (21.6)	100
Philanthropy, voluntarism, grant foundations	241 (95.3)	12 (4.7)	253
Science/technology	28 (77.8)	8 (22.2)	36
Social science	11 (91.7)	1 (8.3)	12
Public and societal	23 (100.0)	0 (0.0)	23
Religion related	79 (96.2)	3 (3.8)	82
Mutual and membership	19 (100.0)	0 (0.0)	3
Unknown	3 (100.0)	0 (0.0)	8
Total	3,037 (92.2)	256 (7.8)	3,293

Source: See table 5.1

from creating hybrid forms may be larger for some nonprofit activities than for others, there are potential advantages to the creation of hybrid forms in a range of different types of nonprofit activity.

Conclusions and Implications

This chapter begins the difficult job of providing a framework for analyzing why nonprofits form hybrid organizations, how these organizations facilitate the strategies of their nonprofit parents, and how these entities operate in the real world. The discussion presented above indicates that the entities within a hybrid structure are tools for the delivery of strategy, that they are usually chosen with the help of a legal expert, and that they are designed to enhance the ability of the nonprofit parent to carry out its mission. While some structures are quite complex, involving multiple for-profit and nonprofit subsidiaries distributed across several geographic locations and delivering several products and services, others are straightforward, as in the case of Vehicles for Change. What all hybrid structures have in common is the requirement that their managers have a higher level of business sophistication than might be found in a freestanding nonprofit and that they can deal well with trade-offs between the commercial and nonprofit objectives of the nonprofit parent.

These entities have not been widely studied in the academic literature, either through the use of large databases or by focusing on more limited case studies. There are several reasons for this lack of coverage. First, differences in the reporting site and in the report forms for nonprofit and for-profit reporting make gathering data on finances and operation difficult. The problem is made more complex by the difficulty of matching the entities constituting a hybrid structure when their names are not similar. Second, the absence of an encompassing theory of when hybrids will develop and where they will grow makes it difficult to build predictive models. Third, the interactions that exist among subsidiaries are difficult to identify and capture. Hence, little is known about the contributions to the nonprofit mission that these entities make. Finally, if better aggregate data were available, governmental policymakers might place greater restrictions on the sector.

The limited evidence available suggests that hybrid organizations still make up a small number of entities among nonprofits, but nonprofits that report holding an interest in at least one for-profit subsidiary account for a significant share of nonprofit expenditures. These entities play an important role in filling in the white space between the nonprofit and for-profit sectors by creating structures that facilitate nonprofit parents' desire to carry out strategies related to their missions. Hybrid organizations are more likely to be found in a limited number of areas within the sector—in culture, education, and health rather than in the social and human services and advocacy areas.

It is likely that these types of structures will grow in the next few years, fueled by the inexorable pressures on nonprofits to find additional sources of revenue and by boards of directors keen on seeing their organization pursue their opportunities to grow more aggressively.[10] As this growth occurs, it is likely that scholars in the nonprofit sector will increasingly find it valuable to turn their attention to these structures and their impact on the blurring of the border between for-profits and non-profits and on the ability of the nonprofit sector to pursue its mission more effectively.

NOTES

The author acknowledges the helpful comments and suggestions made by James Abruzzo, Evelyn Brody, Joe Cordes, Arlene Mirsky, Martin Schwartz, and Beth Yingling. The assistance of the Urban Institute in providing the data is also appreciated. The author is solely responsible for any errors or interpretations in this chapter.

1. Clearly, this is appropriate only for larger nonprofits with the need to solve one or more of the problems discussed here.

2. Note that the term nonprofit refers to organizations granted that status by state law, whereas tax-exempt status is granted by federal law. An important distinction is that a nonprofit may not necessarily have tax-exempt status.

3. Note, too, that an alternative to using the for-profit corporate form is to buy sufficient insurance to insure against risk.

4. It is important that a tax-exempt organization whose staff provides services to a for-profit get appropriately reimbursed by the for-profit, even if it is an affiliate. Otherwise, there is the potential for misuse of the exempt organization's funds. Recently, the Form 990 has begun to require reporting of compensation paid by affiliates.

5. Other dimensions such as communication, overlap of boards, culture, etc. are treated as beyond the ken of this discussion.

6. To get sufficient separation of unrelated business income, a for-profit corporation is normally used rather than a limited liability company, although if the income is "passive" (e.g., certain rents, dividends, interest or royalties), an LLC or LP may be satisfactory.

7. One experienced practitioner who read this section noted that it is most common for a parent to maintain ultimate control by owning 100 percent of the for-profit stock or by electing the board.

8. See Arnsberger (2005). Although an SOI sample was available for 2003, the sample for 2003 was changed so that only organizations with assets of $50 million or greater were sampled with a probability of 1.0.

9. We present data only on for nonprofits with assets greater than or equal to $30 million in assets, and between $10 million and $30 million in assets in order to have cells of reasonable size.

10. See the chapter by Cordes and Steuerle in this volume and Tuckman and Chang (2006).

REFERENCES

Anheier, Helmut K., and Stefan Toepler. 1998. "Commerce and the Muse: Are Art Museums Becoming Commercial?" In *To Profit or Not to Profit: The Commercial Transformation of the Nonprofit Sector,* edited by Burton Weisbrod. New York: Cambridge University Press.

Arnsberger, Paul. 2005. "Charities and Other Tax Exempt Organizations 2002." *Statistics of Income Bulletin,* Fall 2005: 263.

Chandler, Alfred D. 1962. *Strategy and Structure.* Cambridge, MA: MIT Press.

Everson, Mark W. 2004. *IRS Commissioner Testimony: Charitable Giving Problems and Best Practices,* IR-2004-81. http://www.unclefed.com/Tax-News/2004/nr04-81.html.

LaMay, Craig L., and Burton Weisbrod. 1998. "The Funding Perils of the Corporation for Public Broadcasting." In *To Profit or Not to Profit: The Commercial Transformation of the Nonprofit Sector,* edited by Burton Weisbrod (249–70). New York: Cambridge University Press.

Oleck, Howard L. 1988. *Nonprofit Corporations, Organizations, and Associations,* 5th edition. Englewood Cliffs, NJ: Prentice Hall.

Pearce, John, and Richard Robinson. 1991. *Strategic Management: Formulation, Implementation, and Control.* Homewood, IL: Irwin.

Reid, Elizabeth J., and Janelle Kerlin. 2003. "Getting the Biggest Bang for Their Buck: How Tax and Political Regulation Shapes Nonprofit Advocacy." Paper presented at Annual Meeting of the American Political Science Association, Philadelphia, August 28–31.

Sloan, Frank A. 1998. "Commercialism in Nonprofit Hospitals." In *To Profit or Not to Profit: The Commercial Transformation of the Nonprofit Sector,* edited by Burton Weisbrod (151–69). New York: Cambridge University Press.

Thompson, Arthur A., Jr., and A. J. Strickland. 1993. *Strategic Management: Concepts and Cases;* 7th edition. Homewood, IL: Irwin.

Tuckman, Howard. 1998. "Competition, Commercialization, and the Evolution of Nonprofit Organizational Structures." In *To Profit or Not to Profit: The Commercial Transformation of the Nonprofit Sector,* edited by Burton Weisbrod (25–46). New York: Cambridge University Press.

Tuckman, Howard, and Cyril Chang. 2006. "Commercial Activity: Technological Change and Nonprofit Mission." In *The Nonprofit Sector: A Research Handbook,* edited by Walter W. Powell and Richard Steinberg (629–45). New Haven: Yale University Press.

Weisbrod, Burton. 1998a. "Institutional Form and Organizational Behavior." In *Private Action and the Public Good*, edited by Walter W Powell and Elisabeth S Clemens (69–84). New Haven, CT: Yale University Press.

———, ed. 1998b. *To Profit or Not to Profit: The Commercial Transformation of the Nonprofit Sector*. New York: Cambridge University Press.

Young, Dennis. 1981. "Entrepreneurship and the Behavior of Nonprofit Organizations: Elements of a Theory." In *Nonprofit Firms in a Three-Sector Economy*, edited by Michelle White. Washington, DC: Urban Institute Press. Reprinted in Susan Rose-Ackerman, ed., *The Economics of Nonprofit Institutions*, Oxford University Press, 1986.

6

Cross-Sector Marketing Alliances
Partnerships, Sponsorships, and Cause-Related Marketing

Alan R. Andreasen

One of the major forces affecting the financing and performance of the nonprofit sector in the past 25 years has been the growth of partnerships, sponsorships, and cause-related marketing (Daw 2006). This growth is the result of a sea change in the way in which the private sector has viewed its social role (Bloom, Hussein, and Szykman 1995; Smith 1994). Prior to this shift, the major relationships between the sectors were found in executive board memberships, employee volunteering, and traditional corporate philanthropy. Since 1982, there has been a perceptible migration of corporate charity from philanthropy to transactional alliances and, in a growing number of cases, to more complex, integrated relationships (Austin 2000). The major driving force for this shift has been the recognition that corporate–nonprofit partnerships have significant potential for positively affecting the corporate bottom line while addressing important social issues. Today, however, there is only limited evidence of the impact of this shift on either sector.

The sections below will outline the various forms these partnerships can take, report on the scope and value of such relationships, suggest some of the perils to both sides, and, finally, propose a number of research questions that will allow better tracking of the effects of partnerships and sponsorships in the future.

Some History of Corporate Cause Marketing[1]

The shift in corporate philanthropy has a specific point of origin. In 1982, Jerry C. Welsh, then chief of worldwide marketing for American Express Company, agreed to make a 5-cent donation to the arts in San Francisco every time someone used an American Express card and $2 every time someone opened an American Express card account. In three months, the campaign raised $108,000.[2] The success of this unusual venture was not lost on American Express headquarters, which adopted the approach the next year as a nationwide campaign to support the renovation of Ellis Island and the Statue of Liberty. This program was also a great success, with sales using the card increasing 28 percent over the previous year and a total of $1.7 million eventually donated to the renovation project (Wall 1994). In subsequent years, American Express developed the "Charge Against Hunger" program, partnering with Share Our Strength as the principal beneficiary generating $21 million in its first four years.

The lesson for this experience was one that a growing array of businesses quickly learned. What they learned was that partnerships with nonprofit organizations or with specific causes can have important strategic payoffs for corporations. They recognized that nonprofits need not be treated as charities that would be the grateful recipients of corporate generosity—although many relationships would still take that form. A growing number of executives concluded that carefully designed alliances could have important bottom-line payoffs. Partnerships could substitute for other marketing expenditures and, because of this, their funding needn't come from traditional corporate charitable giving funds. This, in turn, meant that enterprising nonprofits could have access to much higher levels of resources than was the case when they sought traditional corporate charitable donations from the community relations or urban affairs departments, at the corporate foundation, or, in some cases, from the private pocketbooks of corporate executives. Kurt Aschermann of the Boys & Girls Clubs of America notes that, in this new corporate environment, enterprising nonprofits have access to multi-million-dollar marketing budgets, not just the tiny amounts of profits traditionally allocated to charitable giving (Cone, Feldman, and Dasilva 2003).

In addition to funding benefits, nonprofit organizations also saw partnerships as a way to obtain more control over their sources of funds and provide access to products and services, new knowledge, and new marketing skills. Income from partnerships and sponsorships would typically come with fewer strings attached than there are to many large traditional grants (Foster and Bradach 2005; see also Ostrower 2005).

Definitions of Key Terms

For present purposes, cross-sector alliances are any formal relationship between a for-profit and a nonprofit organization to pursue a social objective in ways that will yield strategic or tactical benefits to both parties. These alliances are part of, but distinguishable from, the broader term of corporate social responsibility. The latter encompasses all of a corporation's responsibilities to society, including its treatment of its employees and the environment, its accounting and disclosure practices, and its corporate ethics. All of the latter responsibilities often are described as minimizing the potential negative impact of a corporation on society, whereas the alliances discussed here are in major part designed to have a positive impact (as is the goal of traditional corporate giving).

It should be noted that the broad area of cross-sector alliances is replete with confusion in terminology. For example, Richard Earle (2000) uses the term cause marketing in a book with a subtitle that refers to advertising. People often confuse the terms cause-related marketing and social marketing. The latter refers to any attempt to influence the voluntary behavior of target audiences where the goal is to improve the welfare of the individual or society of which they are a part (Andreasen 1994). Social marketers may recruit corporate collaborators in a marketing alliance but need not do so.

Objectives of Alliances

Alliances across sectors can have a number of objectives. Long and Arnold (1995) describe these objectives as preemptive (diffusing a situation), coalescing (bringing together parties with mutual goals), exploratory (new investigations of issues of joint concern), and for leverage (investments to yield higher returns to each party). Galaskiewicz and Colman (2006) divide the objectives into philanthropic, strategic, commercial, and political. In their taxonomy, *philanthropic collaborations* are the traditional transfers of funds from a commercial organization to a nonprofit to further the latter's social objectives. *Strategic collaborations* add exclusive benefits to the firm and are sometimes referred to as strategic philanthropy. *Commercial collaborations* focus on revenues for both sides with limited attention to social welfare. *Political collaborations* "aim at reproducing changing institutional arrangements" (Galaskiewicz and Colman 2006, 181). Frank and Smith (1997) and Torjman (1998) have developed other taxonomies.

This chapter focuses on corporate–nonprofit alliances ("cause-marketing alliances") that have discernable short- or intermediate-term marketing objectives for the corporate partner and yield important payoffs to the nonprofit partner. One might argue that all of the collaborations encompassed by Galaskiewicz and Colman (2006) are designed to ultimately generate corporate sales. For example, the authors include under "political collaborations" what Smith (1994) refers to as "policy marketing," such as when the makers of Crayola crayons promote funding for the arts or when bike manufacturers support the building of bike paths clearly hoping to generate long-term sales for their products. Philanthropic collaborations can have long-term sales implications in cases where "senior management is searching for new, hard-to-imitate, less tangible sources of competitive advantage" (Hess, Rogovsky, and Dunfee 2002, 113). To the extent possible, the focus in this chapter is on collaborations with near- or intermediate-term corporate sales benefits and important benefits to the nonprofit sector.

Gourville and Rangan (2004) provide a useful framework separating out these possible impacts. They posit that both sides in the corporate–nonprofit alliance can receive first-order and second-order benefits. First-order benefits for the corporate partner are sales; the nonprofit organization's first-order benefit is a direct financial payment or the contribution of goods, services, and volunteers. An example of a partnership with only first-order benefits for both sides is a sales-related transaction partnership, where a nonprofit receives a donation every time a corporation makes a sale (Andreasen 1996).

Second-order benefits are gains expected to improve either side's performance in the future. For example, on the corporation's side, a cause-marketing alliance or sponsorship may improve customers' perception of the firm and their attention to company advertising. The alliance may improve company morale or increase the pool of applicants eager to work for the organization. Investors may be more inclined to support the firm (Graves and Waddock 1994), and business partners may be more favorably disposed to engage in nonsocial alliances. A study by IEG of

145 nonprofit managers involved in alliances indicated that for-profits seek the following conditions to engender second-order benefits in return for their support (Association of Fundraising Professionals 2004a; IEG Sponsorship Report 2005):

- Credit on collateral materials (66 percent)
- Category exclusivity (61 percent)
- Program title (40 percent)
- Tickets and hospitality at nonprofit events (30 percent)
- Information from the nonprofit's database

On the nonprofit side, a cause-marketing alliance may yield second-order benefits that come indirectly through donors to the cause and the cause's clients. Alliances may increase awareness of the nonprofit organization among individuals, foundations, and other potential donors and change attitudes toward it. For example, a corporate partnership may suggest that the nonprofit is more innovative or better managed. Other second-order benefits may accrue though effects on clients. New marketing skills flowing from the alliance may yield greater effectiveness, or the alliance itself may directly address client challenges. The Independent Sector recently listed first- and second-order benefits (Cause Marketing Forum 2004c):

- Increased revenue
- Impact on mission
- Enhanced visibility of the cause or the nonprofit's message
- Access to new audiences
- Connections to the corporation's network of employees, suppliers, distributors, and other contacts
- Expertise in marketing or strategy development, and other corporate experience

A Taxonomy of Cause-Marketing Alliances

Cross-sector partnerships can vary on a number of dimensions (see, e.g., Berger, Cunningham, and Drumwright 2004):

1. *Number of partners.* Some alliances are one-on-one but many involve multiple players.

2. *Length of commitment.* Some partnerships are for a single event or promotion. On the other hand, Boys & Girls Clubs of America formed a 10-year partnership with Coca-Cola and a series of three-year partnerships with Procter & Gamble's Crest.
3. *Level of investment.* Many corporate commitments are for a few thousand dollars. However, Boys & Girls Clubs' partnership with Coca-Cola was valued at $60 million, and another partnership with Microsoft was valued at $100 million.
4. *Number of initiatives.*
5. *Brand-level or company-level collaboration.*[3]
6. *Dedicated manager and dedicated marketing budget.* Some partnerships employ these, but some do not.
7. *Fixed or variable donation amounts.*
8. *Grassroots opportunities.* Some partnerships have opportunities for grassroots engagement of company employees and customers.

The following taxonomy offers some sense of the diverse forms marketing-driven collaborations can take (figure 6.1). Similar lists appear elsewhere (Drumwright and Murphy 2001; Kotler and Lee 2005).

Figure 6.1 A Taxonomy of Cross-Sector Marketing Alliances

| Corporation benefits | Nonprofit benefits | |
	First order	Second order
First order	• Sales-related transactions • Licensing • Joint product marketing	
Second order	• Sponsorships • Brand building • Joint issue promotion	• Pro bono advertising collaboration • Other marketing assistance • Strategic volunteering • Board service • Goodwill building partnerships • Mixed programs

1. Alliances that have first-order benefits for both parties
    A. *Sales-related transactional partnerships.* These are the classic partnerships that are often what people mean when they refer to cause marketing (Varadarajan and Menon 1986). They involve commitments by a for-profit enterprise—typically a product manufacturer or a retailer—to donate a specific amount of money (e.g., $1) or a percentage of a sales transaction (or the profit on that transaction) to a nonprofit organization (often with a financial cap). As with Newman's Own products, which boast "all profits for charity," the *entire* profit on such transactions may be donated. Started by actor Paul Newman and writer A. E. Hotchner in 1982 with an investment of $20,000, the Newman's Own Company has donated $175 million in after-tax profits to approximately 1,000 charities in the United States and elsewhere (Newman and Hotchner 2003).

        An important subcategory here comprises affinity credit cards. Affinity cards donate a percentage of credit purchases to designated charities (Schlegelmilch and Woodruffe 1995). Many banks use these cards—which often have fewer features than non-affinity cards—to attract customers. In 2001, Master-Card had 15,000 affinity and co-branded cards worldwide (Fock, Woo, and Hui 2005).

    B. *Licensing.*[4] With licensing, a for-profit pays a fee to a nonprofit for the use of its name or logo. For many years, the American Cancer Society allowed Nicoderm to feature its logo on their packages as an additional motivation to purchase the product and quit smoking. In return for this usage, the American Cancer Society received fees in excess of $1 million. The American Lung Association has had licensing agreements with Advair asthma drug and 3M's Filtrete for whole-house HVAC systems.

    C. *Joint product marketing.* There are occasions when a for-profit and a nonprofit collaborate to introduce a product or service in the hopes of benefiting both parties. One example was the effort by Timberland and City Year to start a line of clothing called "City Gear" to be sold in Timberland outlets (Dees and Elias 1996). Starbucks has partnered with a number of coffee growers to both improve the lives of the growers and market fair-trade coffee in its coffee shops.

2. Alliances that have first-order benefits for nonprofits and second-order benefits for corporations
    A. *Sponsorships.* Sponsorships involve corporate support of some event or activity by a nonprofit that can take the form of cash, products, services, or volunteer help. Events can include one-time ventures, such as the dedication of a building or the opening of an art exhibition, or recurring events, such as awards dinners. A well-known annual fundraising event is the Susan G. Komen Race for the Cure. Share Our Strength partners with American Express, JennAir, and more than 4,000 chefs to create local fundraising events such as Taste of Washington to support food relief programs. Over 18 years, these ventures have collected more than $70 million for 450 groups that fight poverty and hunger.[5] Corporate benefits in these cases are raised awareness, introduction of a new product, opportunities to offer products or services (from their restaurant), acquisition of a direct-mail database, and earned media in television or newspaper coverage (Cornwell and Maignan 1998; Meenaghan 1998). Sometimes, event sponsorship can have both image and political objectives as, for example, in Philip Morris USA's sponsorship of arts events and a tour of the Bill of Rights. Sponsorships may be combined with sales-related transactions (Polonsky and Speed 2001).
    B. *Brand-building diverse involvements.* A small number of corporations have sought to differentiate their organization and their brand offerings in a significant way through a range of charitable activities. Among the best known are Ben and Jerry's, Stoneyfield Farms, The Body Shop, Tom's of Maine, and Timberland (Austin, Leonard, and Quinn 2004; Wallace 2005).
    C. *Joint issue promotion.* Here, a for-profit provides funding support for a nonprofit in addition to carrying out promotion on its own around a particular issue (Keller 2003). A prominent example is Avon, which has promoted breast cancer awareness around the world since 1992 while raising $350 million through its foundation's Breast Cancer Crusade. There are similar efforts by Coca-Cola to use its advertising and promotion skills to fight the AIDS epidemic in Africa, build its brand, and (not incidentally) protect its workforce (Hess, Rogovsky, and Dunfee 2002). A more recent example is the Sierra Club's partnering with Ford

Motor Company to promote the latter's hybrid Mercury Mariner sport utility vehicle (Hakim 2005; see also Hemphill 1996). The American Lung Association has also worked with Toyota on the same issue. In a more trivial example, in 1995 Nabisco changed the shape of its Barnum's Animal Crackers to endangered species and donated $0.05 for every box sold to the World Wildlife Fund (up to $100,000) (Ratnesar 1997).

3. Alliances that have second-order benefits for both parties

In 2001, Drumwright and Murphy proposed a broad definition of corporate societal marketing that includes promotional efforts "with at least one noneconomic objective related to social welfare"—for example, raising awareness or creating favorable attitudes toward some particularly desirable social behavior (Drumright and Murphy 2001, 164). These efforts would include the following:

A. *Pro bono advertising collaboration.* These activities are one of a set of what Bloom and colleagues (1995) call corporate social marketing, which they define as "a corporate initiative where significant amounts of time and know-how of the marketing personnel who work for the corporation are applied toward achieving a major goal of persuading people to engage in a socially beneficial behavior." Drumwright (1996, 71) referred to such efforts as "company advertising with a social dimension." These collaborations involve the donation of communications and marketing skills to specific nonprofit campaigns. The best known of such collaboratives is the work of the Ad Council, a creation of the advertising industry. The Ad Council has a long history of aiding nonprofit organizations and government agencies through pro bono advertising to help fight forest fires and neighborhood crime. Over the years, it has created more than 1,000 campaigns, bringing us such memorable characters as Rosie the Riveter, Smokey Bear, McGruff the Crime Prevention Dog, and Vince and Larry the crash test dummies. The council has also developed advertising slogans that are now widely familiar:

- "Only you can prevent forest fires"
- "A mind is a terrible thing to waste"
- "Help take a bite out of crime"
- "Pollution: It's a crying shame"

The Partnership for a Drug-Free America is a similar national coalition focused primarily on drug use and largely in assistance to the Office of National Drug Control Policy's anti-drug campaign. Both it and the Ad Council operate by recruiting private-sector advertising agencies to prepare campaigns and individual ads on social issues. Other kinds of pro bono advertising support are often available from local agencies.

B. *Other marketing assistance.* Private-sector marketers can offer many kinds of marketing help to nonprofit organizations and social causes other than advertising, such as public relations and marketing research. In the early 1970s, for example, local marketing research professionals helped the Archdiocese of New York track the effects of an "image campaign" designed to recruit future priests (Greyser and Quelch 1992). Other organizations offer research assistance to nonprofits at reduced rates or piggybacked on other studies.

A number of nonprofit programs have benefited from free delivery services, a contribution that has been particularly critical in the case of recent disasters such as the Asian tsunami and Hurricane Katrina. UPS and FedEx occasionally provides its worldwide fleet to assist in the delivery of humanitarian aid. Both clearly benefit from the high visibility and ample photo opportunities that such involvements permit.

Product donations are often a major part of attempts to address a social problem, particularly in health care. Merck has long enjoyed a reputational benefit from providing free drugs to prevent onchocerciasis, or "river blindness." Pfizer recently donated oral antibiotics to fight trachoma, and GlaxoSmith Kline donated albendazole to fight elephantiasis (Hess et al. 2002).

C. *Strategic volunteering.* Lichtenstein, Drumwright, and Braig (2004) point out that some volunteering by corporate employees is not just to meet staff desires for community service but to increase future sales potential for a company's product. Intel employees provide science education classes to Philippines students so that they can use Intel-driven computers someday and inevitably build future demand for its products as well as a future workforce. Meyer (1999) suggests that cause programs that include volunteering can positively affect employee turnover and loyalty. He also suggests that skill-building during these alliances may be an important career benefit for those working with nonprofit partners.

D. *Board service.* For many years, corporate executives have served on nonprofit boards. Such service can often lead to help with the nonprofit organization's marketing efforts while raising the company's profile. A secondary benefit of board membership is that it provides informal opportunities to network with other senior for-profit executives and develop working relationships that could pay off in for-profit and other alliances at a later time. For example, the CEOs of Blockbuster and Coca-Cola, at a board meeting of Boys and Girls Clubs of America, decided to work together on an ad for the clubs that heavily featured Coke's name and that ran exclusively in Blockbuster stores for six months.

E. *Goodwill-building partnerships.* Some nonprofit alliances are indirectly designed to promote favorable responses from local governments that can pave the way—sometimes directly—in access to markets and increased sales for a corporation. In the early days of international family programs in India, distribution of the Nirodh condom brand was carried out by Unilever Brooke Bond Tea and others. These foreign enterprises wanted to create a favorable impression with the Indian government, which had not always been favorably disposed toward foreign-owned enterprises (Harvey 1999). Post, Preston, and Sachs (2002) refer to expenditures for such ventures as the cost of the firm's "license to operate." AT&T in Latin America recently used its communications skills to connect rural hospitals to medical centers and build important in-country goodwill. Gourville and Rangan (2004) also have argued that Wal-Mart's $200 million "Good Works" program probably dampened the effectiveness of local opposition to Wal-Mart's efforts to open stores in new markets and communities. Accumulated goodwill also explains why McDonald's franchises were untouched in the 1992 Los Angeles riots (Smith and Stodghill 1994).

F. *Other ventures.* The Ford Foundation recently documented a series of corporate initiatives involving community development that are hard to classify but that are undoubtedly meant to have sales payoffs for the corporations in addition to the community and nonprofit benefits (Ford Foundation n.d.):

- State Farm's $100 investment in community revitalization that inevitably will produce policy sales.
- Target, with community advice, developed a store specifically for California's immigrant community as a way to tap an underserved market in which it was interested. The nonprofit partner was Neighborhood Housing Services.
- Union Bank of California worked with Operation Hope Inc. to start "Cash & Save" outlets in low-income communities.

G. *Mixed programs.* A number of partnerships, especially long-term and integrated efforts, are multifaceted and defy neat pigeonholing. A good example is Ronald McDonald House Charities, whose basic mission is to provide a home away from home for families of seriously ill children receiving treatment. McDonald's franchisees and company-owned outlets conduct fundraisers worldwide for the 240 Ronald McDonald Houses (part of a separate nonprofit organization, Ronald McDonald House Charities, Inc.) as part of World Children's Day. These outlets also allow the Ronald McDonald Houses to use their restaurants when needed. Employees volunteer at the houses, and the charity partners with other nonprofits. It works with the American Academy of Pediatrics in a national immunization program for kids called "Immunize for Happy Lives"; in 2005, 19 Ronald McDonald Care Mobiles carried out some of these immunizations. The program "brings cost effective, high-quality medical and dental care directly to underserved children in both rural and urban areas. The Ronald McDonald Care Mobiles provide immunizations and health screenings, oral health services, diagnosis and treatment of chronic disease and health education to children who would otherwise go without health care."[6] The parent company also gives its own grants to America's Second Harvest (Kid's Cafes for hungry children), Interplast (treatment of children with cleft palates or cleft lips), Orbis (eye care for children in developing countries), and Reading Recovery (for first-graders with poor reading skills). Other nonprofits participate in many of these programs. For example, there are America's Second Harvest Kid's Cafes in Boys and Girls Clubs. Of course, McDonald's publicizes widely the accomplishments of

Ronald McDonald House, which engenders millions of dollars in indirect promotion of the brand.

Impact of Marketing Alliances

Research on the impact of cross-sector marketing alliances—where it exists—is of four basic types: summary statistics on gross dollar volume of activity, surveys (often by consulting organizations), experimental research (usually by academics), and anecdotes and case studies. The studies identify—and often fail to identify—impacts on either or both partners.

First-Order Benefits for Corporations

Statistical Data

Data on the volume of activity are not available on all of the types of marketing alliances in the taxonomy outlined above. Many corporations have begun such activities. A 2004 survey by PowerPact of leading Fortune 500 product manufacturers and national and regional retailers reported that 100 percent engaged in cause-related marketing; 41 percent of the projects were multiyear, and 95 percent involved a relationship at least 5 years old (Association of Fundraising Professionals 2004b). Such commitment is reflected in the only available data source. The IEG Sponsorship Report has provided data on six kinds of sponsorships for a number of years. Table 6.1 shows results for 2004 and projections for the United States for 2005. Total expenditures are an estimated $12.1 billion for 2005, up 8.8 percent from 2004 (Association of Fundraising Professionals 2005; IEG Sponsorship Report 2005). Internationally, IEG estimates total sponsorship spending in 2005 of $8.4 billion in Europe, $5.8 billion in the Pacific Rim, $2.5 billion in Central and South America, and $1.6 billion in other regions.

Not all of the categories in table 6.1 apply to nonprofit alliances. The figures for sports and entertainment sponsorships are clearly commercial ventures,[7] whereas the "cause" and "arts" categories are undoubtedly cross-sector marketing collaborations. The remaining two categories—festivals and fairs and associations—are less clear. Festivals, fairs, and annual events is a mixed category.[8] The categorization of association and

Table 6.1. Expenditures on Sponsorship for 2004 and 2005 (projected)

	2004 (millions of dollars)	2005 (millions of dollars, projected)
Sports	7,670	8,390
Entertainment tours and attractions	1,060	1,150
Causes	988	1,080
Arts	610	630
Festivals, fairs, and annual events	482	507
Associations and membership organizations	307	339
TOTAL	11,117	12,096

Source: IEG Sponsorship Report (2005).

membership sponsorships is also not clear. It has only recently become a distinct category.

Taking only the figures for causes and the arts, it is clear that the amounts spent are quite significant. If the 2004 revenues of $1,598 million are added to the $12 billion in corporate philanthropic donations (Giving USA Foundations 2005), this represents a 13.3 percent increase in total contributions to the nonprofit sector. The cause category shows particularly dramatic growth, especially when compared with corporate philanthropy.[9] Cause sponsorships amounted to $120 million in 1990, when corporate philanthropy was $7,690 million. However, the percentage increase through 2004 was 823 percent for causes and only 56 percent for corporate philanthropy (IEG Sponsorship Report 2005)! Over the more recent period between 2002 and 2004, cause marketing grew 13 percent, but corporate philanthropy actually declined.

Separate data on licensing revenues indicate that the amounts are more modest but growing. The International Licensing Industry Merchandisers Association reported royalty revenues in the nonprofit category of $40 million in 2004, up 25 percent from 1998.

Anecdotal Results

The popular literature is replete with anecdotal reports of the impacts of cause-related marketing partnerships (Osterhus 1997; Rangan, Karim and Sandberg 1996; Smith 2003). Sue Adkins's *Cause-Related Marketing* (1999) provides a range of examples, primarily from the work of one organization in the United Kingdom, Business in the Community. A second British book, *Brand Spirit,* provides further useful examples (Pringle and Thompson 1999).

Other anecdotal results abound. For example, Ratnesar notes, "Home Depot donated $250,000 in materials to a non-profit home-building group called Christmas in April. So grateful was the group that it subsequently spent twice that much on still more Home Depot goods. Meanwhile, American Express saw its forth-quarter profits jump by 15 percent last year in the midst of its anti-hunger campaign" (1997, 2).

Direct links between cause-marketing alliances to the financial performance of corporations may be difficult to discover. Cornwell and Maignan (1998) suggest that measuring second-order effects on corporate bottom lines will be highly problematic, which was certainly the experience of Margolis and Walsh (2003) in a broader look at cross-sector relationships. Their meta-analysis over 30 years of various studies that have sought to link financial performance to some measure of corporate social performance presumably included some cases of cause-marketing alliances. They found a positive relationship in 42 of 80 studies (53 percent). Social performance led to better financial performance. However, the results are not unequivocal. They also found a reverse causation in 19 studies, giving rise to the argument that a concern for society may come about only after good financial performance allows it to happen.

Positive Second-Order Benefits for Corporations

The rate of growth in cause-marketing alliances certainly implies that corporations think there are major second-order payoffs for cause-marketing alliances and undoubtedly for sponsorships. A number of survey results tend to support that conclusion. They show that citizens (i.e., consumers) generally have more favorable impressions of corporations that engage in social collaborations than of those that do not. The most frequently cited of these studies are those conducted by Cone Communications. The 2004 "Cone/Roper Corporate Citizenship Study" reported that 86 percent of 1,033 adult respondents said they would "switch from one brand to another that is about the same in price and quality if the other brand was associated with a cause" (p. 2). A company's commitment to a social issue would be important for 74 percent in determining which products and services they would recommend to other people (Cone Inc. 2004). Similar results are reported in Golin Harris's 2005 study of corporate citizenship (Golin Harris 2005).[10] MediaLab's Sensor Study of 13,200 people in 20 countries found that 56 percent of respondents noticed whether companies supported causes, 43 percent thought they sold products of good quality, and 53 percent said they would buy products from such companies (Cause Marketing Forum 2004a; see also Endacott 2004).

Research reported on the Business and the Community web site found that 48 percent of consumers in the United States and the United Kingdom said that they switched brands, increased brand usage, or tried to find out about new products that had a social involvement (Business in the Community 2004). The study also reported actual behavioral changes for individuals who were holders of Tesco supermarket affinity cards and were aware of its cause-related marketing programs.

An early study by Webb and Mohr (1998) found that most of their sample was aware of cause-related marketing and, on average, could recall two examples. One-third said that cause-marketing alliances had some effect on their purchases. The intervening mechanism here appeared to be an increase in positive evaluations of the corporate sponsor (see also Brown and Dacin 1997; Ross, Patterson, and Stutts 1992). Participation in sponsored events (a breast cancer race with 70 sponsors) was associated with greater corporate identification and increased likelihood of purchase in a Cornwell and Cote study (2005).

Bhattacharya and Sen (2003), in their study of several kinds of corporate initiatives, including community involvement, found significant heterogeneity across consumers in their reactions to corporate social initiatives. Distinct segments based on their reactions to cause-marketing alliances may exist. Ross, Stutts, and Patterson (1991) found that women may be more responsive to cause-related marketing programs than men. A factor analysis of the detailed responses of 44 consumers by Webb and Mohr (1998) concluded that consumers could be segmented into four groups. *Skeptics* were generally skeptical and negative toward cause-marketing alliances. *Balancers* wish to help causes but analyze such benefits against traditional purchase criteria. *Attribution-oriented* respondents thought more about the cause program, paying particular attention to the firm's motives. *Socially concerned* people were generally positive about cause-related marketing programs. The skeptics' group was the smallest.

Cause-marketing alliances may be particularly appealing to loyal customers of a seller. In an experiment, Lichtenstein and colleagues (2004) mailed two vouchers to 1,000 customers of a national food store chain that could be used for either cash in a store or a donation to a nonprofit that the chain supported. Consumers who identified strongly with the food chain donated 28 percent of the vouchers, a result consistent with findings by Sen and Bhattacharya (2001).

Fock and colleagues (2005), in a survey of Hong Kong students holding a university affinity card, indicated that the prestige of the card predicted loyalty and card use intentions. Schlegelmilch and Woodruffe (1995) reported that banks find affinity cards very useful in expanding their customer base, generating 20 percent of incremental sales growth for U.S. banks in the early 1990s. Success was particularly noticeable for MBNA, which had the largest base of affinity cards and customers in the United States. Reichheld (1993) reported that MBNA's loyalty programs resulted in customer defections at half the industry rate.

A problem with much of the survey data on consumers' attitudes toward corporations involved in cause-related marketing and nonprofit sponsorships is that they are undoubtedly replete with positivity bias. Consumer respondents are likely to feel that one ought to express willingness to support companies that are "doing good." Indeed, the oft-cited Cone studies have this problem—they report high numbers of respondents who say that they would buy products from socially involved firms if their products' price and quality were the same as other companies'. What is not clear is whether they actually carry out this action—especially when options are not equivalent in price and quality. Indeed, Barone, Miyazaki, and Taylor (2000) found that cause-marketing alliance programs will succeed if they do not result in significantly higher prices or lowered quality. However, modest trade-offs are acceptable to the consumer if the cause payoff is great, which is consistent with Strahilevitz (1999), who concluded that the larger the contribution, the bigger the impact.

Charity programs work better than an equivalent price reduction for discretionary purchases (chocolate truffles and theme park tickets); this is not the case for more practical items (Strahilevitz and Meyers 1998). This effect may be true only for small contributions to charity. When offered the choice of a large contribution or a large discount, subjects choose the discount, especially for practical items (Strahilevitz 1999). Alternatively, Singaporean consumers are more likely to pay premium prices for practical rather than hedonic products (Subrahmanyan 2004).

The marketing alliance program will have greater effect if it is perceived to fit well with the corporate sponsor's main mission. Business in the Community (2004, 9) found that consumers for a cause-related marketing partnership to be effective, "the link between the company and the cause must make sense and be clear, or the program may be viewed with suspicion." Pracejus and Olsen (2004) found that a luxury hotel in Washington, D.C., would yield more results that are positive by partnering with the Kennedy Center for the Performing Arts rather than the Children's Miracle Network. Poor fits can lead to consumer criticism that the real objective of the program is "image recovery," as when tobacco companies pledged $1 million in sales of smokeless tobacco products to the National Volunteer Council, or when Exxon supported the Save the Tiger Fund of the National Fish and Wildlife Foundation (Ratnesar 1997).

Other findings from the research literature follow:

- Donations of products by a company yield more responses that are favorable than cash donations (Ellen, Mohr, and Webb 2000).
- Local cause-related marketing partnerships may yield more favorable effects than national programs (Ross et al. 1992).
- The way in which advertisements specify donation amounts affects consumer responsiveness (Pracejus, Olsen, and Brown 2003). Stating donations as a percentage of profits leads consumers to overestimate the amount being donated (thereby risking some backlash or possible Federal Trade Commission regulation).
- If a company has a poor record on social responsibility, "it should choose a nonprofit partner with a cause directly related to the area of criticism, and it should engage in the CSR [corporate social responsibility] initiative as part of a genuine effort to change its ways" (Lichtenstein et al. 2004, 29).

Possible Negative Second-Order Effects for Corporations

Some of the second-order effects for corporate marketers can be negative (Smith and Higgins 2000).[11] For example, some consumers may conclude that the corporation has sacrificed product quality to engage in a social cause (Sen and Bhattacharya 2001).

Consumers may also be very cynical of transparent attempts to win tolerance for unhealthy business practices. Greenpeace criticized General Motors for its tree-planting program as "greenwashing" because the program tries to hide the fact that General Motors has been "a leader in the lobby against fuel efficiency in cars, and that lack of fuel efficiency is one of the primary causes of the greenhouse effect" (Zbar 1993). Despite its considerable investment in nonprofit causes such as the Bill of Rights commemorative promotion, Philip Morris has also faced much criticism of its actions. Many thought that Philip Morris was simply trying to curry support from people for its efforts to stop increased restrictions on smoking (Valentine 1990). Firms can alienate some of their customers by becoming involved in controversial causes. AT&T felt pressure from pro-life groups to drop its support of Planned Parenthood in 1990, which angered pro-choice groups. Recently, *Business-Week* reported threats by the Pro-Life Action League against Mattel for helping raise money for Girls Inc. because the latter supports abortion rights (Maurer 2005).

Joint issue promotion may also hold perils, as Philip Morris's current antismoking campaign suggests. Farrelly et al. (2002) showed that the company's "Think. Don't Smoke" campaign, though generating more attitudes that are favorable toward the tobacco industry, also led to an increase in the odds that a teenager would say they intended to smoke in the next year. Criticism of the firm and its motives followed. In a related study, Szykman, Bloom, and Blazing (2004) reported on people's opinion that Budweiser had ulterior motives for sponsoring a campaign against drinking and driving, although there was no immediate effect on company reputation.

Licensing can hold different perils. SmithKline Beecham (now GlaxoSmithKline) is reported to have paid $2.5 million in a settlement with 12 state attorneys general for falsely implying that the American Cancer Society had endorsed its products (Meyer 1999). The American Medical Association suffered significant membership retaliation as a result of the association's ill-conceived licensing agreement with Sunbeam. A similar membership revolt affected the American Academy of Pediatrics' short-lived partnership with Ross Products, maker of Similac breast milk substitute.

If the marketer is not fully candid with the public, its image may also suffer. American Express is always very clear to say that it is involved in cause-related marketing at least in part because the company hopes to increase sales and employee morale. By contrast, Barnes & Noble ran into considerable public criticism for not being open with the public in a cause-related marketing project. In Minneapolis, the chain ran ads asking people to come to Barnes & Noble to donate books (ideally ones purchased there). What the chain did not tell the public was that the company donated *nothing* to this program. In fact, it kept the profits on the book sales; customers made the donations (Franklin 1993).

If the marketer is not candid with its nonprofit partner, similar bad feelings and bad press can emerge. A good example is the experience of Fleishman-Hillard, a public relations firm, which contacted the Women in Community Service (WICS) program in the early 1990s and said that retailer Limited Express had designated WICS as the recipient of a program it had devised. Under the program, people would bring in used jeans to Limited Express stores for a 25 percent discount on new jeans, and WICS would get the used jeans. Unfortunately, Limited Express neglected to ask WICS if they *wanted* to participate, which they did not, in part because they had no way to make use of the used jeans. Subsequently, Limited Express gave no jeans to WICS, and WICS claimed that Limited Express owed them $110,200 for the use of their brand name in a promotion that sold 3,800 pairs of jeans at an average price of $29. As Carole Cone of Cone Communications noted, "This was just a case of bad business. A good cause-related marketing project is not something shoved down the throat of one party" (Colford 1994).

Excessive righteousness on the part of a corporation that is deeply committed to social problems can cause critics to lie in wait until the corporation shows its first flaw. Drumwright and Murphy (2001) speculate that some companies might generate unrealistically high customer expectations. In an editorial in *Advertising Age,* editor Rance Crain criticized such corporations as The Body Shop, saying "the common denominator of these kinds of companies is that they maintain a holier than thou attitude. But if they should stumble and show any evidence of not living up to their lofty preachings, their customers will hold them strictly accountable, more so than if they operated a more mundane—if less contentious—institution" (Crain 1994).

The corporation also runs the danger of being charged with exploitation. A good example was the effort by Dow Chemicals to include a child with Down syndrome in a commercial for Spray 'n' Wash Stain Stick. Presumably, the company thought that such an ad would make children with Down syndrome more acceptable in the general society. But *Advertising Age* columnist Bob Garfield responded thusly: "Merely to say 'appalling' doesn't serve, because it doesn't capture the sense of utter betrayal we feel at having been suckered into what must be the most crassly contrived slice-of-life in advertising history. Can they possibly be using the notion of 'mentally challenged' as a segue to getting out those really tough stains?" (Garfield 1993, 50; see also Crain 1994).

A similar charge of exploitation exists in reports that corporations spend significantly more dollars promoting partnerships than they actually donate to the charity. For example, in the mid-1990s, Visa carried out a literacy campaign featuring actor Danny Glover that spent $10 million on ads but planned to donate only $1 million to the literacy cause (Ratnesar 1997).

First-Order Benefits for Nonprofit Partners

Unfortunately, the relative newness of the marketing alliance phenomenon means that research evidence on first- and second-order effects for nonprofit organizations is sparse. Case studies and commentaries (e.g., Andreasen 1996) are replete with optimistic hopes and warnings of potential danger but little hard data. Evidence is rare and often anecdotal.

Statistical Results

As noted earlier, cause partnering, licensing, and sponsorship of the arts yield significant revenues to nonprofits—more than $1 billion in 2005 (IEG Sponsorship Report 2005). But a key question is whether this is a net gain for the nonprofit sector, or are these revenues *substitutes* for traditional corporate philanthropy? An indirect measure of the growing importance of corporate partnerships is the growing number of nonprofit organizations that have a significant number of corporate partners. A brief survey of the web sites of the largest nonacademic, nonhospital nonprofits reveals a number of organizations with multiple partners (table 6.2).

Table 6.2 Nonacademic, Nonhospital Nonprofits
with Multiple Corporate Partners

Organization	Number of corporate partners
Habitat for Humanity International	72
Boys & Girls Clubs of America	39
Easter Seals	23
Girl Scouts	27

Survey results

Survey results are of limited help because of the potential positivity bias noted earlier. Some research indicates that consumers would not decrease donations if their charity were involved in a cause-related marketing venture (Basil and Herr 2003; Chaney and Dolli 2001). However, Schlegelmilch and Woodruffe (1995) reported that American respondents to their survey indicated that they may decrease donations to a cause if they use an affinity card for it.

There are limited data on the effect on the philanthropic behavior of corporations. In a survey of 486 CEOs of small to medium-sized businesses supporting the arts in the New York City area, File and Prince (1998) found that cause-marketing motives dominated traditional philanthropic motives and that the majority of CEOs did one or the other, but not both.

Second-Order Benefits for Nonprofit Organizations

Cause-related marketing ads can increase the favorability of an individual's attitude toward a nonprofit organization The Arthritis Foundation found that six types of alliances all had positive effects on perceptions of the foundation with project or event sponsorship having the most effect. Fewer than 5 percent of respondents indicated that it had a negative effect (Cause Marketing Forum 2004b).

Causes may benefit more than brands from alliances. An important mediator is the plausibility of the alliance—that is, the "fit" between the cause and the brand name (Lafferty and Goldsmith 2005). A well-known brand enhances the value of causes whose familiarity is high (American Red Cross) and low (Famine Relief Fund). However, high familiarity makes prior attitudes toward the nonprofit organization more salient (Lafferty, Goldsmith, and Hult 2004). Unfamiliar causes see a bigger attitude improvement than a familiar cause from partnering with a familiar brand (Lafferty and Goldsmith 2005).

Disasters yield more benefits from cause-marketing alliances than ongoing causes (Ellen et al. 2000). And nonprofits may benefit from affiliating with a firm that has recently modified socially undesirable behaviors, although consumers must view the turnaround as real, not cosmetic (Lichtenstein et al. 2004).

Finally, there is the expectation that interactions with the private sector will yield important transfer of valuable concepts and tools that will build nonprofit capacity (Andreasen 2001; Andreasen, Goodstein, and Wilson 2005).

Possible Negative Second-Order Effects for Nonprofits

Becoming involved in cause-marketing alliances carries a number of important risks to nonprofits' revenues and prestige (Polonsky and Wood 2001; Wagner and Thompson 1994).[12] To some extent, these depend on the depth of the relationship. As alliances move from philanthropy through transactions to integration (Austin 2000), the perils to the non-profit organization will increase along the same continuum. However, there are some perils that apply to all alliances.

Nonprofits may waste resources should the alliance fail. For corporations, an alliance may be merely one of many marketing ventures where a failure can be written off as the cost of risk-taking. For nonprofit organizations, especially smaller ones, a failed alliance may drain vital resources and compromise other activities.

The nonprofit may face charges of excessive commercialism.[13] The American Cancer Society has been criticized for being "more interested in cancer profit than cancer preventions" and "more interested in accumulating wealth than saving lives" (Veracity 2005). This is a particular problem with sponsorships in the arts. In a recent museum review, the *New York Times* art critic offered the following comment:

> What's remarkable about the Tut show at the Los Angeles County Museum of Art, for which the museum has effectively sold its good name and gallery space to a for-profit company, is that people still find this arrangement shocking. Outrageous? Sure. It's an abdication of responsibility, integrity, standards. But it's becoming the norm. Money rules. It always has, of course. But at cultural institutions today, it seems increasingly to corrupt ethics and undermine bedrock goals like preserving collections and upholding the public interest. (Kimmelman 2005, AR1)

Cause-marketing alliances may produce only temporary effects. If individuals are prompted to join a nonprofit organization or become a donor because of an alliance partnership—a sponsored event, a dramatic sales-related program, or a joint promotion—the ties to the nonprofit may be shallow and the spike in support temporary.

As with for-profits, there are possible second-order effects from consumer anger about perceived deception about the terms of the cause-marketing alliance relationship. Consumers may be upset if the amount of the donation is obscured or misstated (Olsen, Pracejus, and Brown 2003). There may also be anger if the nonprofit organization is not transparent in naming its corporate partners. The brief survey of top nonprofit web sites noted above found many of them not offering a list of corporate partners. In some cases, for example, Planned Parenthood, this omission may be at the request of the corporations, which fear consumer backlash.

Donors and other supporters may see a transactional alliance as antithetical to the organization's mission. The recent introduction of corporate partnerships in public schools to generate vending-machine revenues has led many parents and social critics to say that schools are feeding their kids to the corporate world and mainly teaching them to be good consumers. Many think this should not be a major (or any) undertaking of school systems even when they are significantly strapped for cash.

Licensing poses particular potential problems. Consumers may become concerned that a nonprofit—especially one involved in health care—has lost its independence and credibility by licensing its logo to a corporation—especially when the corporation demands exclusivity in the relationship. Perhaps the most publicized example of a licensing agreement gone wrong is the 1997 agreement between the American Medical Association (AMA) and Sunbeam, which permitted Sunbeam to put AMA's name on products ranging from blood pressure monitors to heating pads (Collins 1997; Johnson 1999). This was an exclusive agreement; rival products could not use the American Medical Association name. AMA members raised a storm of protest over this agreement, fearing that the AMA name on these products would imply an endorsement or signify that the products were superior to competitors'. The AMA paid Sunbeam $10 million to settle a breach-of-contract lawsuit, and a number of AMA executives resigned.

Joint promotions have other perils. The Arthritis Foundation entered into an agreement with McNeil Consumer Products to market a product to be called Arthritis Foundation Pain Reliever. Although the product was eventually taken off the market because of low sales, at the time many people wondered whether the Arthritis Foundation could be objective when investigating possible cures or treatments for arthritis if it was in a joint venture with a leading over-the-counter drug marketer.

Joint promotions may also put the nonprofit organization at risk of supporters believing they are "selling out." For example, some Sierra Club members may object to the organization's recent alliance with Toyota because the carmaker continues to make gas-guzzling trucks and SUVs.

The private-sector marketer may unduly restrict the nonprofit. The marketer may pressure the nonprofit to not engage in other cause-related marketing ventures or even certain kinds of fundraising that the marketer considers competitive. The corporation (like the government) may insist on detailed and frequent results reports. Where the corporation's expected payoffs are primarily second-order, they may insist on more publicity for the relationship than the nonprofit might ordinarily undertake.

The nonprofit may find itself with a tainted partner. For example, in October 1993, Jenny Craig Inc. announced that it would give $10 for every new enrollment in its weight-loss programs to the Susan G. Komen Breast Cancer Foundation and would spend $7 million on promoting breast cancer awareness. But just before the program was announced, the Federal Trade Commission cited Jenny Craig for engaging in deceptive advertising practices by making unsubstantiated weight-loss claims. Although the Komen Foundation was aware of the pending charges when it entered the arrangement with Jenny Craig, it was hoping that the matter would be settled or dropped before the program was announced.

A successful alliance, especially an integrated one, may cause the nonprofit to shift its mission to more directly meet the corporation's strategic goals. The nonprofit may neglect its traditional fundraising and suffer structural atrophy, as Kimmelman (2005) argues has been the case for arts institutions.

Then there are the many opportunities for frustration and hurt feelings and for wasted time and energy because of culture differences between the two sectors (table 6.3). Often, this conflict results from the power imbalances in the relationship because, as Torjman notes, "Many nonprofit organizations question their ability to be equal players with business partners who may wield substantial economic power and political influences" (1998, 14).

Frustration and hurt feelings may come from a number of sources. Berger and colleagues (2004) set out to understand these potential problems in a detailed set of interviews with corporations, nonprofits, and consultants involved in 11 social alliances. They discovered six potential problems that stem from two sources—cultural differences between the parties and each organization's inexperience working with

Table 6.3 Differences between Social and Commercial Marketers

Social marketers	Commercial marketers
Want to do good	Want to make money
Funded by taxes, donations	Funded by investments
Publicly accountable	Privately accountable
Performance hard to measure	Performance measured in profits, market share
Long-term behavioral goals	Short-term behavioral goals
Often target controversial behaviors	Typically provide noncontroversial products or services
Often choose high-risk targets	Choose accessible targets
Risk-averse managers	Risk-taking managers
Participative decisionmaking	Hierarchical decisionmaking
Relationships based on trust	Relationships often competitive

Source: Andreasen and Drumwright (2001, 104).

institutions and individuals from the other sector. The problems they found follow:

- Misunderstanding, especially early in the alliance. Company managers often did not understand the nature of the nonprofit's mission and internal politics that often argued for different resource allocations. For-profits often had unrealistic or inappropriate expectations—for example, how much time the nonprofits would spend on the alliance. At the same time, they underestimated the time commitment involved. There was often disagreement over objectives and, when measures of success were not agreed upon, reluctance to discuss differences.
- Misallocation of costs and benefits. Many alliances featured perceptions that one side bore too much cost and received too few benefits. Nonprofits saw corporations as having "an insatiable appetite for favorable publicity from the alliance" (Berger et al. 2004, 64). After alliances have been in place for a time, companies sometimes felt that their costs were too great.
- Mismatches of power. The value of the nonprofit's brand and its network of contacts was typically undervalued by the corporation. One-sided exclusivity was often demanded. Further, companies often felt that they could impose a strategy or set of tactics on the

cause-marketing alliance and even meddle in other efforts of the nonprofit. Company managers often seemed to expect instant attention to their questions and needs. Berger and colleagues (2004, 66) noted that "it is not unusual for an alliance to be branded using only the company's name; the nonprofit receives credit only in the small print." Micromanaging by corporations may be greater if their own corporate reputation is on the line.

- Mismatched partners. Partners inevitably differed in styles of management, structure, and goals. Nonprofits focus on long-term results; corporations want instant gratification. Nonprofits often deal with issues involving minorities, the downtrodden, and other populations largely unfamiliar to white-collar corporate executives.
- Misfortunes of time. As time passes, alliances can get stale; key personnel and organizational champions move on and there are no plans for either an exit strategy or the integration and revitalization of old but innovative programs (Austin 2000).
- Mistrust. This can result in undercover sabotage, misdirection, and a lack of candor.

Some Broader Issues for the Nonprofit Sector

A potentially serious problem for the sector as a whole from the growth of marketing alliances is what Andreasen and Drumwright (2001) refer to as cherry-picking. Corporations may be expected to steer clear of controversial issues and focus on challenges with feel-good dimensions. Donna A. Lopiano, chief executive officer of the Women's Sports Foundation recently noted, "Corporations don't want to risk their brand in a fight. . . . They want nice advocacy, not edgy advocacy."

Hundreds of corporations responded to the tsunami disaster and Hurricane Katrina. Causes such as breast cancer attract dozens of partners. The Susan G. Komen Breast Cancer Foundation currently lists 45 corporate sponsors, 17 of which have pledged $1 million. Operation Smile has 32 corporate partners, but AIDS Project Los Angeles lists no corporate partners on its web site.

The excessive attention to a few issues often results in "campaign overload." During the October 2005 national breast cancer awareness month, America was inundated with pink products. In the cosmetics category alone, there were 16 pink products from Estée Lauder, 12 from Avon, 8 from Revlon, and 5 from Sephora (Singer 2005). This proliferation of often trivial connections to an issue has led some nonprofits to urge consumers to be cautious when purchasing products thinking they have a real impact on some social problem. Barbara Brenner, executive director of Breast Cancer Action, noted, "When companies put pink ribbons on their products, they're no longer just selling a sweater or a watch— they're selling the expectation that buying their product is going to make a difference in the fight against breast cancer. Pink ribbon marketing efforts make a significant difference in corporate bottom lines. But the 'portion of the proceeds' that goes to breast cancer is all too often minuscule in comparison" (Breast Cancer Action 2005).

Consumers may be noticing this cherry-picking. The MediaLab Sensor Study mentioned earlier found that 25 percent of consumers felt some events (including commercial events) were too heavily sponsored (Cause Marketing Forum 2004a).

For the broader society, there is the possibility that the increase in corporate funding for marketing alliances may cause the corporation to lose sight of its societal obligations (Polonsky and Wood 2001). That is, rather than giving to good causes to address important social problems, corporations may choose to support only efforts that yield it a bottom-line payoff. For example, rather than giving $100,000 to a critical AIDS campaign in some community, they may promote an event or engage in a sales-related transaction for a "nicer" cause or one where a large customer segment is likely to be responsive (e.g., heart disease or breast cancer issues). The focus on the bottom line resonates with the broader question of the appropriate role for corporations in society (Friedman 1970). As Crane and Desmond (2002, 548) put it, "who should decide and can decide what is in the public's best interests . . . ?" Such issues are beyond the scope of this chapter. (See Crook 2005.)

Partners may not evaluate marketing alliances properly. Foster and Bradach (2005) have recently pointed out that holding an event, engaging in a joint promotion with a corporation, or even starting up a joint marketing effort to generate $100,000 may yield less return in unrestricted funds to the nonprofit's core mission than would a simple $100,000 donation, even after including the costs of getting the money. Their Bridgespan study of nonprofit commercial ventures strongly suggests that nonprofit organizations are not particularly good at assessing the full costs of alliance ventures. This lack of business savvy may cause nonprofits to throw good money after bad investments. It may also make them reluctant to abandon ventures that a corporation wants but that benefits the nonprofit less significantly.

Future Challenges

A critical practical challenge in this domain is ensuring equity for the parties involved in marketing alliances. On the nonprofit side, a number of articles have proposed steps that nonprofit organizations can take to mitigate the possible negative impacts of marketing alliances (Andreasen and Kotler 2003; Austin 2000; Bucklin and Sengupta 1993; Rangan, Karim, and Sandberg 1996). Vigorous promulgation of these cautionary recommendations should be a continuing focus of organizations that are sources of advice in this domain, such as Business for Social Responsibility and Boston College's Center for Corporate Citizenship.

Helpful in this regard would be some way of determining the value of specific marketing alliances and the distribution of value to each side. Gourville and Rangun (2004) propose an interesting framework for addressing this problem based on the concept of first- and second-order benefits. They illustrate the approach by calculating the payoffs from the Sierra Club's partnership with Toyota. They hypothesize the following monetary values for each side:

1. Increased sales of Toyota hybrids resulting in $6 million more in profits
2. A 10 percent reduction in employee turnover yielding training costs reduced by $1 million
3. A saving of $3 million in Toyota's lobbying costs
4. 10,000 new donors joining the Sierra Club as a result of this partnership resulting in $2 million in new donations
5. 2,500 long-time supporters alienated by the alliance withholding $1 million in donations
6. Increases in consumers' awareness of environmental issues and the need for more prudent automobile purchases and usage saves the Sierra Club $1 million in advertising costs

The hypothetical net value of the alliance is therefore $12 million. But what may be troubling is that 83 percent of this value is captured by Toyota and only 17 percent by the Sierra Club. On the other hand, the calculations do not include the costs of the venture. It is possible that Toyota would bear 83 percent of the costs—but probably not. In any case, the availability of such a calculation may cause the Sierra Club to initiate discussions with Toyota for a more equitable allocation of benefits. Its bargaining power, of course, will be constrained by the extent to which the Club has alternative alliances. Clearly, the challenge of improving the metrics in this area is, at minimum, critical to helping individual nonprofits predict the value of future proposed relationships.

Finally, an important line of future research should be to investigate the interaction between corporate spending on the marketing alliances discussed in this chapter and their spending on traditional philanthropy (Seifert, Morris, and Bartkus 2004). Is the former a net addition to the coffers of nonprofit organizations or just a substitute (with sometimes additional burdens)? Is it an addition for some firms and a substitute for others and, if so, what explains these differences? Do some nonprofit sectors benefit more from this innovation than others?

Such questions must be addressed if we are to judge whether this wave of interest in corporate marketing alliances is healthy overall for the nonprofit sector. Certainly, if some substitution effect is occurring—and if the substitution drives corporations to "nicer" social ventures—then what are the implications for civil society? Does this mean that foundations ought to realign their priorities to shore up increasingly neglected topics? Should government back off from some domains and increase involvement in others?

Marketing alliances appear to yield an important new source of revenue for the nonprofit sector. However, scholars are obligated to cast a critical eye on whether or not this development is a mixed blessing.

NOTES

1. This description is excerpted from Andreasen (1996).

2. "Charity Fund-Raising Is a Popular Marketing Tool." *Washington Post,* September 3, 1991, D2.

3. For an overview of branding issues, see Keller (2003).

4. Note that we are not including here the licensing of inventions, patents, and drugs developed by nonprofit universities and hospitals.

5. Share Our Strength's Taste of the Nation, "Behind the Scenes," http://taste. strength.org/site/PageServer?pagename=TOTN_about_index, 2007.

6. Ronald McDonald House Charities, http://www.rmhc.org/mission/care_mobile/index.html, accessed July 14, 2005.

7. Some types of sports sponsorships may be classed as cause marketing—for example, the Walt Disney Company's sponsorship of the Special Olympics.

8. Telephone conversation with William Chipps, senior editor of the IEG Sponsorship Report, January 4, 2006.

9. The Giving USA estimates are based on what corporation financial statements report as charitable giving. Thus, there may be overlap between the estimates of corporate donations and the estimates of cause alliances when the latter are reported as tax deductions.

10. These studies also indicated that perceptions of favorable corporate citizenship would also influence respondents' employment choices and their eagerness to have a company located in their community.

11. Some material in this section is drawn from Andreasen and Kotler (2003).

12. Some material in this section is drawn from Andreasen and Kotler (2003).

13. We do not consider here scientific collaborations between nonprofit universities and corporations that have come under criticism for distorting the scientific process (Hotz 2003).

REFERENCES

Adkins, Sue. 1999. *Cause-Related Marketing: Who Cares Wins.* Boston: Butterworth-Heinemann.

Andreasen, Alan. 1994. "Social Marketing: Its Definition and Domain." *Journal of Public Policy and Marketing* 13(1): 108–14.

———. 1996. "Profits for Nonprofits: Find a Corporate Partner." *Harvard Business Review* 74(6): 47–49.

———. 2001. "Intersector Transfer of Marketing Knowledge." In *Handbook of Marketing and Society,* edited by Paul N. Boom and Gregory T. Gundlach (80–104). Thousand Oaks, CA: Sage Publications.

Andreasen, Alan, and Minette E. Drumwright. 2001. "Ethical Issues in Social Alliances." In *Ethical Issues in Social Marketing,* edited by Alan Andreasen (95–124). Washington, DC: Georgetown University Press.

Andreasen, Alan, and Philip Kotler. 2003. *Strategic Marketing for Nonprofit Organizations,* 6th ed. Upper Saddle River, NJ: Prentice-Hall.

Andreasen, Alan, Ronald C. Goodstein, and Joan W. Wilson. 2005. "Transferring Marketing Knowledge to the Nonprofit Sector." *California Management Review* 47(4): 46–67.

Association of Fundraising Professionals. 2004a. "Charities Not Charging Enough for Marketing, Sponsorship Deals." http://www.afpnet.org/ka/ka-3.cfm?content_item_id=17968&folder_id=2345.

————. 2004b. "U.S. Corporations Embracing Cause-Related Marketing." http://www.afpnet.org/ka/ka-3.cfm?content_item_id=17166&folder_id=1926.

————. 2005. "Nonprofit, Association Sponsorships Expected to Rise in 2005." http://www.afpnet.org/ka/ka-3.cfm?content_item_id=19950&folder_id=2545.

Austin, James E. 2000. *The Collaboration Challenge*. San Francisco: Jossey-Bass.

Austin, James E., Herman B. Leonard, and James W. Quinn. 2004. *Timberland: Commerce and Justice*. Boston: Harvard Business School Publishing.

Barone, Michael J., Anthony D. Miyazaki, and Kimberly A. Taylor. 2000. "The Influence of Cause-Related Marketing on Consumer Choice: Does One Good Turn Deserve Another?" *Journal of the Academy of Marketing Science* 28(2): 248–62.

Basil, D. Z., and P. M. Herr. 2003. "Dangerous Donations? The Effects of Cause-Related Partnering on Donations." *Journal of Nonprofit and Public Sector Marketing* 11(1): 59–76.

Berger, Ida E., Peggy H. Cunningham, and Minette E. Drumwright. 2004. "Social Alliances: Company/Nonprofit Collaboration." *California Management Review* 47(1): 58–90.

Bhattacharya, C. B., and Sankar Sen. 2003. "Consumer–Company Identification: A Framework for Understanding Consumers' Relationships with Companies." *Journal of Marketing* 67(April): 76–88.

Bloom, Paul N., Pattie Yu Hussein, and Lisa Szykman. 1995. "Benefiting Society and the Bottom Line: Businesses Emerge from the Shadows to Promote Social Causes." *Marketing Management* 4(Winter): 8–18.

Breast Cancer Action. 2005. "Breast Cancer Action to Consumers: 'Think Before You Pink.' " http://bcaction.org/index.php?page=050927-2.

Brown, Tom J., and Peter A. Dacin. 1997. "The Company and The Product: Corporate Associations and Consumer Product Responses." *Journal of Marketing* 61(January): 68–84.

Bucklin, Louis P., and Sanjit Sengupta. 1993. "Organizing Successful Co-Marketing Alliances." *Journal of Marketing* 57(April): 32–46.

Business in the Community. 2004. "Brand Benefits." http://www.bitc.org.uk/resources/research/brand_benefits.html.

Cause Marketing Forum. 2004a. "Cause Marketing's Power Shown in MediaLab Study." http://www.causemarketingforum.com/Page.Asp?ID=192.

————. 2004b. "Consumers React Positively to Cause Alliances: Arthritis Foundation Survey Shows." http://www.causemarketingforum.com/Page.Asp?ID=283.

————. 2004c. "Why Are Nonprofits Turning to Cause Marketing?" http://www.causemarketingforum.com/Page.Asp?ID=82.

Chaney, I., and N. Dolli. 2001. "Cause Related Marketing in New Zealand." *International Journal of Nonprofit and Voluntary Sector Marketing* 6(2): 156–63.

Colford, Stephen W. 1994. "Jeans Giveaway Labeled a Poor Fit." *Hartford Courant*, November 25.

Collins, Glenn. 1997. "A.M.A. to Endorse Line of Products." *New York Times*, August 13, A1.

Cone, Carol L., Mark A. Feldman, and Alison T. Dasilva. 2003. "Causes and Effects." *Harvard Business Review* 81(July): 95–101.

Cone Inc. 2004. *2004 Cone Corporate Citizenship Study: Building Brand Trust.* Boston: Cone Inc.

Cornwell, T. B., and L. V. Cote. 2005. "Corporate Sponsorship of a Cause: The Role of Identification in Purchase Intent." *Journal of Business Research* 58:268–76.

Cornwell, T. B., and I. Maignan. 1998. "An International Review of Sponsorship Research." *Journal of Advertising* 27(1): 1–21.

Crain, Rance. 1994. "Social Marketing Misses the Mark." *Advertising Age,* September 26, 22.

Crane, Andrew, and John Desmond. 2002. "Societal Marketing and Morality." *European Journal of Marketing* 36(5/6): 548–69.

Crook, Clive. 2005. "The Good Company." *The Economist,* January 22.

Daw, Jocelyne. 2006. *Cause Marketing for Nonprofits.* San Francisco: Jossey-Bass.

Dees, J. Gregory, and Jaan Elias. 1996. *City Year Case.* Boston: Harvard Business School Publishing.

Drumwright, Minette R., 1996. "Company Advertising with a Social Dimension: The Role of Noneconomic Criteria." *Journal of Marketing* 60(October): 71–88.

Drumwright, Minette R., and Patrick E. Murphy. 2001. "Corporate Societal Marketing." In *Handbook of Marketing and Society,* edited by Paul N. Bloom and Gregory Gundlach (162–83). Thousand Oaks, CA: Sage Publications.

Earle, Richard. 2000. *The Art of Cause Marketing: How to Use Advertising to Change Personal Behavior and Public Policy.* Lincolnwood, IL: NTC Business Books.

Ellen, P. S., L. A. Mohr, and D. J. Webb. 2000. "Charitable Programs and the Retailer: Do They Mix?" *Journal of Retailing* 76(3): 393–406.

Endacott, R. W. J. 2004. "Consumers and CRM: A National and Global Perspective." *Journal of Consumer Marketing* 21(3): 183–89.

Farrelly, Matthew C., Cheryl G. Healton, Kevin C. Davis, Peter Messert, James C. Hersey, and M. Lyndon Haviland. 2002. "Getting to the Truth: Evaluating National Tobacco Countermarketing Efforts." *American Journal of Public Health* 92:901–7.

File, Karen Maru, and Russ Alan Prince. 1998. "Cause Related Marketing and Corporate Philanthropy in the Privately Held Enterprise." *Journal of Business Ethics* 17:1529–39.

Fock, Henry K. Y., Ka-Shing Woo, and Michael K. Hui. 2005. "The Impact of a Prestigious Partner on Affinity Card Marketing." *European Journal of Marketing* 39(1–2): 33–53.

Ford Foundation. n.d. *The Double Bottom Line: Competitive Advantage Through Community Investment.* New York: Ford Foundation.

Foster, William, and Jeffrey Bradach. 2005. "Should Nonprofits Seek Profits?" *Harvard Business Review* 83(2): 92–100.

Frank, Flo, and Anne Smith. 1997. *The Partnership Handbook.* Ottawa, Ontario: Minister of Public Works and Government Services Canada.

Franklin, Robert. 1993. "Help the Needy—And Maybe Merchants, Too." *Minneapolis Star Tribune,* December 24.

Friedman, Milton. 1970. "The Social Responsibility of Business Is to Increase Its Profits." *The New York Times Magazine,* September 13.

Galaskiewicz, Joseph, and Michelle Sinclair Colman. 2006. "Collaboration between Corporations and Nonprofit Organizations." In *The Nonprofit Sector: A Research Handbook,* 2nd edition, edited by Walter W. Powell and Richard Steinberg (108–206). New Haven, CT: Yale University Press.

Garfield Bob. 1993. "This Heavy-Handed Ad Exploits Someone New." *Advertising Age,* May 10, 50.

Giving USA Foundation. 2005. *Giving USA (2004).* Washington, DC: American Association of Fundraising Counsel.

Golin Harris. 2005. *Doing Well by Doing Good 2005: The Trajectory of Corporate Citizenship in American Business.* http://www.golinharris.com/pdf/GH_CCS_2005.pdf.

Gourville, John T., and V. Kasturi Rangan. 2004. "Valuing the Cause Marketing Relationship." *California Management Review* 47(1): 38–56.

Graves, Samuel R., and Sandra A. Waddock. 1994. "Institutional Owners and Corporate Social Performance." *Academy of Management Journal* 37(4): 1034–46.

Greyser, Stephen, and John Quelch. 1992. *Archdiocese of New York.* Boston: Harvard Business School Publishing.

Hakim, Danny. 2005. "With Sierra Club's Help, Ford Pushes a New Hybrid." *New York Times,* July 12, C7.

Harvey, P. D. 1999. *Let Every Child Be Wanted: How Social Marketing Is Revolutionizing Contraceptive Use around the World.* Westport, CT: Auburn House.

Hemphill, T. A. 1996. "Cause-Related Marketing: Fundraising, and Environmental Nonprofit Organizations." *Nonprofit Management and Leadership* 6(4): 403–18.

Hess, David, Nikolai Rogovsky, and Thomas W. Dunfee. 2002. "The Next Wave of Corporate Community Involvement: Corporate Social Initiatives." *California Management Review* 44(2): 110–25.

Hotz, Robert Lee. 2003. "Medical Tests Skewed, Study Finds—Commercial Ties Are Tainting the Outcome of Research at Universities, Yale Investigators Say." *Los Angeles Times,* January 22, A14.

IEG Sponsorship Report. 2005. "'06 Outlook: Sponsorship Growth Back to Double Digits." http://www.sponsorship.com/iegsr/2005/12/26/s7966.asp.

Johnson, Greg. 1999. "Officials Urge Limits on Use of Nonprofit Logos." *Los Angeles Times,* April 7, C1.

Keller, Kevin Lane. 2003. *Strategic Brand Management: Building, Measuring, and Managing Brand Equity.* Upper Saddle River, NJ: Prentice Hall.

Kimmelman, Michael. 2005. "What Price Love? Museums Sell Out." *New York Times,* July 17, AR1, 26. http://www.nytimes.com/2005/07/17/arts/design/17kimm.html.

Kotler, Philip, and Nancy Lee. 2005. *Corporate Social Responsibility.* New York: John Wiley and Sons.

Lafferty, B. A., and R. E. Goldsmith. 2005. "Cause–Brand Alliances: Does the Cause Help the Brand or Does the Brand Help the Cause?" *Journal of Business Research* 58:423–29.

Lafferty, B. A., R. E. Goldsmith, and G. T. M. Hult. 2004. "The Impact of the Alliance on the Partners: A Look at Cause-Brand Alliances." *Psychology and Marketing* 21(7): 509–31.

Lichtenstein, Donald R., Minette E. Drumwright, and Bridgette M. Braig. 2004. "The Effect of Corporate Social Responsibility on Customer Donations to Corporate-Supported Nonprofits." *Journal of Marketing* 68(4): 16–32.

Long, Frederick, and Matthew Arnold. 1995. *The Power of Environmental Partnerships.* Orlando: Harcourt and Company.

Margolis, Joshua D., and James P. Walsh. 2003. "Misery Loves Companies: Whither Social Initiatives by Business?" *Administrative Science Quarterly* 48(June): 268–305.

Maurer, Harry, ed. 2005. "Where Trade Winds Are Blowing." *Business Week,* November 21.

Meenaghan, T. 1998. "Current Developments and Future Directions in Sponsorship." *International Journal of Advertising* 17(1): 3–28.

Meyer, Harvey. 1999. "When a Cause Is Just." *Journal of Business Strategy* 20(6): 27–31.

Newman, Paul, and A. E. Hotchner. 2003. *Shameless Exploitation in the Pursuit of the Common Good.* New York: Nan A. Talese/Doubleday Books.

Olsen, G. D., J. W. Pracejus, and N. R. Brown. 2003. "When Profit Equals Price: Consumer Confusion about Donation Amounts in Cause-Related Marketing." *Journal of Public Policy and Marketing* 22(2): 170–80.

Osterhus, Thomas L. 1997. "Pro-Social Consumer Influence Strategies: When and How Do They Work?" *Journal of Marketing* 61(4): 16–29.

Ostrower, Francie. 2005. "The Reality Underneath the Buzz Of Partnerships: The Potentials and Pitfalls of Partnering." *Stanford Social Innovation Review* (Spring): 34–41.

Polonsky, M. J., and R. Speed. 2001. "Linking Sponsorship and Cause Related Marketing: Complementarities and Conflicts." *European Journal of Marketing* 35(11/12): 1361–85.

Polonsky, M. J., and G. Wood. 2001. "Can the Overcommercialization of Cause-Related Marketing Harm Society?" *Journal of Macromarketing* 21(June): 8–22.

Post, J. E., L. E. Preston, and S. Sachs. 2002. *Redefining the Corporation: Stakeholder Management and Organizational Wealth.* Stanford, CA: Stanford University Press.

Pracejus, J. W., and G. D. Olsen. 2004. "The Role of Brand/Cause Fit in the Effectiveness of Cause-Related Marketing Campaigns." *Journal of Business Research* 57(6): 635–40.

Pracejus, J. W., G. D. Olsen, and N. R. Brown. 2003. "On the Prevalence and Impact of Vague Quantifiers in the Advertising of Cause-Related Marketing (CRM)." *Journal of Advertising* 32(4): 19–28.

Pringle, Hamish, and Marjorie Thompson. 1999. *Brand Spirit.* Chichester, England: John Wiley and Sons, Ltd.

Rangan, V. Kasturi, Sohel Karim, and Sheryl K. Sandberg. 1996. "Doing Better at Doing Good." *Harvard Business Review* 74(3): 42–54.

Ratnesar, Romesh. 1997. "Bottom Line Charity: Doing Well By Doing Good?" *The New Republic,* January 6. http://www.jonentine.com/articles/bottom_line_charity.htm.

Reichheld, Frederick F. 1993. "Loyalty-Based Management." *Harvard Business Review* 71(2): 64–73.

Ross, J. K., L. T. Patterson, and M. A. Stutts. 1992. "Consumer Perceptions of Organizations That Use Cause-Related Marketing." *Journal of the Academy of Marketing Science* 20(1): 93–97.

Ross, J. K., M. A. Stutts, and L. T. Patterson. 1991. "Tactical Considerations for the Effective Use of Cause-Related Marketing." *Journal of Applied Business Research* 7(2): 58–65.

Schlegelmilch, Bodo B., and Helen Woodruffe. 1995. "A Comparative Analysis of the Affinity Card Market in the USA and the UK." *International Journal of Bank Marketing* 13(5): 12–24.

Seifert, Bruce, Sara A. Morris, and Barbara R. Bartkus. 2004. "Having, Giving, and Getting: Slack Resources, Corporate Philanthropy, and Firm Financial Performance." *Business and Society* 43(2): 135–61.

Sen, Sankar, and C. B. Bhattacharya. 2001. "Does Doing Good Always Lead to Doing Better? Consumer Reactions to Corporate Social Responsibility." *Journal of Marketing Research* 38(May): 225–43.

Singer, Natasha. 2005. "Perplexing in Pink." *New York Times,* October 6. http://www.nytimes.com/2005/10/06/fashion/thursdaystyles/06skin.html.

Smith, Craig. 1994. "The New Corporate Philanthropy." *Harvard Business Review* 72(3): 105–16.

Smith, G., and R. Stodghill. 1994. "Are Good Causes Good Marketing?" *Business Week,* March 21, 64.

Smith, N. Craig. 2003. "Corporate Social Responsibility: Whether or How?" *California Management Review* 45(Summer): 52–76.

Smith, W., and M. Higgins. 2000. "Cause-Related Marketing: Ethics and Ecstatic." *Business and Society* 39(3): 304–22.

Strahilevitz, Michal. 1999. "The Effects of Product Type and Donation Magnitude on Willingness to Pay More for a Charity-Linked Brand." *Journal of Consumer Psychology* 8(3): 215–41.

Strahilevitz, Michal, and John G. Myers. 1998. "Donations to Charity as Purchase Incentives: How Well They Work May Depend on What You Are Trying to Sell." *Journal of Consumer Research* 24(March): 434–46.

Subrahmanyan, S. 2004. "Effects of Price Premium and Product Type on the Choice of Cause-Related Brands: A Singapore Perspective." *Journal of Product and Brand Management* 13(2/3): 116–24.

Szykman, Lisa R., Paul N. Bloom, and Jennifer Blazing. 2004. "Does Corporate Sponsorship of a Socially-Oriented Message Make a Difference? An Investigation of the Effects of Sponsorship Identity on Responses to an Anti-Drinking and Driving Message." *Journal of Consumer Psychology* 14(1–2): 13–20.

Torjman, Sherri. 1998. *Partnerships: The Good, the Bad, and the Uncertain.* Ottawa, Ontario: Caledon Institute for Social Policy.

Valentine, Paul W. 1990. "Philip Morris Draws Protest over Bill of Rights Exhibit." *Washington Post,* December 11, B7.

Varadarajan, P. Rajan, and Anil Menon. 1986. "Cause-Related Marketing." *Journal of Marketing* 2:58–74.

Veracity, Dani. 2005. "Is The American Cancer Society More Interested in Cancer Profit Than Cancer Prevention?" http://www.newstarget.com/010244.html.

Wagner, L., and R. L. Thompson. 1994. "Cause-Related Marketing: Fundraising Tool or Phony Philanthropy?" *Nonprofit World* 12(6): 9–13.

Wall, Wendy L. 1994. "Companies Change the Ways They Make Charitable Contributions." *Wall Street Journal,* June 21, 1, 19.

Wallace, Nicole. 2005. "Blending Business With Charity Can Be 'Head-Busting' Work." *Chronicle of Philanthropy,* April 28, 35.

Webb, D. J., and L. A. Mohr. 1998. "A Typology of Consumer Responses to Cause-Related Marketing: From Skeptics to Socially Concerned." *Journal of Public Policy and Marketing* 17(2): 226–38.

Zbar, Jeffrey D. 1993. "Wildlife Takes Center Stage as Cause-Related Marketing Becomes a $250 Million Show for Companies." *Advertising Age,* June 28, S-1.

7

Innovative Foundation Financing
The Annie E. Casey Foundation

Burton Sonenstein and Christa Velasquez

As investors, lenders, guarantors, depositors, loss insurers, stockholders, creditors, information suppliers, and patient capital—foundations have the capacity to influence market behavior. Foundations can shape capital flows and capital costs; influence the speed and scale of investment and development; underwrite the costs of new more constructive financial products; and reduce the risks faced by private investors when they invest in people, places, projects, purposes that have not been seen as competitive or prudent opportunities.
—Douglas W. Nelson, president, Annie E. Casey Foundation

For thousands of years, private philanthropies have funded projects to advance social missions. In ancient Greece, wealthy individuals created theaters, stadiums, aqueducts, and other amenities for community benefit. Charitable bequests were formalized under Roman law as early as 150 B.C. In the 20th century, such American industrialists as Andrew Carnegie and John D. Rockefeller strengthened philanthropy by aiming it at the roots of problems to create permanent solutions (Frumkin 2002). As it shifts emphasis from delivering services to catalyzing social change, 21st century philanthropy is again being transformed. A special focus here will be on foundations' newer, innovative financing mechanisms—going beyond simple grantmaking to increase, leverage up, and reutilize the financial resources available to support their missions.

Many foundations have realized that grantmaking alone can scarcely begin to address the social challenges before us. Whatever their importance, grants are small relative to such measures as government spending or national income. For instance, at the national level foundations had approximately $511 billion in assets and made $32 billion in grants in 2004 (Foundation Center 2006). Compare those numbers with data from Steuerle and Hodgkinson (2006), who indicate that nonprofit organizations as a group received almost $100 billion in government grants in 2003 and more than $700 billion in program service revenues (income from fees and charges paid by clients of nonprofits). Similarly, at the local level, foundation grants by themselves tend to be modest relative to total cost associated with addressing large-scale social problems. Hence foundation leaders recognize that if their resources are to be put to maximum use, they must go beyond grantmaking and approach initiatives with a broad array of financing vehicles, a strategy for attracting large coinvestments from public, private, and philanthropic sources of capital, and a development plan to align all stakeholders and sources of capital.

One consequence of these efforts is that foundations increasingly are coming to realize the potential of financing tools traditionally associated with the business sector. In its social investing, the Annie E. Casey Foundation (AECF) ventures beyond traditional foundation grant funding to mirror the private-sector financing efforts of private banks and institutions, which are continually open to new financing structures and tools. Over the past decade, AECF has expanded the number of ways it has been able to use its financial resources to further its mission by filling financing gaps, providing capital at affordable rates, and attracting coinvestors.

Social and Program-Related Investment: Rationale and Brief History

The current and growing foundation interest in social investing reflects a much broader public interest in socially responsible investing that has evolved over time. The modern impetus for socially responsible investing in the United States grew out of the anti-apartheid movement. Beginning in the 1960s, American college students pressured their universities to "divest" from corporations doing business in apartheid South Africa. Momentum gathered until, between 1985 and 1990, some 200 U.S.

A Brief Glossary of Terms

There is no general consensus on terminology. The authors' attempt to define the terms in this chapter is relative to the Annie E. Casey Foundation's experience only.

Social Investment

An umbrella term for any investment with both financial and social goals. The tax code does not define what constitutes a social investment, which is not specific to foundations. At the Annie E. Casey Foundation, social investing signifies the whole range of creative tools available to foundations beyond traditional grants and regardless of their rate of return. These include deposits, program-related investments, and market-rate investments.

Mission-Related Investment

A term not defined by the tax code but one that usually applies to foundations; at the Annie E. Casey Foundation, mission-related investment refers to investments with a market-rate return on a risk-adjusted basis that also produces some social return or benefit.

Program-Related Investment (PRI)

A term applied solely to private foundations that is defined by the tax code. A PRI is made primarily for social purpose with a below-market rate of return on a risk-adjusted basis. An investment qualifies as a PRI only if it meets three tests: (1) the primary purpose is to accomplish one or more of the foundation's charitable purposes, (2) no significant purpose is producing income or property appreciation, and (3) no purpose is influencing legislation, participating or intervening in a political campaign, or engaging in other lobbying activity legally off-limits to foundations. Provided the investment meets these three criteria, a PRI may be made to either a for-profit or nonprofit organization.

corporations closed operations in South Africa, and 26 states, more than 150 universities, and scores of cities divested their funds in companies and banks doing business there (Investors' Circle 2001). Investors' Circle, a network of "angel investors" (wealthy individuals providing capital for start-ups) dedicated to sustainability, calls this "the 20th century's first mass movement of . . . international capital in response to a non-financial social issue" (Investors' Circle 2001). The success of the anti-apartheid divestiture movement made it safe and sound for investors to consider social along with financial outcomes, and socially responsible investing took off.

Mission-related investing, a subset of socially responsible investing, encompasses a variety of approaches foundations use to fuse their missions with their investments. Some philanthropies use this term to refer to any investments that both generate a return and serve their social mission. Others use the term only to refer to investments that generate returns at or near market rates. At AECF, *social investing* signifies the whole range of creative tools available to foundations beyond traditional grants.

A particular variant of social investing strategies takes the form of making what the tax code classifies as program-related investments (PRIs). To preserve its tax-exempt status, a U.S. foundation must annually distribute 5 percent of its endowment to programs that further its social mission. Typically, these distributions are in the form of grants. At the same time, a foundation must invest its endowment, or corpus, to maximize return on investment; most also seek to create a perpetual or long-term sustainable funding stream. On pain of severe penalties, the foundation also has a fiduciary duty to protect its assets and avoid jeopardizing investments or making investments that might imperil its assets. Although it may seem counterintuitive, no law requires foundations to steer investments toward their social goals: if it wanted to, a health care organization could buy shares in a tobacco company.

On the flip side, Internal Revenue Service (IRS) regulations permit foundations to make below-market-rate loans, guarantees, and equity investments to finance projects or organizations. These disbursements, PRIs, can be counted toward the 5 percent minimum payout distribution. PRIs count toward payout because the primary purpose is charitable and not financial. Mission-related investments do not count toward payout because the primary purpose of the investment is financial return.

According to the Internal Revenue Code, an investment qualifies as a PRI only if it meets three tests: (1) the primary purpose is to accomplish one or more of the foundation's charitable purposes, (2) no significant purpose is producing income or property appreciation, and (3) no purpose is influencing legislation, participating or intervening in a political campaign, or engaging in other lobbying activity legally off-limits to foundations (IRC §4944(c) and Treasury Regulations §53.49443(a)).

Although a PRI can be one of the most powerful and flexible financing options at foundations' disposal, the legal distinctions are important, and many private foundations—worried about separating fiduciary duty from philanthropic giving—have faced internal challenges to implementing social investing strategies. Among the most conservative foundation leaders, for instance, such financial strategies appear to blur the fine line between the foundation's investment and programmatic functions. For this reason, not all foundation presidents, trustees, and investment officers are comfortable with PRIs.

Many investments also require financial expertise and industry experience that a particular foundation may lack. Moreover, investments such as PRIs require significant legal documentation, due diligence, and reporting, which can overwhelm smaller foundations, though opportunities to pool resources with other organizations and investing through financing intermediaries can help mitigate these problems.

Despite these limitations, many foundations today undertake diverse types of PRIs. These foundations employ a variety of approaches for selecting, implementing, and structuring deals and manage the PRI-making process in ways that influence the relationship between grant-making and investing staff, the structure or terms of investments, or the level of engagement with an investee organization during the term of the investment. Along with mission-related deposits and market-rate mission-related investments, PRIs have the potential, for a variety of reasons addressed in this chapter, to bring about social change on a scale that grantmaking alone cannot.

Although historically foundations have used these instruments mainly to finance community economic development and affordable housing, they hold increasing appeal for underwriting or financing programmatic advances in education, the environment, and arts and culture. Early pioneers of PRIs have been joined in the past 10 years by such foundations as the F. B. Heron Foundation, the Meyer Memorial Trust, and the Skoll Foundation. Recently, an affinity group of grantmakers interested in PRIs formed the PRI Makers Network to respond to the need for more information, technical assistance, and collaborative funding opportunities. The network comprises grantmakers who use PRIs and other investments to accomplish their philanthropic goals (as well as those interested but not currently making PRIs), and its mission is to provide a forum for networking, professional development, collaboration, and outreach to funders.

Trends in Social Investing: Mission-Related and Program-Related Investments

Foundations have shown increasing interest in social investing in recent years. Between 1990 and 2001, the number of foundations engaged in PRIs rose from 57 to 105, and the number of PRIs rose from 161 to 340. The amount invested in PRIs between 1990 and 2001 rose from $91.9 million to $246.2 million, an increase of a little more than 200 percent after adjusting for inflation (Foundation Center 2006). Several reasons can explain this increased traction:

- The rise of "intentional investment." Foundation investment staff make decisions daily in working to build the corpus. Some foundation investment management firms acknowledge that many foundations want to do more than simply protect and grow the corpus; they also want to more closely align investments with their missions.

- The desire to put more resources in the service of philanthropic mission. Only a small percentage of foundations' wealth goes to charitable activities in a given year. Assuming grantmaking of about 5 percent of assets means that roughly 95 percent is invested in return-generating activities. Yet few of these activities relate to any charitable social or mission-related goals. Thus, some see traditional investment patterns of foundations as a missed opportunity; finding practical ways to increase mission-serving funds is among philanthropy's primary challenges today.

- The need to increase resources for mission-critical organizations or projects. There is an emerging mindset of utilizing more foundation resources for mission purposes, such as increasing the payout rate beyond the legally required 5 percent. Most of the social, human, health, economic, and environmental problems that foundations address cannot be conquered without spending far more than foundations traditionally have. Most foundations could grant their entire endowments to their most successful projects and still not accomplish their missions. As awareness of the limits of traditional funding increases, so too does interest in social investment.

- Growing interest in leveraging additional dollars. What ultimately happens in America to people, places, and causes—economic opportunity, climate stabilization, historic preservation, education, race relations, antipoverty campaigns, or efforts to fortify family structure—depends less on philanthropy's focus than on the behavior of government and private markets. For this reason, foundations have increasingly come to understand, social investing presents unprecedented opportunities to engage and leverage these stakeholders.

- Growing interest in simultaneously meeting payout requirements and recycling funds. Social investments such as PRIs allow foundations to meet or exceed payout requirements *and* to use the money repeatedly. Although investments such as PRIs cannot and should not ever replace grants—in many cases, for example, the nature of a project is such that funds simply *cannot* be repaid—they can lengthen the life and return on investment for foundation assets. Some foundations do use PRIs as a way to meet payout requirements, and their combined grant and PRI distributions equal 5 percent. AECF makes PRIs in addition to a 7.8 percent payout rate and encourages other foundations to make PRIs in addition to their current level of grantmaking.

This change in thinking did not come about overnight. As early as 1968, the Taconic Foundation "formed a consortium of Ford and other foundations that pooled funds to make PRIs" (Ford Foundation 1991, 5). Over the years, other foundations followed suit. The John D. and Catherine T. MacArthur Foundation's first PRI financed the purchase of Shorebank common stock in 1983 (Fanton 2008). Now one of the nation's most successful community development financial institutions, Shorebank was at the time a small community bank focused on investments in the surrounding—and rapidly deteriorating—community in Chicago. Based on the community-oriented focus of the bank, the investment qualified as a PRI. Today, the MacArthur Foundation controls a PRI investment pool of $200 million, approximately 5 percent of its corpus, with PRIs to more than 100 nonprofit and for-profit organizations in the United States and abroad.[1]

The Double-Bottom-Line Concept

When social investments are made, foundations look to two bottom lines: the social return and the financial return. The latter includes the return or preservation of capital in addition to interest, dividends, or gains on investments. For instance, an investment in a financing fund that lends money to child care providers to purchase or improve their centers will generate the social return of creating more quality child care slots, potentially creating child care jobs, and increasing the income of the providers. The financial return can be generated from interest payments and the return of capital. Like the dual-return aspects, there are also two types of risk: the financial and programmatic. Financially, the foundation runs the risk of losing some or all of its investment. Programmatically, the project or organization could fail to meet the programmatic goals—in this example, not producing the projected number of child care slots, jobs, or increases in providers' income. A PRI could be financially successful but programmatically disappointing or programmatically successful but a financial loss. It is worth noting that a third bottom line many foundations and individuals increasingly seek is environmental return.

Approaches to Social Investing

Social investing is not a "one-size-fits-all" proposition. What may be right for a $3 billion private foundation with a grantmaking staff of 150 may not be effective for a smaller regional or family foundation with no paid staff. Foundations of all sizes often find it beneficial to coinvest with other private and governmental investors. Fortunately, foundations can choose from an increasingly wide variety of investment approaches that allow foundations of varying sizes to participate at different levels of commitment and to attract different sources of funds. These methods include investments made directly to an organization (known as direct investments) and wholesale investments—that is, investments through financial intermediaries such as loan or investment funds.

Direct Investments

Foundations may choose to invest directly in a nonprofit or social purpose business rather than using an intermediary entity to place its funds. These foundations find that direct investment complements their foundation philosophy, culture, mission, and resources better than devotion of the entire portfolio to passive investment. The direct approach enables a foundation to maintain a closer relationship with the investee organization and retain more control over the subsidized activity and the capacity building of the organization than is typical with an intermediary organization.

To make direct investments, investors typically must possess or retain financial expertise and industry experience. Investments such as PRIs also require a great deal of legal documentation, due diligence, and reporting, which can be expensive or time consuming. Unless the foundation can mount an ongoing PRI program, small singular investments or "one-offs" can inhibit diversification and increase overall risk. Moreover, the foundation's program interests and personnel may change before investments such as PRIs run their course. The Annie E. Casey Foundation has chosen not to make direct investments, but many foundations invest directly in projects or organizations important to their work. Many foundations will provide bridge financing to maintain operations and sometimes even mortgage financing for nonprofit facilities of mission-critical grantees. Other foundations may invest directly into a company that will create jobs or socially beneficial products or services.

The Rockefeller Foundation's Program Venture Experiment (ProVenEx fund) invests directly in companies as well as indirectly through financial intermediaries that overlap with the foundation's philanthropic goals. One of ProVenEx's investments is in a biopharmaceutical company that is undergoing pivotal clinical trials for a microbicide that could prevent the transmission of HIV/AIDS. ProVenEx made its initial investment in this company in 1999 as an early-stage investor, when the financial risk was highest, because the company's microbicide product was considered to be among the most promising candidates to meet a significant public health need. A publicly traded pharmaceutical company has since acquired this company, which now has potential access to capital markets to develop its portfolio of microbicide products (World Economic Forum 2005).

Intermediaries

A lack of capacity to solicit, screen, perform due diligence, and monitor social investments is not limited solely to small foundations. Even in large foundations, program officers may lack the requisite financial skills, investment officers have limited time to implement such instruments, or both. In these cases, intermediaries can help meet these challenges. An increasing number of commingled loan and investment vehicles enable foundations to more efficiently share risk, management, and outcome measurement.

Community development financial institution (CDFI) intermediaries are especially useful to foundations. As context, it is helpful to understand that in 1977, the Community Reinvestment Act opened the door to legislation and regulations that require the commercial financial industry, particularly depository institutions with assets of $250 million or more, to help meet the credit needs of the communities in which they operate, including low- and moderate-income neighborhoods. Every five years, federal agencies evaluate each depository institution's record and assign a rating that is taken into account when institutions apply for deposit facilities and when mergers and acquisitions are approved or denied. The Community Reinvestment Act provided the impetus for direct lending and investing by commercial depository institutions and for creating CDFIs chartered to invest in the financial health of low-income communities.

After the Community Reinvestment Act passed, the community development industry mushroomed, creating a new market for financial goods and services to serve low-income communities and individuals. In 1994, the federal government created the CDFI Fund to channel funding to individual CDFIs and their partners through competitive applications. Because CDFIs serve customers and communities with little access to traditional financial services, they are a critical vehicle for targeting funds and services to low-income communities and their residents. And because CDFI intermediaries channel investments to local nonprofit organizations for the investor, they also help foundations cut down time spent diversifying, managing, and monitoring their portfolios. Intermediary investments effectively allow foundations to channel funds through CDFIs, which provide the on-the-ground expertise and managerial infrastructure.

Investments in CDFIs present some drawbacks that foundations must weigh. These investments allow less direct control over the individual deal and its fit with the foundation's social mission than do direct investments. In some instances investors pay intermediary management fees, which are typically in the 1–3 percent range of capital committed. In other situations, the intermediary earns revenue through the spread, or the difference between the cost of capital (interest paid on the PRI to the foundation) and the price the intermediary charges to its borrower. An intermediary's spread varies depending on the organization, the type of lending or investing it is doing, and any provisions set by the foundation investors. CDFI spreads typically range from as low as 1–2 percent to 10 percent. The liquidity of investments in CDFIs varies with the structure and terms of investment agreements. If the foundation makes a loan and the CDFI uses the money as outlined in the loan agreement, it gets repaid upon maturity according to the investment terms. If the CDFI is using the funds for purposes outside those prescribed in the loan agreement, the CDFI is in default and the foundation can demand immediate repayment. If the investment is in a community development venture capital or private equity fund, investors are invested for the life of the fund (usually 10 years) unless the fund managers use the PRI proceeds for something outside of what is allowed by the partnership agreement. This structure is the same for any traditional venture capital or private equity fund without a social purpose.

In support of AECF's work on strengthening children and families and in generating jobs, in 2004 it made a $1 million PRI to Cascadia Revolving Fund in Seattle, Washington, for its Child Care Fund, which helps Washington and Oregon child care providers pay for program improvements by offering low-interest loans and technical assistance to those who do not qualify for traditional bank financing. Such improvements can help providers get licensed to care for more children, boost operating margins, and improve their long-term business prospects. Cascadia expects to finance the creation of 175 child care slots in King County, Washington, with the proceeds of the PRI.

Another AECF investment supports the development of affordable housing in the Lower San Antonio neighborhood of Oakland, California, one of the Bay Area's most diverse communities. Its population is approximately 34 percent Asian, 27 percent Latino, 23 percent African American, and 12 percent white. Homeownership rates this neighborhood are low, with 81 percent of residents renting and more than 43 percent of households spending 30 percent or more of their income on housing. Homeownership is clearly out of reach for most of these residents. The rental market for multifamily housing is also tight, with vacancy rates at 4.5 percent.

To address the affordable housing shortage, AECF supported the creation of the Lower San Antonio Community Fund, a $10.25 million revolving loan fund managed by the Northern California Community Loan Fund. The new fund will disburse both loans and grants for predevelopment and site-acquisition financing for affordable housing projects in the neighborhood. AECF made a $2 million PRI and a $250,000 grant. The PRI will finance specific real estate projects with financial returns expected accordingly, and the grant funds are to provide funding for pre-site controls (e.g., appraisals, environmental impact studies), predevelopment (e.g., title fees, demolition), and increased loan-loss reserves.

Other loan and grant investors include the Evelyn and Walter Haas, Jr. Fund, Northern California Community Loan Fund, Low Income Investment Fund, and Local Initiatives Support Corporation. Nonprofit housing developers that belong to an AECF-supported local real estate council can borrow from the Lower San Antonio Community Fund, which is expected to finance approximately 200 new units of affordable housing in the community. In the first 17 months of operation, the fund has financed the development of 278 units of affordable housing and 18,000 square feet of commercial space.

Double-Bottom-Line Venture Capital or Private Equity Funds

In another form of the intermediary approach, double-bottom-line efforts can be professionally managed by venture capital funds. These funds can pursue local and regional social objectives by seeking entrepreneurial opportunities in businesses that, for example, hire local residents or locate facilities in low-income areas. Charitable investors often choose these investments, which promise both attractive financial returns and mission-related outcomes. To the extent that such double-bottom-line funds can achieve market rate, or near–market rate returns, even more institutional investors, including public pension funds, are likely to find them attractive.

One example of a double-bottom-line venture is the New York City Investment Fund, a $96 million private fund with a civic mission. The key investment criterion is that the proposed project is likely to generate benefits for New York City and its communities. Priorities include preservation or creation of affordable housing, job creation, revitalization of distressed areas, and innovative ideas or products that position New York at the cutting edge of a growth economy. Another example, the Wisconsin Rural Enterprise Fund, was formed through partnerships with rural cooperatives, local economic development organizations, and financial institutions. Managed by the Northwest Regional Planning Commission and Wisconsin Business Innovation Corporation, this fund exists to foster new markets, higher-wage jobs, and economic diversification throughout rural Wisconsin, where the availability of venture capital is scarce. The fund invests primarily in early-stage science-based agriculture and high-tech wood product businesses.

The Bay Area Equity Fund is a fund in which the Annie E. Casey, F. B. Heron, Ford, and MacArthur foundations invest. This fund invests in companies that generate near–market rate returns and positive social and environmental returns—for example, jobs for community residents, health benefits, or environmentally friendly business practices—for targeted low-income neighborhoods in the San Francisco Bay Area. Reflecting the Bay Area's economic strengths, the fund favors growth companies in the technology, health care, and consumer goods and services sectors. It invests mainly in private, mid- to late-stage companies in or near low- to moderate-income neighborhoods of the 10-county Bay Area.

Managed by JPMorgan Chase, the Bay Area Equity Fund has raised $75 million in capital through investments from major banks, insurance companies, foundations, corporations, and private individuals.[2] It is structured in two tiers. The economic growth tier invests in companies that need between $3 million and $5 million in equity investments. The strategic equity tier invests in smaller companies needing up to $1 million. Regional cross-sector partnerships with two nonprofits—the Bay Area Council and the Alliance for Community Development—sponsor this fund. These nonprofits focus on the development of the Bay Area and help generate investment opportunities for the fund and provide technical assistance to portfolio companies.

Since its inception in 2004, the Bay Area Equity Fund has invested approximately $34 million in 17 companies, creating 978 jobs, of which 589 are entry-level positions. It has also joined with a portfolio company—the term used to describe companies in which the fund invests—to convene meetings of corporate, government, and nonprofit entities to coordinate initiatives designed to engage citizens in their communities.

Multiplying Up: Investment-Leveraging and Syndication

Even when a foundation invests directly or through intermediaries, the grants, loans, and investments it can provide are apt to be inadequate to the project at hand typically because the amount required is simply beyond the resources of a single foundation. Two related financing techniques—leveraging and syndication—provide ways of multiplying the amount of money available to finance the investment or project at hand. "Leveraging" refers to efforts to use a foundation's investments or its cash and credit to encourage other investors to take part. "Syndication" describes a group of investors, known as a syndicate, who invest together in a large project.

A prime example of a program-related investment is AECF's work in Indianapolis, where social investments resulted in the Indianapolis Charter Schools Facilities Fund. AECF and the Local Initiatives Support Corporation have each guaranteed $1 million of the fund, which leveraged $20 million from JPMorgan Chase (formerly Bank One). The fund will finance 15 new charter school facilities that will serve approximately 2,800 students.

Foundations are increasingly interested in syndicating investment opportunities. Many foundations, for example, have expressed interest in investing in national funding vehicles for affordable housing. The development of such vehicles allows foundations to invest in a pool along with other like-minded investors, with the managing organization reinvesting funds at the local level. Innovative variations on this theme include creating pools of capital from investments by organizations across the country that local community development entities can deploy to finance land acquisition, provide shared equity mortgages, and finance charter school construction.

National capital vehicles provide an efficient way for a range of public and private investors to participate in financing transactions. Varying levels of participation, risk, and return mean that foundations, banks, and other institutional investors can all find appropriate investing opportunities. These financing vehicles aggregate significant capital for rapid and specialized deployment (i.e., reinvestment) and create opportunities for standardized loan terms and documentation, which significantly streamlines the work a foundation must do. For foundations, this approach can make the investment more practical and cost efficient.

The Benefits of Innovative Financing

As these concepts and examples suggest, foundation assets can be a powerful tool for organizations that lack the assets or credit history needed to qualify for affordable financing from mainstream financial institutions. A foundation can be a powerful ally by leveraging the strength of its own balance sheet to arrange for or guarantee bank financing. Moreover, a foundation commitment—basically a vote of confidence—can catalyze other strategic funders in the philanthropic, public, and private sectors. For foundations, social investing may meet the 5 percent payout requirement and offer a range of benefits, including the following:

- Interest on PRIs can help offset the need for high returns on corpus investments. If a foundation's PRIs are funded out of its budget and counted toward the 5 percent payout requirement, financial returns that are generated supplement corpus investment returns. Like grants, PRIs count toward payout, but unlike grants, they earn a financial return. PRI earnings are treated like all other investment income and therefore adds to the overall return on the endowment.

- Foundations with large endowments and large payout requirements can often use PRIs as a legitimate holding bin for funds that must be disbursed while grantmaking strategies are still being defined.
- Programmatically, innovative financial investments can bring foundation objectives to scale by facilitating increased investment from other sources and enabling reuse of the original funds over time.

Many foundations have discovered that social investing creates a more collaborative, synergistic, and mutually accountable relationship with grantees. Extending a loan, providing a guarantee, or making an equity investment also gives a foundation an economic stake in the organization's performance. In these cases, foundations are far more likely to lend their own expertise, provide operational advice, intervene in crises, and sit on governance boards.

From a programmatic standpoint, these social investments are also often a means to complement grant support to further the mission; provide larger amounts of support for a specific project (e.g., a $2 million grant for affordable housing may not be feasible, but a loan guarantee for that amount might be); and build the accountability, repayment, and sustainability skills of grantees so that they can implement better business practices or engage other sectors for support.

Social Investing in Practice
at the Annie E. Casey Foundation

AECF first allocated $20 million in 1998 for social investing, including mission-related deposits, PRIs, and market-rate investments that support the its mission. In 2002, it established a formal social investments program, and in 2004 the trustees increased the social investing allocation to $100 million. Now a wide range of social investments benefit both the endowment and the programmatic activities. In other foundations, of course, social investing may follow different paths.

Today, rather than substituting PRIs for grants, AECF draws its $100 million social investing allocation from endowment-investment capital. The social investment staff is located within the foundation's finance department and works closely with program staff to package deals. This work is carried out within the context of a coordinated grantmaking strategy designed to build local organizations' capacity to carry out their own missions complementary to that of AECF.

AECF prefers to coinvest with other organizations whenever possible as a way to mitigate risk and to influence other stakeholders. Typically, the foundation invests 10 percent or less of a project or fund's total financing, and private institutional investors, bank investors, and other philanthropic organizations and public sources provide the rest.

AECF joins other foundations such as the F. B. Heron Foundation in making mission-related deposits to federally insured depository institutions (primarily community development banks, credit unions, etc.) that deliver financial products and services in targeted neighborhoods. Structured as insured certificates of deposit or share certificates, the capital provided by the AECF can strengthen relationships with financial institutions and enable financial institutions to strengthen their presence and the services they provide in underserved neighborhoods.

The grantmaking and programmatic staff at AECF identify opportunities for social investments. The social investment staff then works with program staff to underwrite and structure each investment. This approach meets both our social and fiduciary objectives. Since 1998, AECF has made 36 social investments (21 mission-related deposits and 15 program-related investments). Although the financial return expectations vary by individual investment, depending on the instrument (guarantee, debt, equity) and other considerations, they range from 1 percent to percentages in the low teens, with a goal of an overall portfolio return of 3–5 percent. The overall return expectation for the traditional endowment investment portfolio is 9 percent.

Although most foundations do not measure the return of their social investment portfolios relative to their costs, foundations may consider investment opportunity costs, default costs, and programmatic opportunity costs of making a program-related investment. Investment opportunity cost is the difference in return on a PRI or the same amount invested in a regular, nonsocial investment. On the surface the comparison will favor a nonsocial investment. However, the PRI has an unseen benefit. An outstanding PRI is not included in the asset base used to calculate a foundation's legally required 5 percent payout. Because of this, a PRI has a 5 percent head start on a regular investment (Lingenfelter 1997).

Default costs, or the investment losses, tend to receive more attention than the other costs. Some foundations have been making PRIs for many decades, but others, like the Annie E. Casey Foundation, are relatively new to the field and there currently are no reliable data on the historical performance of PRIs. Anecdotally we know that certain types of investing (investing directly in companies or highly experimental projects) generated high levels of losses, that other types of investing are of lower risk (deposits or investing in intermediaries for affordable housing), and that PRI portfolios in general have been generating modest positive returns.

Programmatic opportunity cost is the difference between the programmatic return of one investment over another, be it a PRI or a grant. For grants, which are not recycled back to the foundation, the programmatic opportunity cost is permanent. For PRIs, which are repaid to the foundation less any defaults or losses, the opportunity cost is temporary. Despite the possibility of redeploying the repaid funds for other programmatic opportunities, each PRI, like each grant, must be measured on its programmatic merit (Lingenfelter 1997).

AECF considers a range of impact criteria when evaluating a potential social investment. The proposed investment does not have to rate high against all evaluative criteria if the overall combination of factors looks right. For example, AECF might consider a higher-risk investment if it is proven to have a particularly high impact on AECF's grantmaking objectives. Criteria for evaluation of potential investments include the following factors: programmatic fit, potential program impact, financial strength of organization, financial feasibility of proposed project, strength of management, geographic coverage of "Casey places," leverage of additional funds, potential influence on systems or policies, innovation, and replication.

In its PRIs, AECF ventures beyond traditional foundation grant funding and is continually open to new financing structures and tools. Over the past decade, AECF has expanded the number of ways it has been able to leverage its financial resources. It has found ways to help organizations access and deploy low-cost borrowing, used its investments to attract coinvestors, utilized grant financing and loan guarantees to absorb first-loss-type risks, and made below-market loans to lower the overall cost of capital for project financing. At the same time, AECF and other foundations must deploy these tools under different and often stricter requirements than private capital providers face, because foundations have a greater fiduciary responsibility to the public reflected only in part in legal regulations.

The largest and most extensive of AECF's innovative financing efforts has been associated with its $15 million loan guarantee for East Baltimore

Development, Inc.—which has catalyzed approximately $100 million of additional investment by a large network of local, state, federal, private, and public funds that participate through loans, loan guarantees, investments, and grants to finance the first phase of an 80-acre community revitalization project including a life sciences park, mixed-income housing, a community school, and other retail and social service facilities (see box 7.1). Most urban redevelopment projects of this type have seldom been a focus of foundations, largely because of their scale, but almost all large real estate projects involve significant loan financing, not to mention dealing with governmental bodies, rules, subsidies, and taxes. These factors essentially position the foundation into the innovative financing arena if it wants to play on this field at all.

Measuring the Impact of Social Investments

For PRIs, aligning grantmaking strategies with social investing strategies is crucial, as the programmatic outcomes are just as or even more important than the financial return on investment. Similarly, the approach to evaluation should be rigorous and creative, designed to respond to a community's unique needs and a recipient organization's capacities to respond.

In the case of the East Baltimore project, AECF has funded a comprehensive data tracking system to document and measure the social outcomes of the project. The case management system documents the experience of relocated residents for three years and measures outcomes in access to services, employment, health, education, and asset building. EBDI STAT provides monthly reporting of statistics relating to the progress of the project and the impact on residents, such as the jobs created for residents and minorities. AECF's goal is to demonstrate with data that large-scale urban revitalization does not only have to be about real estate and gentrification, but also about providing tangible benefits and improved outcomes for the current residents and disadvantaged families in the community.

Some of the results achieved in the first phase of the East Baltimore project are encouraging. The application of "responsible relocation" has generated largely positive outcomes for the homeowners and renters relocated in phase I. A survey of those relocated residents indicates a high level of satisfaction and documents that most of the relocations were into neighborhoods with higher property values, better school systems, and

Box 7.1. Transforming East Baltimore

East Baltimore was once an economically healthy, thriving community, where families enjoyed a deep sense of community pride. And while the residents remain one of the community's greatest resources, over time the neighborhood has suffered from years of disinvestment, blight, and crime. As a result, for East Baltimore's families, employment, health, educational achievement, adequate housing, and crime and safety indicators rank among the city's lowest.

Large-scale urban revitalization requires investing hundreds of millions of dollars over 10 to 20 years. To attract the multiple sources of city, state, federal, and private capital, a catalytic and creative approach to financing large-scale social development is needed.

The Annie E. Casey Foundation (AECF) stepped up to the plate in East Baltimore not only because its headquarters are only a few miles away, but also because it takes a "place-based" approach to social change, concentrating on some of America's most troubled neighborhoods and communities. In East Baltimore, it has deployed grants and a wide range of financing tactics and strategies to trigger and sustain large-scale neighborhood stabilization and revitalization. These grants served multiple purposes, including leveraging up private sources of capital, making a commitment to residents affected by the change, and mainly employing risk capital for the social good by providing a catalyst for public and private investments that otherwise were unlikely to be made.

Led by East Baltimore Development, Inc. (EBDI), the nonprofit organization established to administer the project, the East Baltimore redevelopment project strives for "responsible redevelopment"—employing economic, community, and human development strategies to optimize benefits for area residents, businesses, and the surrounding neighborhoods.

Eighty acres adjacent to the Johns Hopkins Hospitals and Medical Centers in East Baltimore are being redeveloped. Some $800 million in investments will be raised to create a 2-million-square-foot life sciences technology park, 1,500 new and renovated mixed-income housing units, and 4,000 to 6,000 new jobs over 10 to 15 years.

To finance a project of this size, the foundation had to think and act big. In 2003, the foundation leveraged its own balance sheet to arrange for an initial $15 million in debt financing for EBDI. The foundation guaranteed the loan to EBDI to finance the phase I land acquisition, demolition, and infrastructure improvements on a 30-acre parcel where the first life science buildings and housing were to be built. With the foundation's support, EBDI secured the $15 million loan and an additional $3.9 million new markets tax credit forgivable loan from a large commercial bank—both on more favorable terms than it could have secured on its own.

This initial financing enhanced the credibility of EBDI and the project, enabling EBDI to select a prominent master developer and secure substantial funding from federal, state, city, and private sources.

(continued)

Box 7.1. *(continued)*

These investments complemented a multi-year grantmaking initiative that will bring as much as $20 million in grants over 10 years to East Baltimore to improve the quality of life for new and existing residents and to establish new standards for responsible relocation. For example, the Annie E. Casey Foundation committed $5 million in grant funds to match a Johns Hopkins grant to create the Supplemental Benefits Fund. The fund enhanced the financial benefits and case management services available from public sources for the relocation of 400 homeowners and renters from the project area. Casey and Hopkins also committed to several years of operating support for EBDI. This early-stage high-risk commitment to significant large-scale support catalyzed more than $100 million of public and private investments by other funders, including the City of Baltimore, the State of Maryland, Johns Hopkins University, and local and national philanthropies. EBDI has successfully completed the phase I relocation and has commenced construction of the first life science building and housing units. In many ways, the East Baltimore project demonstrates just how powerful innovative foundation financing can be in tapping into private and public sources of capital, serving the interest of residents whose lives are disrupted in redevelopment projects, and engaging in redevelopment—a type of activity traditionally outside of a foundation's grantmaking purposes.

---

lower crime rates. Homeowners have gained substantial equity in their new homes. A new demolition protocol was developed and implemented to reduce the harmful impacts of lead dust and other contaminants in the environment.

In principle, the outcomes of a project such as that in East Baltimore could be subjected to a formal cost-benefit analysis that relates specific investments to social outcomes. In practice, undertaking such an analysis is not feasible but it is possible to track and measure these outcomes and attribute them to an intentional effort to target investments to improve the outcomes of residents and disadvantaged families in large-scale redevelopment—to make them beneficiaries, not victims, of the process.

The Annie E. Casey Foundation measures the impact of its social investments on two levels:

1. **Population-level impact** focuses on community-wide improvements, which can include increased access to services, reductions in poverty, public policy that responds to the needs of families,

improved infrastructure, rising property values or increases in jobs, homeownership, or earnings. In many cases, the foundation partners with research institutions to collect objective data on macro-level outcomes in targeted neighborhoods because individual investee organizations are unlikely to have the capacity or resources to undertake this type of assessment.

2. **Deal-specific impact** is written into the covenants of individual investment agreements. These agreements are established case by case depending on the recipient organization's competencies and include such quantifiable targets as numbers of affordable housing units developed, small businesses financed, and jobs created. These outputs are measured continually as part of each organization's reporting requirements.

As in traditional grantmaking, measuring the social return on a PRI or mission-related investment is difficult, and there are no industry standards or best practices. Foundations continue to struggle with developing an approach that is both measurable and manageable, and several key issues need to be addressed (Clark et al. 2004).

Foundations make PRIs to address the financing gap that public capital markets will not fill. Although there has been a push to standardize and expand investment to a larger scale, PRIs often are unique, one-off deals in a wide range of program areas. Foundations make investments for a myriad of reasons, and two foundations that have invested in the same organization or project may have different social impact measures. Nonstandard deals with multiple social goals make the development of widely accepted impact indicators difficult.

Even if a foundation has identified the indicators it hopes to track, collecting that data could be a costly and time-consuming effort. AECF conducts population-level surveys in its targeted communities as part of its ongoing Making Connections initiative, which helps identify areas for investment and impact of the foundation's investments. This large-scale data gathering and analysis is not something that most PRI recipients and many foundations would be able to undertake.

Researchers in all program areas struggle with determining causality: did one action or intervention cause a particular outcome, a completely different intervention, or a combination of interventions? In the case of the Annie E. Casey Foundation, its Making Connections initiative concentrates the foundation's resources—grantmaking, technical assistance, and other supports—on a target community. PRIs are simply one tool or intervention to generate successful outcomes for families.

Conclusion

Why should foundations be willing to move beyond traditional grant-making to deploy a more expansive set of financing tactics and strategies to achieve their missions? Large-scale change often requires large-scale initiatives that will attract coinvestors and ensure the sustainability of the change by involving vested cross-sector stakeholders. Although foundations cannot expect to persuade private for-profit investors to become more charitable, the philanthropic sector's control of approximately $500 billion can influence market behavior. Foundations are only beginning to glimpse the possibilities and the potential of the catalytic role of their endowments. Through careful experimentation, scaling up successful efforts, and outreach among members of the foundation community, the philanthropic sector can begin to realize its fuller potential.

NOTES

1. MacArthur Foundation web site.

2. DBL Investors web site, "DBL Investors: Double Bottom Line Venture Capital Investing," http://www.dbinvestors.com.

REFERENCES

Clark, Catherine, William Rosenzweig, David Long, and Sara Olsen. 2004. "Double Bottom Line Project Report: Assessing Social Impact in Double Bottom Line Ventures." New York: Rockefeller Foundation.

Fanton, Jonathan. 2008. "Building Institutions for Social Change: The Case for Buy-and-Hold Philanthropy." Presented at the PRI Makers Network Conference, New Orleans, Louisiana, January 31.

Ford Foundation. 1968. *New Options in the Philanthropic Process: A Ford Foundation Statement of Policy.* New York: Ford Foundation.

———. 1991. "Investing for Social Gain: Reflections on Two Decades of Program-Related Investments." New York: Ford Foundation.

Foundation Center. 2006. *Foundation Yearbook.* New York: Foundation Center.

Frumkin, Peter. 2002. "Not Every Victim Ought to Be a Charity Case." *Washington Post,* November 17.

Investors' Circle. 2001. *Mission-Related Investing: Strategies for Philanthropic Institutions.* San Francisco: Investors' Circle. http://www.investorscircle.net/index.php?tg= fileman&idx=get&inl=1&id=1&gr=Y&path=Essays&file=Northwest+Area+ Foundation+final+report.pdf.

Lingenfelter, Paul E. 1997. "Program Related Investments: Do They Cost or Do They Pay?" In *Program Related Investments: A Technical Manual for Foundations,* edited by Christie I. Baxter. New York: John Wiley.

Steuerle, C. Eugene, and Virginia Hodgkinson. 2006. "Meeting Social Needs: Comparing Independent Sector and Government Resources." In *Nonprofits and Government: Collaboration and Conflict,* edited by Elizabeth Boris and C. Eugene Steuerle (81–106). Washington, DC: Urban Institute Press

World Economic Forum. 2005. *Private Investment for Social Goals: Building the Blended Value Capital Market.* Geneva, Switzerland: World Economic Forum. http://www. weforum.org/pdf/Initiatives/BVI_ExecutiveSummary.pdf.

8

Nonprofit Labor
Current Trends and Future Directions

Eric C. Twombly

Nonprofit organizations operate in labor-intensive industries. In higher education, for example, nonprofit colleges and universities not only depend on instructors to teach classes and executives to provide managerial leadership, but they also rely on support staff to assist in research, administration, and technology. The fields of arts and culture, social services, health care, research, and advocacy also rely heavily on their workers—both paid and voluntary—to supply programs, goods, and services to diverse consumers and constituencies. On the whole, the labor-intensive nature of the nonprofit sector warrants a competent and committed labor force.

The importance of nonprofit labor is also reflected in national and local statistics. The Independent Sector and the Urban Institute (2002) report that there were about 10.9 million paid employees in the charitable sector in 1998, representing about 7.1 percent of paid employment in the United States, up from 5.3 percent in 1977. In some localities, the importance of nonprofit staff is particularly great. For example, nearly 25 percent of private employment in the District of Columbia is in nonprofit organizations (Nonprofit Roundtable of Greater Washington 2005). Volunteer labor in the nonprofit sector is substantial. In 1998, 109.4 million people—or 56 percent of all Americans—provided an estimated 19.9 billion hours of voluntary labor to the sector (Independent Sector 1999). Brown (1999) estimates that the annual monetary value of labor donations to the charitable sector is between $200 billion and $300 billion.

This chapter focuses on the effects of blurring sector boundaries on the market for nonprofit labor. On employer demand for labor, many nonprofits have become more entrepreneurial, moving into commercial ventures to supplement their revenue (Dees and Anderson 2003; James 2003; Weisbrod 1998) and raising the need for employees that can manage complex organizations with multiple income sources. At the same time, many for-profit firms have entered traditionally nonprofit-dominated industries (Frumkin and Andre-Clark 2000; Ryan 1999; Salamon 2002), providing wider occupational opportunities for traditional nonprofit employees. From the perspective of current and potential employees of nonprofit organizations, the adoption of more businesslike modes of operation among nonprofits also has the potential to change the mix of pecuniary and nonpecuniary aspects of nonprofit employment.

Alongside these developments, government has added to the complexity of the nonprofit staffing environment not only by demanding greater accountability of charitable organizations (Lampkin and Hatry 2003), which require workers that can evaluate and monitor agency services, but also by developing or expanding public service programs, such as AmeriCorps and Senior Corps, that give people the option to exercise their altruistic tendencies outside of the nonprofit sector.

The chapter explores the nexus between blurring of the boundaries and the market for nonprofit labor from several perspectives. The next section draws on studies of wage-setting in nonprofits to explore the relationship between nonprofit organizational form and labor compensation of nonprofit employees.

An implication of this literature is that blurring of the boundaries is likely to place upward pressure on cash compensation of nonprofit employees for several reasons. On the supply side, it is likely that prospective employees of nonprofits will demand higher wages to work for nonprofits because, as many nonprofits become more like their for-profit counterparts, the "nonpecuniary rewards" of working for a nonprofit may become smaller. The shifts toward commercialism, entrepreneurship, and businesslike practices in the nonprofit sector, coupled with new social ventures by for-profit entities and public-sector opportunities, have the potential to create a host of new opportunities for employees who once may have chosen to work for nonprofits but who now can easily work in the for-profit or public sectors with a pro-social or altruistic orientation. On the demand side, nonprofits also have increasing needs to hire professionally trained staff with the expertise to operate charities in highly competitive markets. In addition, as nonprofits are compelled to operate in more businesslike ways, their ability to provide nonpecuniary rewards and other noncash perks to employees may be reduced.

The chapter also examines how projected changes in the U.S. labor market will affect the nonprofit sector. Specifically, we draw on forecasts by the U.S. Bureau of Labor Statistics (BLS) to argue that expected population growth and shifts in labor force participation and particular occupations will have a significant effect on the ability of nonprofit organizations to attract and retain qualified workers during the next decade.

Theories of Nonprofit Labor and Compensation

Research on nonprofit labor and compensation serves as a useful starting point to examine the potential impact of organizational and policy changes on nonprofit staffing. Charitable organizations function in a "mixed economy," where they coexist with for-profit firms and government entities providing relatively similar goods and products in a wide variety of industries (Weisbrod 1988).

An important question from the standpoint of labor economics is why workers choose nonprofit employment over other institutional settings. If, for example, a nonprofit and a for-profit child care center provide similar programs, but the nonprofit pays less, why would a worker forgo the additional wages at the for-profit to work for the nonprofit?

The question is more than academic. Because nonprofits depend greatly on labor to supply programs and services, they must be able to attract and retain qualified employees, which has two consequences. First, nonprofits compete with the for-profit and public sectors on the open market for staffing. Second, to be successful in this competition for labor, nonprofits must exhibit some set of characteristics—pay, working conditions, and so forth—that are more attractive to potential employees than for-profits or government offer.

Two theoretical perspectives have guided research into these issues: one emphasizes the interplay between altruism and the nature of nonprofit goods and services, and the other focuses on the nature of property rights in enterprises without explicit ownership rights. Although each takes a different approach to explain labor market behavior in the nonprofit sector, both bodies of research provide important clues about how nonprofits attract and retain workers.

Donative Behavior and Worker Preferences

One strand of the literature on nonprofit labor markets takes its starting point from the fact that, in contrast to a typical for-profit enterprise, a nonprofit organization offers intrinsic rewards that can—up to a point— substitute for cash compensation. The implication is that employees may be willing to work for lower wages in the charitable sector because they care about the production of goods and services with social value more than workers in the for-profit sector (Preston 1989). Hansmann (1980) also argued that quality can play a role in self-selection of employees into sectors, in that some employees will sort themselves into the nonprofit and for-profit sectors based on their desire to produce quality services or their desire for financial gain.

One can see the potential effects of donative behavior when looking across industries. Consider a college senior who will soon graduate with a marketing degree and who has a set of preferences on social action and community building. All other factors being equal, the student might take a job working in a nonprofit advocacy organization instead of a position with for-profit retail organization—and forgo additional wages that might come from working for a proprietary firm.

A number of empirical studies have examined whether nonprofit workers are systematically willing to accept lower cash remuneration in exchange for nonpecuniary job satisfaction. Weisbrod (1983) finds that public interest lawyers receive 20 percent less in annual wages than private-sector lawyers, which he identifies as a heterogeneity of worker preferences. Ruhm and Borkoski (2000) note more limited evidence of labor donations, although they find insignificant wage penalties when statistically controlling for industry. Leete (2001) also finds marginal support for the notion of donative labor by uncovering significant differences between nonprofit and for-profit wages in select industries. In contrast, upon reanalyzing Weisbrod's data on public interest and private-sector attorneys, Goddeeris (1988) finds little support of wage penalty for non-profit lawyers (see also Mocan and Tekin 2003).

Thus, although there is some empirical evidence that, other things being equal, employees at nonprofits are willing to "donate" a portion of their labor services in the form of lower wages, the results are not uniform. Leete (2001) for example, cautions that even when wage differentials are observed, a number of economic forces may be contributing to such differentials. Still, the presumption that workers may be willing to accept less cash compensation when working for nonprofits meshes with the growing body of literature that finds that the altruistic preferences of employees—and the belief in the mission of nonprofits as organizations that are vested in providing public goods—can positively affect recruitment and retention in nonprofit organizations (Mason 1996; Onyx and MacLean 1996; Rycraft 1994). Indeed, a recent study finds that, when compared with federal or corporate employees, nonprofit workers are more satisfied with the chance to accomplish something worthy and perceive that they are personally helping organizations achieve their mission (Light 2002).

Viewed as a whole, the existing research suggests that some workers are responsive to the organizational form (i.e., nonprofit vs. for-profit) of their employer and will sort themselves into sectors on the basis of preferences and motivations. Indeed, intrinsic benefits—such as working for a nonprofit because one believes that its executives are less likely than a for-profit's to spend lavishly on themselves—appear to play a large role in nonprofit staffing. Because nonprofits have long been the dominant force in "caring" industries, where the expression of community or prosocial mission is evident, they may have had an advantage in attracting and keeping qualified employees who place a premium on social values. However, as discussed below, shifts in the organizational and policy environment over the past decade have begun to transform what it means to work for charitable organizations and what options are available for workers.

Property Rights and Nonprofit Labor

As noted in previous chapters in this volume, an important organizational feature of nonprofit enterprises is the existence of the non-distribution constraint. Like for-profit organizations, nonprofits have governing boards and executive staffs. But unlike for-profits, they cannot issue stock and are legally barred from distributing economic residuals to executives, staff, or other stakeholders (Hansmann 1980). The non-distribution constraint in the nonprofit sector can create economic inefficiencies, because charitable leaders may have a substantial incentive to use financial resources to obtain nonpecuniary benefits (Friesner and Rosenman 2001; Preston 1988).

One potential result of the lack of ownership resulting from the non-distribution constraint is that nonprofits may have higher average operating costs than for-profits in identical industries, making them less competitive in the marketplace but potentially more attractive to workers. Indeed, Preston (1989) notes that because nonprofit leaders face less incentive to operate efficiently, nonprofits can potentially pay higher compensation *within specific industries* than their for-profit competitors. Borjas, Frech, and Ginsburg (1983) found some support for this conjecture in their study of nursing homes, claiming that because of attenuated property rights, workers are able to obtain economic rents from their nonprofit employers. More recently, Mocan and Tekin (2003) found some support for the hypothesis that attenuated property rights can lead to a positive intra-industry labor compensation differential for nonprofits, after adjusting for the self-selection of workers into sectors and for full-time and part-time status.

Considerable disagreement remains, however, on the relative importance of ownership form on sectoral wage differences. Holtmann and Idson (1993), for example, find that important factors in explaining an observed positive wage differential for nonprofit nursing homes are the use of higher-quality labor by nonprofit nursing homes and the ability of registered nurses to switch from nonprofits to their for-profit competitors.

Changes in Organizational Form and Nonprofit Compensation

The work on nonprofit–for-profit compensation differentials offers several important insights about wage setting in the nonprofit sector. On one hand, nonprofit organizations produce goods and services that provide intrinsic rewards to their workers, which allows nonprofits to pay lower cash compensation. However, within particular industries (such as day care, health care, or education) that include both nonprofit and for-profit producers of the same (or similar) good or service, workers can enjoy the same nonpecuniary satisfaction from producing "caring" goods or services regardless of whether they work at a nonprofit or a for-profit, and as a result may be less likely to trade off lower cash compensation for greater job satisfaction. At the same time, the presence of the nondistribution constraint and lack of explicit ownership may create enough budgetary slack within nonprofit organizations to permit nonprofit enterprises to pay higher compensation than their nonprofit competitors in those same industries.

While the effect of organizational form on relative compensation of nonprofit and for-profit workers cuts both ways, it has some fairly direct implications for how blurring of sector boundaries is likely to affect the market for nonprofit labor. To the extent that blurring of the boundaries causes more nonprofits to resemble for-profit enterprises, potential employees of nonprofit organizations should become less willing to trade off lower cash compensation for the nonpecuniary advantages of working at a nonprofit. At the same time, insofar as adoption of more businesslike practices at nonprofits reduces budgetary slack, nonprofits may also face greater challenges in meeting potentially higher expectations of current and prospective employees for higher cash compensation.

A Changing Environment for Nonprofit Labor

The literature on determinants of relative compensation in the nonprofit and for-profit sectors provides a useful framework for broadly understanding the motivations and preferences of nonprofit workers on sector-wide changes in the operations and characteristics of nonprofit organizations. This section attempts to place this literature in the context of organizational and policy trends of the past two decades that have redefined the nonprofit universe and its relationship with the for-profit and public sectors. Taken together, these changes in business strategy by nonprofits and for-profits, coupled with several public policy initiatives that target nonprofit activity, are creating a new environment for nonprofit labor.

New Modes of Business in the Nonprofit Sector

One of the most important changes in the nonprofit sector in the past two decades is the greater application of standard business practices, such as strategic financial planning and organizational self-assessments (Bryson 1995; Kaplan and Norton 1996) and the pursuit of new forms of revenue (Weisbrod 1998). Nonprofit entrepreneurship by itself is not new. In fact, nonprofit leaders historically have been quite adept at piecing together multiple funding sources to support their operations. Human service organizations, for example, often receive revenue from charitable con-tributions, government grants and contracts, user fees, and third-party payments. Many arts and cultural organizations depend on a mix of membership dues, revenue from ticket sales, and, for larger groups, returns on endowments to fund their events. In the field of research, nonprofit organizations may receive contract and grant income from a host of funders in government, philanthropy, and the business sector.

What is different today from two decades ago is the prevalence of commercial activities in the charitable sector (James 2003; Salamon 2002; Tuckman 1998; Young 1998). Commercialism among nonprofits generally means the pursuit of revenue through the sale of goods or ser-vices that do not specifically relate to their charitable mission. Examples of commercial pursuits abound: hospitals running gift shops, YMCAs offering health club services, and nonprofits lending their "brand" to for-profits in exchange for revenue (Andreasen 1996). Although empirical evidence on how much commercialism has actually grown in the sector is spotty, filings of unrelated business income tax forms by nonprofits to the Internal Revenue Service (IRS) have increased, suggesting that more organizations are involved in business-related ventures (Rushton 2007).

The expansion of commercial activities has accompanied other struc-tural shifts in the charitable sector. Many nonprofits have broadened or refined their marketing approaches through targeted solicitations; seek-ing consumers who have the ability to pay for goods and services; devel-oping online giving mechanisms; and hiring professional fundraising organizations to generate financial support. Meanwhile, nonprofits have become more entrepreneurial and aggressive in the pursuit of traditional sources of money, such as government contracts. During the past two decades, whether wholeheartedly or with trepidation, the nonprofit sec-tor has moved toward a culture of entrepreneurship rooted in commer-cial enterprise (Salamon 2002).

Increased Competition with For-Profit Organizations

As nonprofits became more businesslike, for-profit organizations moved into traditional charitable fields, such as child care and mental health, and into specific industries, such as home health care. In these areas, nonprof-its had tended to dominate the production of goods and services, but since the early 1980s, nonprofits have seen their market share erode (Hirth 1997, 1999). For instance, between 1982 and 1997, the share of child care jobs held by nonprofit organizations fell from 60 to 28 percent (Salamon 2002). Declines in health care have been particularly sharp. From the mid-1980s to the late 1990s, the nonprofit share of rehabilitation hospitals dropped from 70 to 35 percent (Gray and Schlesinger 2002). Now, in many industries, nonprofits and for-profits compete for revenue, clients, and other inputs. Moreover, not only have nonprofits lost market share in some fields, but some claim that nonprofits, particularly in the field of human services, are no longer the best qualified to supply traditional charitable services (Ryan 1999).

Meanwhile, some for-profit firms use programs or strategies that explicitly embrace social responsibility, further blurring the distinctions between for-profits and nonprofits. Ben and Jerry's Ice Cream has long made social responsibility a part of its core business strategy. Target, Inc. donates a percentage of its sales to community-based organizations and features financial contribution to social causes in its marketing strategy.

In the end, the entry of proprietary firms into traditionally charitable fields of service, coupled with business strategies rooted in social responsibility, has raised questions about the extent to which consumers—and workers—can distinguish between nonprofit and for-profit organizations.

Shifts in Government Attention toward Nonprofits

Fueled in part by the flow of billions of dollars of public funds into the charitable sector and high-profile scandals at the United Way of America, the Nature Conservancy, the James Irvine Foundation, and other nonprofits, policymakers and regulators have paid increased attention to nonprofit organizations. Not only has government called for greater accountability and performance measurement of nonprofit programs, but the IRS has increased examination of wage practices in the sector, designed in part to expose excessive payments to nonprofit executives and board members. While calling for greater outcome measurement, government has also reduced the direct—and often long-term and stable—funding of charities in many policy areas in favor of indirect policy mechanisms, such as vouchers and managed-care payment systems, which increased competition for funding and complicated the ability of nonprofits to financially plan for the future (Gronbjerg and Salamon 2002). These fiscal stressors can cause nonprofit organizations to rethink their staffing options, leading some to outsource their labor needs, particularly in human resource management, or to create multiple part-time positions without employee benefits in lieu of full-time slots with employee benefits. These methods may shed costs and increase organizational efficiency. There is anecdotal information that outsourcing has become more prevalent in the sector in recent years, although there is limited systematic information on how much outsourcing has taken place.

Another important public policy initiative has been the development and expansion of public service work programs that aim to increase civic participation. For example, AmeriCorps, established under the National and Community Service Trust Act in 1993, provides a multitude of opportunities for young people to serve in community-based nonprofits, faith-based organizations, and public agencies in exchange for government financial support for higher education. The program has wide political support, evidenced by the 2003 Strengthen AmeriCorps Program Act, which called for a substantial increase in funding, enabling a substantial increase in the number of AmeriCorps members. Other government-promoted community service programs include Senior Corps and Learn and Serve America.

A New Era for Nonprofit Labor

Although systematic empirical evidence is limited, shifts in nonprofit and for-profit practices and changes in government attention and policy have the potential to significantly change the character of the nonprofit labor market. First, nonprofit organizations face more competition for qualified labor, not only among themselves, but also with for-profits and government. In some fields, for-profit firms and nonprofits offer similar employment options, allowing individuals to choose where to work on the basis of not only their desire to produce public goods, but also on factors such as compensation and working conditions, which were less pertinent in times when nonprofits dominated these industries. For example, a social worker with experience in caseload management now has greater options to move between nonprofits and for-profits while producing goods with non-excludable public benefit. Another example relates to health care: registered nurses can more easily shift between nonprofits and for-profits because of the near-indistinguishable nature of their work in these two types of medical settings.

Government, too, proves to be a formidable competitor for labor. There is some evidence that the child care industry is losing qualified staff to public school systems that offer better wages and benefits and more stable work hours (see De Vita, Twombly, and Montilla 2002). Moreover, although as of yet there are no hard data that document their impact on the nonprofit labor market, public service programs are also likely to have important effects on attracting—or diverting—potential employees to the nonprofit sector. On the one hand, the availability of AmeriCorps scholarships may bring attention to the value of working in nonprofits to those who may not have considered them. On the other hand, Ameri-Corps volunteers may be more likely to work at well-known charities, leaving smaller community-based organizations to scramble for qualified and motivated workers. Moreover, public service programs have the potential to attract employees to government who may have otherwise sought work in the nonprofit sector. In the end, shifts in the organizational and policy environment appear to have produced more choices for workers to exercise their altruistic or pro-social preferences—a factor that theory suggests helps bring workers into the charitable sector.

Second, the demands on the nonprofit workforce have grown substantially in the past two decades (see Cryer 2004; Light 2000). On the executive level, managing nonprofits has become a complex endeavor. In today's competitive environment, nonprofit executives need to balance the demands of clients, government, other funders, and their boards of directors with the ability to raise funds from multiple and unstable sources. Many nonprofit leaders also must be able to recruit and effectively use volunteer labor while meeting staff demands for supportive working conditions, compensation, and potential for personal and professional growth. Meanwhile, there is growing pressure on nonprofit executives to implement systems that show the effectiveness of their programs and services. The cumulative impact of these factors is the demand for nonprofit executives with greater technical competence and leadership skills than in previous eras.

Frontline staff of nonprofit organizations also face new demands. The shift of responsibility to implement public programs from government to private organizations has increased the discretion of employees in the nonprofit sector. In human services, frontline workers are routinely responsible for the allocation of benefits and work opportunities for people leaving welfare. One positive result of these demands may be the greater vesting of some nonprofit workers in the mission of their organizations, which theory suggests can help to boost employee retention rates. But recent evidence suggests that these new demands have adversely affected many executives and on-the-ground workers, spurring burnout and turnover in the sector (Howe and McDonald 2001). For example, in a survey of employees of nonprofit human service organizations, Light (2003) found that more than four in five workers strongly or somewhat agreed that it is easy to burn out in the work they do.

The nature of nonprofit work, particularly in industries that involve caring for disadvantaged populations, can also discourage workers, making it harder for them to maintain their commitment to the mission of the organization. Indeed, Light (2003) found that three of every four human service employees said their work was frustrating. Discouragement and frustration, coupled with the changing roles and expectations of nonprofit workers, can increase the likelihood of their migration to other sectors and occupations where their skills are applicable.

Even volunteers are not immune to organizational complexity, which has limited their ability to lead nonprofit organizations and set in motion the professionalization of nonprofit staff (Smith and Lipsky 1993). Focusing specifically on social service provision, because of the complicated nature of funding streams and the difficult social and economic needs of social service clients, agency volunteers were unable to effectively manage their nonprofits' operations (Salamon 1995). As a result, nonprofits began to hire paid leaders and staff, which facilitated the professionalization of the human service workforce (Annie E. Casey Foundation 2003). Since then, the need to develop a professionalized workforce to address competitive challenges and organizational complexity has become a hot button in the nonprofit sector, and educational credential and professional training matter more now than in the past. One needs to look only at the rapid development of training institutes for nonprofit employment and the growth of management programs in graduate schools in the United States for anecdotal evidence of the reach of the new professionalism into the charitable sector (see Mirabella and Wish 1999; Wish and Mirabella 1998). What is more, the content of many nonprofit management programs tends to reinforce the importance of for-profit business models and application of strategic planning and measurement tools to operate today's nonprofit sector (Haas and Robinson 1998).

Recent Trends in Nonprofit Employment

The movement toward professionalism in the nonprofit workforce has coincided with a period of relatively strong employment growth in the charitable sector. For example, certain public policies have increased the availability of workers in professions common to the nonprofit sector. The training and work requirements in the 1996 federal welfare reform legislation have led to expansion of qualified labor in the child care industry. Moreover, with U.S. Bureau of Labor Statistics data, the Independent Sector reports that from 1997 to 2001, the average annual growth rate in nonprofit employment was 2.5 percent, compared with 1.8 percent in the for-profit sector and 1.6 percent in government. Salamon (2004) corroborated the relatively strong employment growth in the charitable sector. In fact, his research suggests that between 2000 and 2003 the nonprofit sector was the only net source of expanding employment in many areas of the United States.

Compensation in the nonprofit sector has increased as well, albeit modestly. The Chronicle of Philanthropy, for example, noted the relatively small increase in the pay of nonprofit executives following the economic downturn in 2000–2002 (Gose 2004). A compensation survey by PRM Consulting found that wages increased in health and social service organizations by 2.9 percent and in educational nonprofits by 3.2 percent (Kerkman 2003). Moreover, recent research suggests that some nonprofits offer more generous benefit packages (see Bryan 2005) than for-profit organizations and tend to excel at providing work-life polices, such as paid maternity leave (Pitt-Catsouphes et al. 2004). There are methodological problems with this research, including response bias that limits the generalizability of these findings to the sector as a whole, and the lack of comparable for-profit information. Nevertheless, these studies provide some tentative support that some nonprofit industries are focusing on the importance of providing benefits to their workers.

Despite relatively strong employment growth and steadily increasing wages, there are warning signs for the nonprofit sector. The greatest pressure may stem from the ability of nonprofits to differentiate themselves from their for-profit and public-sector competitors. Because the nature of nonprofit activity is labor intensive, organizations need to find ways to capitalize on workers' desires to fulfill the need to provide public goods while keeping pace with compensation trends in the market. These tasks may be difficult in practice, because there appears to be a shortage of qualified labor (Light 2002), stemming from the competitive forces and complexity of organizational demands on workers described above. For example, Wyszomirski (2002) noted substantial vacancy rates in leadership positions at prominent arts institutions, which is attributable in part to the availability of alternative employment opportunities that may serve the needs of pro-social executives while providing a less stressful work environment. And even among current executives, survey data suggest that more than one-third of nonprofit managers plan to leave their positions within two years, and roughly one-half indicate they will not pursue another leadership position (Peters and Wolfred 2001). Equally problematic is that the apparent labor gap is not confined to paid employees. It applies to volunteers as well. Indeed, Hager and Brudney (2004) determined that more than 90 percent of organizations in their survey population could use the services and time of more volunteers.

Future Directions in Nonprofit Labor

While nonprofit organizations currently face several challenges in human resource development and management, key economic and demographic factors over the next decade will continue to reshape the landscape of nonprofit employment and voluntarism. For some nonprofits, these factors will make their current labor issues more acute. By the same token, broad economic and demographic shifts may provide strategic opportunities for well-managed and entrepreneurial nonprofits. Drawing on data and analysis by BLS, we describe each key factor and the implications for nonprofit labor below.

First, the U.S. population is projected to grow relatively slowly over the next several years. In fact, the current annual rate of population growth is an estimated 0.9 percent, a proportion that is consistent with the 10-year span of 1994–2004, but one that is lower than in previous periods (Saunders 2005). Overall, slow population growth tends to correlate with the slow expansion of the labor market, which, when coupled with various policy and organizational factors that will likely continue to expand the nonprofit sector, can create new competitive pressures for organizations in the recruitment and retention of qualified employees.

Second, the relatively low number of people younger than age 25 entering the U.S. labor force and increasing numbers of persons older than age 55 remaining in the labor market suggest that the median age of the labor force will rise during the next decade. These interacting effects are reflected by Toosi (2005), who reports that the median age of the U.S. labor force was nearly 38 in 1994, roughly 40 in 2004, and will likely be nearly 42 by 2014. Moreover, although a large number of persons born between 1946 and 1964—commonly referred to as baby boomers—will retire and "early retirement" will likely become more commonplace, labor market participation of older Americans is projected to increase during the next decade. Toosi (2005) estimates that labor participation rates for those 55 years of age and older will rise from 30.5 percent in 2004 to 37 percent in 2014. The projected increase for those age 65 and older is similarly strong, jumping from 11 percent in 2004 to 16 percent in 2014. Although aging typically leads to withdrawal from the workforce, advances in the health and training of the workforce—coupled with shifts in government policy to eliminate mandatory retirement age and make later the age in which retirees can claim full social security benefits—will help keep older people in the labor market longer than in previous eras.

The third factor that will likely affect nonprofit labor is that occupations with the largest projected growth are concentrated in industries where nonprofits have a relatively large presence. For example, the health care industry will increase its employment. Nonprofits play a large role in the provision of health services, particularly to the elderly, and Hecker (2005) projects that the health care sector will add nearly 1.8 million professional jobs between 2004 and 2014, amounting to a 26 percent increase. Nearly two-thirds of these new jobs will be for registered nurses. Support jobs in the health care industry are also projected to grow strongly, gaining 1.2 million positions by 2014, equaling an increase of nearly 34 percent from 2004.

Taken together, these findings suggest an important dynamic of the emerging labor market for nonprofits: the most highly paid and the least-paid workers will grow relative to others. Professionals in health-related occupations will rise in numbers, as will the service workers who support hospitals and other health-related providers.

Community and social services occupations are also projected to increase. The community-level and social services fields are projected to gain 463,000 jobs from 2004 to 2014, equaling an increase of more than 30 percent. Social service groups form the largest numeric type of organization in the nonprofit sector. Indeed, in 2003, more than 50,000 social service organizations—roughly 23 percent of the total sector—filed a Form 990 with the IRS (De Vita, Twombly, and Auer forthcoming).

What are the likely implications of these trends for nonprofit labor? First, competition for management, professional skills, and teaching skills will likely lead to rising compensation for nonprofit organizations and their for-profit competitors, a cost that some nonprofits may have trouble absorbing. In addition, the changing demographic composition of the labor market suggests that older workers may receive incentives to remain in their skilled positions, implying that differentials for increased years of experience will rise in both nonprofit and for-profit businesses. The balance that is struck, however, between employment in nonprofits and for-profits, particularly for older members of the workforce, clearly depends on the competitiveness of both sectors in offering explicit compensation, satisfaction with work, and other implicit benefits of the workplace. And while the credentialization of positions in health, education, and social service organizations makes it likely that explicit compensation will be the major force determining who works in the nonprofit sector, job satisfaction can substitute for compensation (Helliwell and Huang 2005), particularly in the nonprofit sector (Letts, Ryan, and Grossman 1999). This last finding suggests that wherever skilled workers practice their craft, management of human resources, clear communication of mission to employees, and correlation between work assignments and meeting the mission will influence workers' willingness to accept lower compensation (a donative behavior that is not limited to nonprofit organizations).

These trends also have important implications for nonprofits' use of volunteers. Despite relatively higher rates on labor market participation, the retirement of the baby boomers may offset some of the competitive and compensatory pressures nonprofits face in the pursuit of qualified labor. For some nonprofits, the ability to attract and retain older persons as volunteers—or even as part-time or contract workers—can be a boon to organizational productivity and cost effectiveness. Still, the BLS's American Time Use Survey in 2004 reported a relatively modest prevalence of voluntary activity in the United States. And although BLS data show that those who are not employed are more likely to contribute their time than are employed individuals, the data cannot substantiate that the movement in the coming years of people into not-employed status—whether by choice or involuntarily—will create a windfall of volunteer activity for nonprofits. In the end, nonprofit organizations will need to think strategically about where to find, how to manage, and how to retain volunteers.

Conclusion

This chapter examines the current state of nonprofit labor in the context of substantial organizational and policy shifts during the past two decades and discusses the potential direction of the nonprofit labor market over the next several years. Several findings emerge. One is that the blurring of the sectors seems likely to create new opportunities for potential nonprofit workers. Meanwhile, as the operation and the production of goods and services in the nonprofit sector have become more similar to those in the for-profit field, the jobs of nonprofit managers and frontline staff have become both more complex and more similar to jobs in the for-profit sector. Finally, projected economic and demographic trends will raise the need for nonprofits to act strategically and creatively in securing qualified labor.

As theory implies, mission matters to both paid staff and volunteers in many industries in the charitable sector. As a result, nonprofits must develop new and strategic methods to positively reinforce the commitment of existing employees and differentiate themselves from for-profits and government to attract new ones. There is some evidence that nonprofits are struggling to recruit the next generation of workers while managing the roles and responsibilities of current staff and volunteers (Cryer 2004; Hager and Brudney 2004). Faced with a current shortage of labor and competition for employees with for-profits and government, nonprofits must redouble their recruitment and retention efforts.

Moreover, the charitable sector needs to develop mechanisms that ensure that the expanded entrepreneurship and the application of business tools commonly associated with for-profit organizations do not alienate its workforce. Some have argued that the movement toward commercialism has threatened the charitable character of the nonprofit sector (Salamon 2002; Weisbrod 2004), which raises questions of whether commitment to mission will be traded for bottom-line business approaches. One can speculate—but cannot say with empirical certainly— that new business strategies in the charitable sector may alter the desirability of nonprofits as places of employment for those attracted to the sector for altruistic or pro-social reasons.

REFERENCES

Andreasen, Alan R. 1996. "Profits for Nonprofits: Find a Corporate Partner." *Harvard Business Review* 74(6): 47–49.

Annie E. Casey Foundation. 2003. *The Unresolved Challenge of System Reform: The Condition of the Frontline Human Services Workforce.* Baltimore, MD: Annie E. Casey Foundation.

Borjas, George J., H. E. Frech III, and Paul E. Ginsburg. 1983. "Property Rights and Wages: The Case of Nursing Homes." *Journal of Human Resources* 18:231–46.

Brown, Eleanor. 1999. "Patterns and Purposes of Philanthropic Giving." In *Philanthropy and the Nonprofit Sector in a Changing America,* edited by C. T. Clotfelter and T. Ehrlich (212–30). Bloomington: Indiana University Press.

Bryan, Sharnell. 2005. "Charities Outdo Businesses on Worker Benefits." *Chronicle of Philanthropy* 17(6): 47.

Bryson, John M. 1995. *Strategic Planning for Public and Nonprofit Organizations.* San Francisco, CA: Jossey-Bass Publishers.

Cryer, Shelly. 2004. *Recruiting and Retaining the Next Generation of Nonprofit Sector Leadership.* New York: New York University's Wagner School of Public Affairs.

Dees, J. Gregory, and Beth Battle Anderson. 2003. "Sector Bending: Blurring Lines Between Nonprofit and For-Profit." *Society* (May/June): 16–27.

De Vita, Carol J., Eric C. Twombly, and Jennifer Claire Auer. Forthcoming. *The Nonprofit Human Service Sector.* Washington, DC: The Urban Institute.

De Vita, Carol J., Eric C. Twombly, and Maria D. Montilla. 2002. *Toward Better Child Care Worker Compensation: Advocacy in Three States.* Washington, DC: The Urban Institute.

Friesner, Daniel, and Robert Rosenman. 2001. "The Property Rights Theory of the Firm and Mixed Competition: A Counter-Example in the U.S. Health Care Industry." *International Journal of the Economics of Business* 8(3): 437–50.

Frumkin, Peter, and Alice Andre-Clark. 2000. "When Missions, Markets, and Politics Collide: Values and Strategy in the Nonprofit Human Services." *Nonprofit and Voluntary Sector Quarterly* 29(1): 161–83.

Goddeeris, John H. 1988. "Compensating Differentials and Self-Selection: An Application to Lawyers." *Journal of Political Economy* 96(2): 411–28.

Gose, Ben. 2004. "Executive Pay Rises Modestly." *Chronicle of Philanthropy* 16(24): 31–48.

Gray, Bradford, and Mark Schlesinger. 2002. "Health." In *The State of Nonprofit America,* edited by Lester M. Salamon (65–106). Washington, DC: Brookings Institution Press.

Gronbjerg, Kirsten, and Lester M. Salamon. 2002. "Devolution, Marketization, and the Changing Shape of Government–Nonprofit Relations." In *The State of Nonprofit America,* edited by Lester M. Salamon (447–70). Washington, DC: Brookings Institution Press.

Haas, Peter J., and Maynard G. Robinson. 1998. "The Views of Nonprofit Executives on Educating Nonprofit Managers." *Nonprofit Management and Leadership* 8(4): 349–62.

Hager, Mark A., and Jeffrey L. Brudney. 2004. *Volunteer Management Practices and Retention of Volunteers.* Washington, DC: The Urban Institute.

Hansmann, Henry B. 1980. "The Role of Nonprofit Enterprise." *Yale Law Journal* 89: 835–901.

Hecker, Daniel E. 2005. "Occupational Employment Projections to 2014." *Monthly Labor Review* 128(11): 70–101.

Helliwell, John, and Haifang Huang. 2005. *How's the Job? Well-Being and Social Capital in the Workplace.* NBER Working Paper 11759. Cambridge, MA: National Bureau of Economic Research.

Hirth, R. 1997. "Competition Between For-Profit and Nonprofit Health Care Providers: Can It Help Achieve Social Goals?" *Medical Care Research and Review* 54(4): 414–38.

———. 1999. "Consumer Information and Competition Between Nonprofit and For-Profit Nursing Homes." *Journal of Health Economics* 18(2): 219–40.

Holtmann, A. G., and Todd L. Idson. 1993. "Wage Determination of Registered Nurses in Proprietary and Nonprofit Nursing Homes." *Journal of Human Resources* 28(1): 55–79.

Howe, Phillip, and Corrine McDonald. 2001. *Traumatic Stress, Turnover and Peer Support in Child Welfare*. Washington, DC: Child Welfare League of America.

Independent Sector. 1999. *Giving and Volunteering in the United States: Findings from a National Survey*. Washington, DC: Independent Sector.

Independent Sector and the Urban Institute. 2002. *The New Nonprofit Almanac and Desk Reference: The Essential Facts and Figures for Managers, Researchers, and Volunteers*. San Francisco: Jossey-Bass.

James, Estelle. 2003. "Commercialism and the Mission of Nonprofits." *Society* 40(4): 29–35.

Kaplan, Robert S., and David P. Norton. 1996. "Using the Balanced Scorecard as a Strategic Management System." *Harvard Business Review* 74(1): 75–85.

Kerkman, Leah. 2003. "Health, Education Workers Win Pay Raises, Study Finds." *Chronicle of Philanthropy* 15(24): 42.

Lampkin, Linda M., and Harry P. Hatry. 2003. *Key Steps in Outcome Management*. Washington, DC: The Urban Institute.

Leete, Laura. 2001. "Whither the Nonprofit Wage Differential? Estimates from the 1990 Census." *Journal of Labor Economics* 19(1): 136–70.

Letts, Christine W., William P. Ryan, and Allen Grossman. 1999. *High Performance Non-profit Organizations: Managing Upstream for Greater Impact*. New York: John E. Wiley & Sons.

Light, Paul C. 2000. *Making Nonprofits Work: A Report on the Tides of Nonprofit Management Reform*. Washington, DC: Brookings Institution Press.

———. 2002. *The Content of Their Character: The State of the Nonprofit Workforce*. Washington, DC: The Brookings Institution.

———. 2003. *The Health of the Human Services Workforce*. Washington, DC: The Brookings Institution.

Mason, David E. 1996. *Leading and Managing the Expressive Dimension: Harnessing the Hidden Power Source of the Nonprofit Sector*. San Francisco: Jossey-Bass.

Mirabella, Roseanne M., and Naomi B. Wish. 1999. "Educational Impact of Graduate Nonprofit Degree Programs: Perspectives of Multiple Stakeholders." *Nonprofit Management and Leadership* 9(3): 329–40.

Mocan, Naci H., and Erdal Tekin. 2003. "Nonprofit Sector and Part-Time Work: An Analysis of Employer-Employee Matched Data on Child Care Workers." *Review of Economics and Statistics* 85(1): 38–50.

Mocan, Naci H., and D. Viola. 1997. *The Determinants of Child Care Workers' Wages and Compensation*. NBER Working Paper 6328. Cambridge, MA: National Bureau of Economic Research.

Nonprofit Roundtable of Greater Washington. 2005. *The Business of Doing Good in Greater Washington: How the Nonprofit Sector Contributes to the Region's Economy.* Washington, DC: Nonprofit Roundtable of Greater Washington.

Onyx, Jenny, and Madi MacLean. 1996. "Careers in the Third Sector." *Nonprofit Management and Leadership* 6(4): 331–45.

Peters, Jeanne, and Timothy Wolfred. 2001. *Daring to Lead: Nonprofit Executive Directors and Their Work Experience.* San Francisco: Compass Point.

Pitt-Catsouphes, Marcie, Jennifer E. Swanberg, James T. Bond, and Ellen Galinsky. 2004. "Work-Life Policies and Programs: Comparing the Responsiveness of Nonprofit and For-Profit Organizations." *Nonprofit Management and Leadership* 14(3): 291–312.

Preston, Anne E. 1988. "The Effects of Property Rights on Labor Costs of Nonprofit Firms: An Application to the Day Care Industry." *Journal of Industrial Economics* 37:335–50.

———. 1989. "The Nonprofit Worker in a For-Profit World." *Journal of Labor Economics* 7(4): 438–63.

Ruhm, Christopher J., and Carey Borkoski. 2000. "Compensation in the Nonprofit Sector." NBER Working Paper 7562. Cambridge, MA: National Bureau of Economic Research.

Rushton, Michael. 2007. "Why Are Nonprofits Exempt from Corporate Income Tax?" *Nonprofit Voluntary Sector Quarterly* 36(4): 662–75.

Ryan, William P. 1999. "The New Landscape for Nonprofits." *Harvard Business Review* 77:127–36.

Rycraft, J. R. 1994. "The Party Isn't Over: The Agency Role in Retention of Public Child Welfare Caseworkers." *Social Work* 39:7580.

Salamon, Lester M. 1995. *Partners in Public Service: Government-Nonprofit Relations in the Modern Welfare State.* Baltimore, MD: Johns Hopkins University Press.

———. 2002. "The Resilient Sector: The State of Nonprofit America." In *The State of Nonprofit America,* edited by Lester M. Salamon (3–64). Washington, DC: Brookings Institution Press.

———. 2004. "A Misleading View of Employment Trends." *Chronicle of Philanthropy* 16(23): 39–40.

Saunders, Norman C. 2005. "A Summary of BLS Projections to 2014." *Monthly Labor Review* 128(11): 3–9.

Smith, Steven R., and Michael Lipsky. 1993. *Nonprofits for Hire: The Welfare State in the Age of Contracting.* Cambridge, MA: Harvard University Press.

Toosi, Mitra. 2005. "Labor Force Projections to 2014: Retiring Boomers." *Monthly Labor Review* 128(11): 25–44.

Tuckman, Howard P. 1998. "Competition, Commercialization, and the Evolution of Nonprofit Organizational Structures." *Journal of Policy Analysis and Management* 17(2): 175–94.

Weisbrod, Burton A. 1983. "Nonprofit and Proprietary Sector Behavior: Wage Differentials Among Lawyers." *Journal of Labor Economics* 1(3): 246–63.

————. 1988. *The Nonprofit Economy*. Cambridge, MA: Harvard University Press.

————. 1998. "The Nonprofit Mission and Its Financing: Growing Links between Non-profits and the Rest of the Economy." In *To Profit or Not to Profit,* edited by Burton A. Weisbrod (1–24). New York: Cambridge University Press.

————. 2004. "The Pitfalls of Profits." *Stanford Social Innovation Review* (Winter).

Wish, Naomi B., and Roseanne M. Mirabella. 1998. "Curricular Variations in Non-profit Management Graduation Programs." *Nonprofit Management and Leadership* 9:99–109.

Wyszomirski, Margaret. 2002. "Arts and Culture." In *The State of Nonprofit America,* edited by Lester M. Salamon. Washington, DC: Brookings Institution Press.

Young, Dennis R. 1998. "Commercialism in Nonprofit Social Service Associations: Its Character, Significance, and Rationale." *Journal of Policy Analysis and Management* 17(2): 278–87.

9

Measuring the Nonprofit Bottom Line

Linda M. Lampkin and Harry P. Hatry

F unders and donors have called upon nonprofits to provide more-systematic measurement of their performance in achieving their mission, and to use such information in deciding how to allocate their resources among competing uses. Some have described such changes as moving nonprofits toward more systematic or businesslike ways of making decisions.

In the case of for-profit businesses, common performance measures are profit and return to investors, along with related indicators such as market share and gross sales/revenues. Competition in the marketplace creates incentives for businesses to pay attention to these measures in making decisions about business strategies and operations. Businesses face strong incentives to maximize profit by producing the greatest value at the lowest possible cost, and financial and capital markets hold individual businesses accountable for performance. Shares must increase in value or shareholders will sell them, and noncompetitive organizations will face incentives and mechanisms for mergers and acquisitions.

In contrast to for-profit enterprises, nonprofits are "in business" to fulfill their missions, normally some form of public interest. The primary objective of a typical nonprofit is neither profit nor shareholder return, but achievement of goals for the common interest—the very reason for choosing nonprofit (tax-exempt) status. Moreover, although nonprofits must also compete for resources with other nonprofits, and in some cases with for-profit businesses, the nature of such competition differs from that among for-profit businesses. Most notably, nonprofits have stakeholders, not stockholders; they receive funds from clients, grant makers, and individual donors instead of customers and financial institutions. Consequently, nonprofits face a different bottom line than do for-profit businesses, as well as different incentives to maximize that bottom line.

Despite these differences, nonprofits will act more like their for-profit counterparts to the extent that they invest time and resources in developing more systematic measures of performance and use such measures to guide their operations and planning. In doing so, managers, stakeholders, and funders of nonprofits might be said to focus on a nonprofit *outcome margin* rather than a *profit margin*. This focus could be measuring the number of low-income clients finding decent jobs, reducing teenage violence in particular neighborhoods, increasing test scores of tutored or mentored youth, or improving client status.

A few nonprofit sectors, such as health care, have considerable experience with developing and using outcome measures, but for many nonprofits outside these sectors, developing, let alone using, such indicators is relatively new territory. This chapter focuses on the broadening role of outcome measurement among nonprofits as a means of assessing performance and of guiding operational decisions. We discuss why nonprofits are increasingly called upon to develop and use more-systematic measurement of outcomes; current practices in the use of such measures; and the challenges nonprofits face when developing and using such measures.

Pressures for Outcome Measurement

Although advances in computer technology now permit data to be more easily collected and processed, systematically measuring outcomes in the nonprofit sector requires time, effort, and some cost, especially to start up such a process. To be sure, individual nonprofits face internal incentives to invest time and resources in such activities. Nonprofit organizations need to pay attention to their performance of administrative and management tasks, as do businesses. The number of professionally trained managers in the nonprofit sector has increased in recent years, and these professionals are often interested in benchmarking, best practices, and performance management.

At least as important as technological advancement, however, are external pressures for outcome measurement, including increased competition among nonprofits for financial resources, greater government oversight, and the need for greater accountability. Nonprofits' key stakeholders—individual donors, foundations, or government funders—also increasingly believe in nonprofits striving for maximizing value (however defined) while minimizing costs.

The growth of the number of public charities (69 percent more were registered with the U.S. Internal Revenue Service in 2006 than in 1996[1]) has been dramatic and shows no signs of abating. In fact, in 2006, the number of new applications for tax-exempt status as a public charity grew to over 83,000,[2] meaning that more and more organizations are competing for charitable donations (Frumkin 2001). Ignoring a spike in 2005 prompted by responses to natural disasters, charitable giving overall has increased at a much slower rate—only 2.3 percent in inflation-adjusted dollars from 2003 to 2004 and 1.0 percent from 2004 to 2005. In fact, giving to human services organizations actually declined by 1.1 percent in inflation-adjusted dollars from 2003 to 2004 and by 9.2 percent from 2004 to 2005 (Giving USA Foundation 2005, 19).

Set against the backdrop of more nonprofits competing for a fixed (or slowly growing at best) pool of contributions, the clients, funders, and other nonprofit stakeholders are increasingly pressing nonprofits for information on results. The call for better measurement of outcomes has come from government (stimulated by the Government Performance and Results Act at the federal level and legislation in many states), from private foundations, and from third-party funders such as the United Way.

As stewards of donated funds that enjoy favorable tax status, foundations are facing more public scrutiny as the media and Congress discuss more stringent regulations. Some funders, such as community foundations and local affiliates of the United Way organizations, rely on donors and need to be able to convince potential donors of the value of their performance. Funders are increasingly asking grantees for increased accountability and better reporting—reporting on *how well* their money was spent, not just *how* it was spent. Some foundations, like the William and Flora Hewlett Foundation, require logic models from all grantees.

According to Carla Dearing, president and CEO of the Community Foundations of America, "In order to track and articulate their effectiveness, community foundations have to go to a more granular level, breaking data about grantee performance into manageable chunks that can be tracked and analyzed. Only by doing so will they be able to tell stories of community impact, and have the data needed to back up those claims" (Orosz, Phillips, and Knowlton 2003, 21).

In a 2003 national survey of 1,192 foundations (including corporate, community, and independent foundations), 28 percent reported that they always required grantees to collect information on outcomes of their work (Ostrower 2004, table 2). The proportion requiring outcome reports varied by asset size, ranging from 22 percent for foundations with assets of $10 million or less to 36 percent with those with assets greater than $400 million.

United Way of America and a number of its local affiliates have long been a leader in encouraging—or requiring—the use of outcome measurement by grantees.[3] In April 2006, United Way of America estimated that approximately 400 local affiliates required reporting on outcomes from their approximately 20,000 community-based nonprofit grantees.[4] Some community foundations—for example, those in Chicago, Cincinnati, New Haven (CT), Baton Rouge (LA), Omaha (NE), and North Carolina—have begun requiring performance measures for each grant.

Greater need and opportunities for nonprofits to diversify their revenue base create additional incentives for nonprofits to pay more attention to performance measurement. With a tenet of "steer, not row," government has engaged in a massive outsourcing of its service delivery, with widespread public support ranging from those who advocate the benefits of competition to those who think small, community-based groups will be more likely to receive funding in this environment (Frumkin 2001). Yet, even as government outsourcing creates more opportunity for nonprofit revenues, it also opens up an entire new market for business. Government agencies used to automatically award service contracts to reputable, committed community nonprofit institutions, but no more. Their newly adopted "business" mindset has government making contract decisions on the basis of who appears to be the least expensive and most efficient provider, without considering the nonprofit or for-profit status of the potential contractor.

The Current State of Nonprofit Outcome Measurement

As noted above, for-profit businesses have a number of "ready-made" outcome indicators that directly relate to the for-profit bottom line and that permit comparisons of bottom-line indicators to be made across competing firms. The parallel information for nonprofits (which is often not as readily available) is outcome information that permits comparisons of different organizations providing the same services.

Some national associations of nonprofit organizations have attempted to provide such comparative information—for example, American Red Cross, Boys and Girls Clubs of America, and Volunteers of America. This means that organizations providing the same services must regularly collect data in approximately the same way on a common set of indicators. Such comparative information can motivate lower-performing organizations to make improvements and can spur the search for best practices.

A national survey by the Independent Sector in 1997 found that 46 percent of nonprofit organizations (out of 654 respondents) reported that they routinely collected data on changes in client condition at or after completion of services (31 percent of very small organizations and 81 percent of very large organizations) (Wiener, Kirsch, and McCormack 2002). To our knowledge, there has been no follow-up national survey. Thus, it is difficult to estimate the number or percentage of nonprofit organizations currently undertaking some form of systematic regular outcome measurement.

Financial Reporting and Outcome Measurement

Reporting on both government and nonprofit activities has always included details on the use of the funds, but the focus has changed over time. Initially, the focus was financial accountability, usually covering outputs such as number of brochures distributed or number of clients served. The availability of financial data on nonprofits from the annual IRS Form 990 has made it easier to compute simple ratios that are seen as an indicator of efficiency—for example, overhead costs as a proportion of program expenses. But that type of calculation gives no value to the very qualities that make nonprofits unique—the commitment to social ends and values. In fact, effectiveness is a much better measure of the value created by nonprofits than any calculation of costs. If nonprofits compete for funds purely on the basis of efficiency, then what ensues is a race to the bottom, and the overall nonprofit mission may suffer.

A number of national associations have undertaken efforts to provide guidance to their affiliates for regular tracking of the outcomes of their programs, including the American Red Cross, Boys and Girls Clubs of America, Volunteers of America, CARF (The Rehabilitation Commission), and Council on Quality and Leadership in Support for People with

Disabilities. In addition, a number of funding and accreditation organizations have specified standards for monitoring performance, sometimes including information on client characteristics and perhaps client satisfaction (box 9.1) (Plantz, Greenway, and Hendricks n.d.). These efforts have tended to count the resources put into the program (inputs such as money, staff, and supplies) and the direct products of the program activities (outputs).

In addition, outside consultants occasionally conduct formal evaluations after some projects. Increasingly, however, the emphasis is on calling for funded organizations to report regularly on results, not just financial measures or program outputs. The financial and output measures yield little information on program effects. Outcome measurement focuses on this aspect of performance.

Outcome Measurement and Modeling of Program Effects

An increasingly common tool to begin outcome measurement is outcome sequence charts (also known as logic models), a diagrammatic representation linking a program's inputs (the resources brought to a specific

---

Box 9.1. Examples of Standards Requiring Reporting on Nonprofit Program Results

Organization (Source)	Standard for Reporting on Results
American Council for Voluntary International Action (http://www.interaction.org/ content/pvostandards/)	7.1.9. "A member shall have defined procedures for evaluation, both qualitatively and quantitatively, its programs and projects. These procedures shall address both the efficiency of the use of inputs, and the effectiveness of the outputs, i.e. the impacts on the program participants and the relationship of these impacts to the cost of achieving them."
Association of Fundraising Professionals (http://www.afpnet.org)	"The Accountable Nonprofit Organization . . . clearly states its mission and purpose, articulates the needs of those being served, explains how its programs work, how much they cost and what benefits they produce."

Box 9.1. *(continued)*

Organization (Source)	Standard for Reporting on Results
	"Quality [is indicated by] Evaluating the total organization and all its outcomes on an ongoing basis."
BBB Wise Giving Alliance (http://www.give.org/standards/ newcbbbstds.asp)	"Standards for Charitable Accountability— Measuring Effectiveness 6. Have a board policy of assessing, no less than every two years, the organization's performance and effectiveness and of determining future actions required to achieve its mission. 7. Submit to the organization's governing body, for its approval, a written report that outlines the results of the aforementioned performance and effectiveness assessment and recommendations for future actions."
Charities Review Council of Minnesota (http://www.smartgivers.org/ AccountabilityStandards.html)	Standard 1C. "Through the annual report or other communications available to donors, the organization provides specific, objective information about its accomplishments related to its stated mission."
Combined Federal Campaign (http://www.opm.gov/cfc/ opmmemos/index.asp)	§950.203 Public accountability standards "The organization must be . . . a human health and welfare organization providing services, benefits, or assistance to, or conducting activities affecting, human health and welfare. The organization's application must provide documentation describing the human health and welfare benefits provided by the organization within the previous year." "The organization must . . . Certify that contributions are effectively used for the announced purposes of the charitable organization."

(continued)

Box 9.1. *(continued)*

Organization (Source)	Standard for Reporting on Results
Evangelical Council for Financial Accountability (http://www.ecfmembers.org/ PDF/BestPractices.pdf)	Standard #4—Use of Resources "Every member organization shall exercise management and financial controls necessary to provide reasonable assurance that all resources are used (nationally and internationally) to accomplish the exempt purposes for which they are intended."
Independent Sector (http://www.independentsector. org/issues/accountability.html)	"Adhering to accountability standards promotes self-regulation within the sector. By codifying standards of ethical behavior and responsible stewardship, an organization creates a benchmark against which to measure the performance of their board, staff, volunteers, members, and associates. Issue areas that such standards should cover include mission, governance, legal and regulatory compliance, ethical practices including avoiding conflicts of interest, responsible stewardship of resources (both financial and other), disclosure policies, human resource policies regarding inclusiveness and diversity, and program evaluation."
Standards for Excellence: An Ethics and Accountability Code for the Nonprofit Sector (http://www.standardsfor excellence.org)	C. Program Evaluation "(1) A nonprofit should have defined, cost-effective procedures for evaluating, both qualitatively and quantitatively, its programs and projects in relation to its mission. These procedures should address programmatic efficiency and effectiveness, the relationship of these impacts to the cost of achieving them, and the outcomes for program participants. Evaluations should include input from program participants. "(2) Evaluations should be candid, be used to strengthen the effectiveness of the organization and, when necessary, be used to make programmatic changes."

problem), first to its logical outputs (the quantity of work activity completed), and then to the sequence of outcomes expected (results of the program). Going through the process of developing such diagrams can help a nonprofit organization clarify thinking about the program, determine what outcomes the program is expected to accomplish, and suggest the indicators needed to track progress against those outcomes.

However, this is just a starting point. A nonprofit organization needs to select specific data collection procedures to obtain the data on each outcome indicator, provide a basic process for tabulating the data and performing at least basic data examination/analysis, and then use the data for helping manage and improve services. These steps are unfamiliar ground for many nonprofit organizations. The data processing effort alone can cause some organizations major problems. Fortunately, the advent of inexpensive computers and software, along with the growing facility of our population in using computers, means that data processing should not be a major problem. However, the other steps can appear daunting to some, probably many, nonprofit organizations. Few nonprofit organizations have personnel familiar with the technical side of outcome measurement (or program evaluation). Social service personnel, unlike many in the business sector, tend not to be numbers people.

External Guidance and Standards

Guidance to nonprofit organizations has come, as noted earlier, through national organizations (probably the most useful source thus far) in getting the attention of nonprofits, (at least those affiliated with the national organizations) plus a smattering of materials differing widely as to the level of their specificity.[5]

Government funders have also developed their own approaches. For example, organization rating systems such as the federal government's Baldrige award process (to reward "performance excellence") and the federal Office of Management and Budget's PART process combine scores for both non-program-related process criteria and results into one overall score—with actual results counting for less than 50 percent of the total score.[6] (Both programs, however, also reported the scores for each individual component.)

Most of the standards have focused on the presence of process elements but are now beginning to call for some measures of outcomes or effectiveness. The word "effectiveness" has the strong implication that the program was the cause of the result that occurred. Unfortunately, in the real world, it is seldom that any organization and its programs can take full credit for any result. Invariably many other factors could have, and probably did, cause or at least contribute to the result. Although the program may have been a contributor to the outcome, the extent of this contribution is extremely hard to measure. Even the most sophisticated in-depth evaluations seldom are able to make clear causal claims. Thus, the word "outcome" is often used in place of "effectiveness" by those reporting results. The use of "theories of change," including outcome sequence charts (logic models), can help provide some confidence that the organization had an important contribution to the outcomes but can not assure it.

Outcome Measurement and Program Operations

Little evidence currently exists on the usefulness of the outcome measurement movement, a limitation that also applies to most management information processes, not just outcome measurement. Even though it may require added cost and new management processes, the systematic collection and use of program outcome data do appear to have the potential for substantial payoffs. In a survey of nearly 400 health and human service organizations in the United States in 2000 (United Way of North America 2000), program directors reported agreeing or strongly agreeing that implementing program outcome measurement had helped their programs in the following ways:[7]

- Focusing staff on shared goals (88 percent)
- Communicating results to stakeholders (88 percent)
- Clarifying program purpose (86 percent)
- Identifying effective practices (84 percent)
- Competing for resources (83 percent)
- Enhancing record keeping (80 percent)
- Improving service delivery (76 percent)

On the basis of their experiences, 89 percent of these directors said they would recommend program outcome measurement to a colleague.

On the negative side, many nonprofit organizations have responded to the calls for reporting on results and, especially, "impacts" with dismay about the resources required—time, money, computer software and hardware, staff expertise. They may try to set up an outcome measurement system and actually find too much information—so many indicators are available and in use for similar programs that it is overwhelming to assess their quality and usefulness. More often, the problem is too little information, as the measurement of outcomes is relatively new in many areas.

The feasibility of doing special program evaluations (instead of, or in addition to, regularly tracking outcomes) is questionable. Asking nonprofit organizations, especially small ones, to do such evaluations is probably asking too much. Although some such evaluations may be useful in furthering knowledge and the understanding of what works best, they should almost always be undertaken by specialists and should cover more than the program of one organization.

A major data-gathering problem for many nonprofit service organizations is that important outcomes for many services are not expected until after the client has stopped receiving those services. For example, the extent of success of drug and alcohol abuse treatment programs, employment programs, and mental health programs cannot be reasonably determined until months after their clients have completed the service. Few nonprofit organizations systematically follow up former clients to find out their progress.

Moving toward Outcome Management

Greater use of outcome and performance measurement would enable nonprofit managers and their potential funders to make decisions about programs based on information in addition to primarily financial data such as that found on IRS Form 990. However, nonprofit organizations have cited a number of barriers and obstacles to implementing sound outcome measurement systems. Concerns about the practical feasibility of greater use of performance and outcome measures are understandable, especially considering the state of the knowledge that most nonprofit organizations and their staffs currently have about outcome measurement and outcome management. Some concerns are relatively easy to address; others are not.

Too Difficult and Expensive

Some nonprofits feel that outcome measurement is just too difficult and that the time and resources required detract from direct service delivery.

The need to follow up with clients after they have left the program to assess sustained changes in behavior or condition presents potential time and cost problems.

One technique that nonprofits have found useful to measure outcomes is adapted from the business sector—surveys of customers. Even for environmental programs, surveys may be useful for obtaining feedback from potential polluters (whether households or businesses) on whether the program's efforts have contributed to more environment-friendly behaviors.

Nonprofit organizations may perceive such surveys as being difficult and expensive to conduct. Surveys are likely to be expensive if they are done under contracts with survey firms (that do rigorous but typically costly work), and if funders require considerable precision in the outcome data. If the survey requirements are less rigorous, then the organization staff (preferably guided by an appropriate consultant) may be able to collect and analyze the data themselves. Short questionnaires can be administered by mail (when appropriate). Small incentives (such as donated movie tickets and restaurant certificates) could encourage clients or former clients to respond. Most nonprofits have good relations with their clients and might obtain better response rates than a survey firm or researcher. Social worker staff will be more interested if the follow-up effort is part of an aftercare process.

Whereas businesses use surveys as market research tools to find out what customers want and customers' attitudes toward their products and services, nonprofits use them to identify needs and then to find out the extent to which their service helped clients. Businesses use the information to increase sales, whereas nonprofits assess the extent to which their programs, services, and activities are helping the beneficiaries and to help identify areas that need to be improved. And while businesses focus on increasing sales to customers, nonprofits must deal with multiple stakeholders, requiring the tracking of additional indicators. An example is giving consideration to the special needs of vulnerable populations, an additional dimension that nonprofit organizations typically address.

Terms Diverse, Confusing, and Contradictory

The definitions of inputs, outputs, and outcomes (and intermediate versus end outcomes) and their roles are sometimes not clear and may vary from program to program.[8] It can be difficult to measure some outcomes directly, so an organization may use proxies for those outcomes. Such proxies can have widely differing amounts of evidence that give confidence as to the extent to which the proxy can be expected to yield the desired outcome. For example, a program's objective may be to enable clients to avoid a certain kind of behavior in the future. However, because of the perceived difficulty in following up with clients for a period of time after their departure, programs typically assess only changes in the client's knowledge about the behavior's risks and attitudes toward the behavior. Unfortunately, the degree to which increased knowledge and improved attitudes leads to the desired change in behavior is seldom known and may not be a good proxy for the desired behavior change, such as reduced drinking, smoking, or illegal drug use.

A classic example of the use of proxy outcome indicators occurs in child immunization programs. Many people are likely to consider the indicator "percent of children properly immunized" solely as an output; however, because the evidence is so strong that immunizations prevent certain diseases, many other people are likely to consider this indicator as an outcome. The ultimate outcome, of course, is that the incidence of these diseases is dramatically less for immunized persons. However, the usefulness of the latter indicator for child health program managers is highly limited because of the long time lag before the indicator can be properly calculated.

Contradictory and Multiple Outcome Measurement Requirements

Funders often require reporting that places an onerous burden on nonprofits with multiple funders. Some organizations start from scratch to design their outcome measurement systems, except for those affiliated with a national association that provides guidance on appropriate indicators. The identification of a basic set of outcome indicators, along with the development and testing of reliable, valid, and low-cost procedures for measuring those outcomes for the various functions nonprofit organizations perform, might considerably ease the work required for nonprofits attempting to set up their own processes to track outcomes.[9]

No outcome indicators will apply universally to all programs (even within a particular service area). Thoughtful, well-researched sets of core outcome indicators for each type of service and, for programs not covered by any of these sets, a flexible, practitioner-oriented framework of indicators might help bring outcome measurement to the next stage of general acceptance and use by funders (including government and foundations) and nonprofit organizations.

The Attribution Problem

Even the best outcome measurement does not solve the problem of identifying how much of the outcomes achieved are actually a result of the nonprofit program. In-depth program evaluations (especially those using randomized designs) attempt to do this, but often the causality/attribution issue cannot be resolved even then. Such evaluations are typically quite costly and can require many months, if not years, to carry out. Some larger nonprofits or those with specific funding for that purpose may undertake them occasionally, but they are rare. Findings from such in-depth evaluations thus have limited usefulness in helping nonprofits make timely choices about program improvements.

Instead, the sector needs to rely on less sophisticated analysis, on tools such as outcome sequence charts and theories of change, and even on common sense to provide evidence that a substantial linkage exists. Even small nonprofits need to develop some capacity to undertake at least basic analysis of their outcome data. Even simply comparing client condition at the time of entry into the program and at the time of exit (or, even better, some months after exit) can add to the organization's confidence that it had a significant role in the change. Many local mental health programs, for example, have been undertaking such analyses for many years, with tools developed through federal government funding.

As the outcome measurement process becomes more familiar and more comfortable, its use can be expanded to experiment with different approaches to service delivery. For example, an organization might randomly assign clients to different services (perhaps a curriculum with different content or two four-hour sessions versus one eight-hour session) and then use the outcome data to assess each approach. This procedure could provide strong evidence of which approach produced better outcomes.[10]

Possible Misinterpretation and Misuse of Data

Even with sound outcome measurement procedures, nonprofit organizations have problems interpreting the findings. Are the levels reported good or bad? Comparisons and benchmarks—ones that enable an organization to compare its latest results to those of other organizations—can help indicate whether or not possible action is called for. Within the organizations, there are some readily available benchmarks. These include comparisons (a) to outcomes from previous reporting periods, (b) to targets that the organization may have established at the beginning of each year for each outcome indicator, and (c) by client and service characteristics (if the organization breaks out the outcome data for clients by client residence, income level, gender, age group, handicap status, or number and type of sessions attended, etc.).

It is more difficult to find levels of outcome achieved by other organizations providing similar services with similar outcome indicators. Although this comparison is attractive in theory, it is often difficult to implement because of lack of agreement on outcome indicators and data collection procedures. Without standard-setting bodies (an unlikely possibility for the nonprofit sector), the most practical way to arrive at a commonly accepted set of performance metrics is to help practitioners develop and accept them. To do so, practitioners would be considerably helped if a model or candidate set of such core outcome indicators (with recommendations on data collection procedures) were available, or at least guidance (such as a common framework) to help them develop their own. These will enable the data to start flowing in a structured way so that they can be aggregated and analyzed. Inevitably, the indicators will need to be refined.

If reasonably comparable data are available on any outcome indicators, this will better enable each program area to seek out effective practices. Perhaps a national organization could examine outcome data from comparable programs and seek information from high-level performers as to what they are doing so well—a search for "best" or, at least, "successful" practices.

For example, to assess and learn from results of different school-related programs that try to improve student performance (such as tutoring or mentoring programs), the program staff needs to agree on the appropriate outcome indicators. If they agree that student scores on standardized tests are appropriate program outcome indicators, then comparisons of outcome indicators across the different programs can encourage improvements. Data on the costs of various program alternatives would further enlighten the comparisons among alternative programs.

As various program staff review their outcome indicators, a list of common concerns of the programs becomes obvious. Often, programs seek changes in knowledge, attitudes, behavior, and status or condition of clients or participants. Most programs should track a common set of quality-of-service characteristics, such as the service's timeliness, accessibility, physical location, and helpfulness of the staff. Because of the incredible diversity within the nonprofit sector, it would be a very difficult task to develop a core set of candidate indicators for all types of nonprofit programs. However, a more generic standard framework for developing outcomes could be helpful to programs seeking to create outcome measurements where none are already available.

Developing a Common Outcomes Framework

An example of such a framework is shown in box 9.3. For example, although a researcher may be able to find information on program outcomes with a web-based key word search, the results are likely to be undifferentiated—overwhelming in volume and time-consuming to assess for relevance. And the search results might vary significantly with different search terms.

However, a common framework of outcomes can provide a systematic listing with context and additional relevant content; a user would be able to learn efficiently about the subject and find the best resources. This would help funders and nonprofit organizations think in a more structured way about how to measure their contributions to society and their roles as change agents. Over time, this process can help document effectiveness and also better manage their resources.

Although there currently is no shortage of outcomes and their indicators in some program areas, there is no centralized grouping of them or assessment of their quality that serves as a resource for organizations that wish to develop outcome measurement systems. And because of the vast range of programs and services nonprofits provide, major gaps exist in available outcome indicators.

As noted earlier, outcome sequence charts (also called logic models) for programs—linking how the program activities lead to the desired outcomes—are often the starting point.[11] After outcomes are listed, measurable indicators for each of those outcomes would be developed. A number of sources (see box 9.2) can help to develop a list of criteria for indicators for use in the development of a common framework and for use in identifying outcome indicators for any particular service. Some sources are summarized below. Most of these cover other operational components (financial sustainability, etc.) as well as program outcomes.

Box 9.2. Examples of Criteria for Quality Outcome Indicators

Source	Criteria
Murray, Vic. "The State of Evaluation Tools and Systems for Nonprofit Organizations"[a]	Specific, observable, measurable, unambiguous; must measure some important aspect of the outcome that no other outcome measures
United Way of America[b]	SMART (Specific, Measurable, Achievable, Relevant, Time-bound)
Western Australia Mental Health Information Development Plan[c]	Applicable (address important dimensions that are useful to the service providers); acceptable (brief and user friendly, with easily understood language and clear format); practical (suitable for routine use with minimal cost and training, and simple scoring and interpretation); reliable (same results when used by different people); valid (quantify and measure what it is designed to measure); sensitive to change (reflects meaningful client changes)
The Urban Institute and The International City Managers Association (ICMA)[d]	Appropriate and valid (relate to the objectives and really measure what needs to be measured); unique (measures some characteristics that no other measure covers); complete (list of measures covers most objectives); comprehensible (easily understood); controllable (related at least in part to the program); cost effective to collect; timely (obtained soon enough that action can be taken); accurate and reliable
Financial Standards Accounting Board[e]	Unbiased, comparable, complete, consistent, with feedback value, material (of significance), neutral, of predictive value, relevant, predictive, reliable, valid, timely, understandable, verifiable.

---

a. Murray (2001, 40–4)

b. United Way of America (1996)

c. Consumer Outcomes in Mental Health, Western Australia. n.d. "About Outcome Measures." http://www.mhidp.health.wa.gov.au/one/outcome.asp.

d. Hatry et al. (1992, 2–3)

e. Financial Accounting Standards Board (1980, 2002)

Box 9.3. Standard Framework of Nonprofit Program Outcomes

Program-Centered Outcomes

Reach

Outreach
Common indicators:

Percentage of target constituency enrolled
Percentage of target constituency aware of service
Participation rate
Number of service requests per month

Reputation
Common indicators:

Number of favorable reviews/awards
Number of community partnerships
Percentage of constituents satisfied

Access
Common indicators:

Percentage of target constituents turned away
Percentage of target constituents reporting significant barriers to entry
Percentage of services offered at no charge

Participation

Attendance/utilization
Common indicators:

Acceptance rate
Percentage of capacity enrolled/registered
Percentage who enroll for multiple services/offerings
Attendance rate
Average attendance rate at events
Percentage of capacity filled at event
Number of subscriptions
Renewing memberships/subscriptions
Percentage of subscribers who are also donors

Commitment/engagement
Common indicators:

Percentage who continue with program past initial experience
Percentage of participants considered active
Percentage of constituents utilizing multiple services/offerings
Referral rate

Graduation/completion
Common indicators:

Percentage who successfully complete program
Percentage who report immediate needs met
Recidivism rate (back into program)
Average length of time in program
Percentage who continue to next level

Box 9.3. *(continued)*

Satisfaction

Quality
    Common indicators:

Number of favorable reviews/awards
Percentage reporting improved attitude/feeling
Constituent satisfaction rate
Referral rate

Fulfillment
    Common indicators:

Percentage reporting needs met
Percentage of target constituents served
Completion rate

Participant-Centered Outcomes

Knowledge/Learning/Attitude

Skills (knowledge, learning)
    Common indicators:

Percentage whose scores improved after
    attending
Percentage that believe skills were increased
    after attending
Percentage increasing knowledge (before/after
    program)

Attitude
    Common indicators:

Percentage showing improvement as reported
    by parent, teacher, coworker, other
Percentage showing improvement as reported
    by participant

Readiness (qualification)
    Common indicators:

Percentage feeling well-prepared for a particular
    task/undertaking
Percentage meeting minimum qualifications for
    next level/undertaking

Behavior

Incidence of bad behavior
    Common indicators:

Incidence rate
Relapse/recidivism rate
Percentage reduction in reported behavior
    frequency

Incidence of desirable activity
    Common indicators:

Success rate
Percentage that achieved goal
Rate of improvement

(continued)

Box 9.3. *(continued)*

Maintenance of new behavior
    Common indicators:
        Number weeks/months/years continued
        Percentage change over time
        Percentage moving to next level/condition/status
        Percentage that do not reenter the program/
            system

Condition/status

Participant social status
    Common indicators:
        Percentage with improved relationships
        Percentage who graduate
        Percentage who move to next level/condition/
            status
        Percentage who maintain current level/condition/
            status
        Percentage who avoid undesirable course of
            action/behavior

Participant economic condition
    Common indicators:
        Percentage who establish career/employment
        Percentage who move to long-term housing
        Percentage who maintain safe and permanent
            housing
        Percentage enrolled in education programs
        Percentage who retain employment
        Percentage with increased earnings

Participant health condition
    Common indicators:
        Percentage with reduced incidence of health
            problem
        Percentage with immediate positive response
        Percentage that report positive response post-
            90 days

Community-Centered Outcomes

Policy

  Awareness/understanding of issue
    Common indicators:
        Percentage of target constituents aware of issue
        Number of people reached through
            communications
        Percentage of target constituents taking desirable
            action
  Stakeholder support of issue
    Common indicators:
        Number of stakeholders convened
        Percentage of key stakeholders as partners

Box 9.3. *(continued)*

Influence on agenda
   Common indicators:

Number of legislative contacts
Percentage of supporting votes secured
Percentage of legislators aware of issue

Public health/safety

Risk of threat
   Common indicators:

Percentage of public aware of issue
Percentage of public taking precautions
Number of options/contingency plans
Time spent planning

Civic participation (to be developed)

Increase participation
   Common indicators:

Number of people participating in event
Percentage increase in turnout
Number of people volunteering

Economic (to be developed)

Increased opportunities
Support for economic growth/development
Economic sustainability

Environmental (to be developed)

Cleanliness
Safety
Aesthetics
Preservation

Social (to be developed)

Awareness of an issue
Incidence of undesirable activity
Incidence of desirable activity

Organization-Centered Outcomes

Financial (to be developed)
Management (to be developed)
Governance (to be developed)

Source: http://www.urban.org/center/CNP/projects/outcomeindicators.cfm

CCAF-FCVI Inc. Framework for Performance Reporting[12]

This includes the following 12 attributes of effectiveness:

- Management direction (are program objectives clear and understood?)
- Relevance (does program still make sense for the problem?)
- Appropriateness (are the program design and level of effort logical for the problem?)
- Achievement of intended results (have goals and objectives been achieved?)
- Acceptance (are stakeholders satisfied?)
- Secondary impacts (did the program have other consequences, intended or unintended, positive or negative?)
- Costs and productivity (what is the relationship among costs, inputs, and outputs?)
- Responsiveness (does program have the capacity to adapt to external changes?)
- Financial results (does program account appropriately for revenues, expenditures, assets, and liabilities?)
- Working environment (is the work environment for staff appropriate; do staff have necessary information, capacity, and motivation?)
- Protection of assets (are assets appropriately safeguarded?)
- Monitoring and reporting (are key results of organizational and program performance identified, reported, and monitored?)

American Council for Voluntary International Action

This large alliance of United States–based international development and humanitarian nongovernmental organizations with more than 160 members operating in every developing country has developed and promotes its Private Voluntary Organization Standards for its member organizations. Its 27 pages cover many aspects, including governance, practice, finance, resources, public policy, and program.[13] Specifically, the standards for programs require that they do the following:

- Facilitate self-reliance, self-help, popular participation, and sustainability, to avoid dependency;
- Be designed, implemented, and evaluated by participants from all groups affected, to the maximum extent possible;

- Give priority to working through local and national groups, encouraging their creation and strengthening those that exist;
- Respect and foster human rights and respect dignity, values, history, religion, and culture of people served;
- Focus on those at risk without discrimination and give priority to strengthening capacity of most vulnerable groups;
- Promote advancement and empowerment of women;
- Consider the full range of potential impacts upon the host country;
- Share program knowledge and experience;
- Adhere to professional standards in specific fields of activity (such as disaster response, refugee assistance, child sponsorship); and
- Have defined procedures for evaluation, both qualitatively and quantitatively, to address impacts on the program participants and the relationship of these impacts to the cost of achieving them.

This last standard calling for "defined procedures for evaluation" does not clearly address the use of "outcomes indicators" that can help measure effectiveness in achieving goals. A member organization trying to meet this standard would need additional guidance on whether an outcome tracking system would meet the standard.

United Way of America

This organization describes itself as dedicated to leading its 1,400 community-based members (who are independent, separately incorporated, and governed by local volunteers) in making a measurable impact in every community in America. It has done groundbreaking work on outcome measurement and provides extensive resources on its web site for use by members and nonmembers.[14] It focuses on program outcomes and provides some broad general categories that are useful for taxonomy development. Outcomes are changes or benefits in the following (Plantz, Greenway, and Hendricks n.d.):

- Knowledge
- Attitude
- Values
- Skill
- Behavior

- Condition
- Status

The order of this listing also represents a series of outcomes for many programs, each one leading to the next. For example, after attending a lecture on the health risks of smoking, the outcome of knowing more about the dangers of smoking (change in knowledge) may lead to an outcome of wanting to stop smoking (change in attitudes), which may lead to the ultimate goal of quitting smoking (change in status). The listing above serves as a chain that links initial outcomes to intermediate outcomes to end outcomes for many programs.[15]

Outcome Measurement and Resource Allocation

Outcome measurement is focused on past and current performance. Once developed, however, such measures are also useful in principle for making choices about the future.

Outcome Measurement and Budgeting

Looking at the outcome information during the planning and budgeting process allows the organization to better allocate funds and set priorities. Nonprofit resources are almost always limited. Knowing the outcomes of various programs will help when decisions are made to expand, contract, or eliminate programs. Particularly successful programs might be expanded or, alternatively, more resources might be given to less successful ones so that corrective actions can be taken. Historical outcome data can make projections of what is achievable with the funds requested. Without outcome data, it is much more difficult to make these decisions.

When targets for programs have been set and data have been collected throughout the year, more realistic planning for the next year can be completed. If, for example, outcomes have been poor for a particular class of clients, the organization might want to develop a plan to correct this over a specific time frame.

These data can also inform budget projections. When the outcomes achieved with prior years' budget allocation are known, then more accurate estimates of what funds are needed to achieve certain levels of outcomes can be calculated. If analyses of outcome data have identified the need for changes, then budget requests can include any costs of the needed changes.

If the nonprofit organization undertakes a long-range strategic planning process, the outcome data can provide a strong starting point. Such information identifies strengths and weaknesses with the organization's services or clients. The plan can incorporate future targets for key outcome indicators against which annual progress can be measured.

Budgeting in general typically begins with a projection of expected revenues, sometimes a difficult projection for nonprofits to make. The data from an outcome measurement system would identify past results that can serve as the starting point for estimating the likely results achievable with the expected available resources.

Outcome Measurement and Assessing Economic and Social Value

To most efficiently and effectively allocate resources, organizations need to make choices among alternative ways to use their resources. The business sector, with its sole focus on the bottom line of profits, tends to do this explicitly and systematically, examining each option's probable effects on revenues and costs. Nonprofit organizations, with their need to be responsive to numerous stakeholders instead of stockholders, tend to make their choices in a considerably less systematic way.

Three related approaches to this more complex social decisionmaking process are available that, in principle, could help organizations make resource allocation choices. These are discussed below. The first two approaches have been most commonly used by governments, especially the federal government,[16] and have some promise for use in the nonprofit sector. However, they require somewhat sophisticated procedures and have seldom been used on a regular basis by nonprofit organizations (and even less often by small ones). As nonprofit organizations become more familiar and comfortable with outcome information, at least the larger nonprofit organizations may find these approaches useful. Each of theses three procedures can be used both to assess past performance and to evaluate future programs options.

Cost-Effectiveness Analysis

This type of analysis is likely to be the most readily adaptable to nonprofit organizations. The costs of individual services, programs, or activities are linked to the various outcomes for those services, programs, or activities. An organization needs an outcome measurement process that provides the outcome data and an accounting process that can distinguish the costs of each program or activity, even if only roughly.

When used to compare different ways to deliver services, cost-effectiveness analysis requires that the organization define thoroughly each alternative being considered so that each alternative's resource requirements and likely outcomes can be estimated. The outcomes can consist of any number of quantitatively measurable outcomes. If important outcomes cannot be measured, they can at least qualitatively be considered. Decisionmakers then have a number of outcome indicators to help them make their choices.

The basic steps include (1) selecting the alternative service approaches to assess; (2) estimating the costs of each alternative; (3) identifying the key outcome indicators and estimating the values that each alternative would achieve; and (4) combining estimates of resource cost with the outcome estimates to compare the cost-effectiveness of various programs.

If the program has one outcome indicator that is the key, crucial outcome for the program, the findings can be expressed as a single cost-effectiveness ratio, "the amount of outcome achieved per dollar," for example, "number of persons employed six months after employment services ended." Many programs, however, have multiple outcomes to consider and multiple client groups for whom separate measurements are needed. (Note that it is not likely to be meaningful to attempt to split the costs into those applicable to each outcome, because the outcomes will likely occur simultaneously.)

As a tool for guiding resource use, cost-effectiveness analysis can be quite useful for assessing which way of achieving a common objective is the most cost-effective (e.g., the relative effects of after-school programs vs. weekend programs on reducing juvenile delinquency). Cost-effectiveness analysis will not, however, reveal whether any given program produces social value in excess of its costs.

Cost-Benefit Analysis

This approach goes a step beyond cost-effectiveness analysis by imputing monetary values to the outcomes of the program. Cost-benefit analysis has most often been used to provide information for decisions about major government public works (such as dam construction) and regulatory programs. It can be used prior to the beginning of a program, to help in the decision to use scarce resources for one program or another, or after program implementation to contribute to learning about whether a particular type of program has been worthwhile.

Similar to business reports that list revenues and net profits, cost-benefit analysis translates all measurements into one common unit, dollars. The common unit allows for a calculation of cost-benefit ratio and the net dollar difference between the estimated costs and the estimated benefits. This can, at least on the surface, considerably ease the decisionmakers' decision—if they have confidence in the numbers. The assignment of dollar values incorporates the value judgments of those assigning dollar values to outcomes measured in nondollar units.

While the pressure for efficiency and effectiveness in both the government and nonprofit sectors grows, many issues make cost-benefit analysis very difficult.[17] The feature of cost-benefit analysis that makes it both distinctive and controversial is its requirement that program outcomes be monetized. For some outcomes, this may not be feasible, and considerable disagreement can exist about how the outcomes can, or even should, be translated into dollar equivalents. For example, what is the monetary value of getting a person to stop using illegal drugs, to get a child to stay in school for another year, or to reduce air or water pollution by certain amounts? Although economists have made some inroads into some of these determinations, inevitably the decisions on monetization and the application of a monetary metric to nonprofit outcomes can be very controversial (Cordes and Coventry 2007). Reducing all the information to a simple ratio can also lead to the loss of detailed information on the major components of programs and their outcomes, such as the individual outcome data and program costs.

Social Return on Investment and Similar Metrics

These approaches are similar to cost-benefit analysis but shift the use from one time, ad hoc decisions about investments to regular tabulations of social returns (Olsen 2003; Roberts Enterprise Development Fund 2001). The primary applications thus far have been in programs aimed at improving employment opportunities for disadvantaged persons. As in the previous tools, calculating the social return on investment for a nonprofit starts with data obtained from a performance measurement system (or from a program evaluation). As with cost-benefit analysis, a variety of expenditure data, and perhaps estimated added tax revenues (attributed to the program being examined), are then included.

These procedures have the same advantages (yielding one number representing the worth of the program) and disadvantages (often making leaps of faith to estimate the dollar worth of the outcome). It should be noted that the organization that first used social return on investment has now ceased using it, but it does continue to use and report on values derived from a performance measurement process (Roberts Enterprise Development Fund 2005).

Conclusion

The pressure for better measurement in the nonprofit sector is coming from many directions, including foundations and individual donors, governments, nonprofit managers, board members, and volunteers.

Considerable attention has been given within the nonprofit organization world to performance measurement, including its benefits and its handicaps. At present, meaningful implementation appears to be highly limited (though evidence is badly missing as to the extent of implementation of performance measurement in nonprofit organizations). A number of steps are needed to encourage and help nonprofit organizations implement practical procedures that will both meet the demands of funders and help the nonprofit organizations manage their work and improve their services to clients and the community. These steps include the following:

- More training and education in performance measurement and, particularly, how it can help organizations improve their services
- Development of a common framework and basic core outcome indicators for measuring outcomes for specific program areas
- Assistance in identifying and implementing practical data collection procedures and in undertaking basic analyses of the outcome information to make the information useful to the organization
- Making external benchmarks available to service providers in specific program areas
- Use of comparative outcome information across the country in individual service areas to help identify and disseminate information on successful practices and effective theories of change

We quote from Jim Collins (2005, 7–8):

> To throw our hands up and say, "But we cannot measure performance in the social sector the way you can in business" is simply lack of discipline. All indicators are flawed. . . . What matters is not finding the perfect indicator, but settling upon a *consistent and intelligent* method of assessing your output results, and then tracking your trajectory with rigor.

The bottom line for nonprofit organizations should be successfully helping clients and their communities—making them better off. Nonprofit organizations certainly want to do this. Regularly collected outcome information has the potential for providing meaningful evidence of program outcome and, even better, for helping the nonprofit organizations improve their abilities to help their clients and communities. But the time, money, and effort spent on outcome measurement will be wasted if the resulting information is merely sent to a funder and is not used to help improve the programs. Outcome measurement, along with outcome management (the use of the information to help make improvements), has considerable potential to improve the nonprofit bottom line but has a long way to go.

NOTES

1. The Urban Institute's National Center for Charitable Statistics, table "Number of Nonprofit Organizations in the United States, 1996–2006," http://nccsdataweb.urban.org?PubApps/profile1.php?state=US.

2. IRS Databook 2006, table 24. "Tax-Exempt Organization and Other Entity Applications or Disposals, by Type of Organization and Internal Revenue Code Section, Fiscal Year 2006," http://www.irs.gov/pub/irs-soi/06databk.pdf.

3. United Way of America's 1996 report "Measuring Program Outcomes: A Practical Approach" has sold more than 100,000 copies.

4. Telephone interview with Margaret C. Plantz, director of Community Impact Programs, United Way of America, April 5, 2006.

5. The foremost publication in the nonprofit sector thus far is the previously cited United Way of America's 1996 report "Measuring Program Outcomes: A Practical Approach." Examples of more recent national association material includes the very detailed Boys and Girls Clubs of America's "Youth Development Outcome Measurement Tool Kit"; the Girl Scouts of the U.S.A.'s 1997 "Girl Scout Outcomes Study Procedures Manual"; and Big Brothers Big Sisters of America's 2001 "Program-Based Outcome Evaluation." Guidance materials published by organizations other than the national associations include the Rensselaerville Institute's 2004 "Outcome Frameworks: An Overview for Practitioners" and the Urban Institute's 2004 six-part series on "Outcome Management for Nonprofit Organizations."

6. See the latest "Criteria for Performance Excellence" pamphlets issued annually by the National Institute of Standards and Technology and the "PART" materials posted on the OMB web site.

8. For example, in an opinion commentary in the April 6, 2006, issue of *Chronicle of Philanthropy* ("The Limits of Usefulness"), Kennard T. Wing gives the example of a woman who runs a literacy organization and understood that "grantmakers don't want to support literacy per se" and that "she has to show that, having learned to read, wonderful things happen to her clients."

9. The Urban Institute and the Center for What Works have developed prototype sets of core outcome indicators for a number of specific program areas plus a common framework of outcome indicators that might serve as a starting point for nonprofits whose services do not fall into one of the detailed program areas. More information is available at http://www.urban.org/center/CNP/projects/outcomeindicators.cfm.

10. This experimental design and other basic analysis procedures that nonprofit organizations can use are discussed in more detail in Harry P. Hatry, Jake Cowan, and Michael Hendricks, "Analyzing Outcome Information: Getting the Most from Data," The Urban Institute, Washington, DC, 2004, http://www.urban.org/publications/310973.html.

11. For example, see appendix A in Hatry et al. (2003).

12. See http://www.ccaf-fcvi.com for more information.

13. See http://www.interaction.org/content/pvostandards.

14. See Outcome Measurement Resource Network at http://national.unitedway.org/outcomes/.

15. See Hatry and Lampkin (2003) for more information on deciding what and how to measure.

16. For detailed descriptions of these first two approaches, see Kee (2004) and Michel (2001).

17. See Boardman et al. (1996, 7, 12).

REFERENCES

Boardman, Anthony E., David H. Greenberg, Aidan R. Vining, and David L. Weimer. 1996. *Cost-Benefit Analysis: Concepts and Practice.* Upper Saddle River, NJ: Prentice Hall.

Collins, Jim. 2005. "Good to Great and the Social Sectors: Why Business Thinking Is not the Answer." Boulder, CO: Jim Collins.

Cordes, Joseph, and Coventry. 2007. "Using Cost Benefit Analysis to Measure the Impact of Nonprofits: Promises, Implementation, and Limitations." Washington, DC: George Washington University.

Financial Accounting Standards Board. 1980. Statement of Financial Accounting Concepts no. 2. Norwalk, CT: Financial Accounting Standards Board.

———. 2002. "The Focus of Private Sector Financial Reporting on Measures of Performance." Norwalk, CT: Financial Accounting Standards Board.

Frumkin, Peter. 2001. "Going Beyond Efficiency." *Nonprofit Quarterly* (July): 20–23.

Giving USA Foundation. 2005. *Giving USA (2004)*. Washington, DC: American Association of Fundraising Counsel.

Hatry, Harry, and Linda Lampkin. 2003. *Key Steps in Outcome Management*. Washington, DC: The Urban Institute.

Hatry, Harry, P., Philip S. Schaenman, Donald M. Fisk, John R. Hall, Jr., and Louise Snyder. 1992. *How Effective Are Your Community Services?* Washington, DC: International City Managers Association.

Hatry, Harry, P., Jake Cowan, Ken Weiner, and Linda M. Lampkin. 2003. "Developing Community-Wide Outcome Indicators for Specific Services." Washington, DC: The Urban Institute.

Kee, James E. 2004. "Cost-Effectiveness and Cost-Benefit Analysis." In *Handbook of Practical Program Evaluation*, 2nd ed., edited by Joseph S. Wholey, Harry P. Hatry, and Kathryn E. Newcomer. San Francisco: Jossey-Bass.

Michel, R. Gregory. 2001. "Decision Tools for Budgetary Analysis." Chicago: Government Finance Officers Association.

Murray, Vic. 2001. "The State of Evaluation Tools and Systems for Nonprofit Organizations." In *Accountability: A Challenge for Charities and Fundraisers*, edited by Putman Barber. *New Directions for Philanthropic Fundraising*, Number 31, Spring, published by Jossey-Bass.

Olsen, Sara. 2003. "Social Return on Investment: Standard Guidelines." Center for Responsible Business Working Paper 8. Berkeley: University of California.

Orosz, Joel J., Cynthia C. Phillips, and Lisa Wyatt Knowlton, eds. 2003. *Agile Philanthropy: Understanding Foundation Effectiveness*. Allendale, MI: Grand Valley State University, Dorothy A. Johnson Center for Philanthropy and Nonprofit Leadership.

Ostrower, Francie. 2004. "Attitudes and Practices Concerning Effective Philanthropy: Survey Report." Washington, DC: The Urban Institute. http://www.urban.org/publications/411067.html.

Plantz, Margaret C., Martha T. Greenway, and Michael Hendricks. n.d. "Outcome Measurement: Showing Results in the Nonprofit Sector." http://national.unitedway.org/outcomes/resources/What/ndpaper.cfm.

Roberts Enterprise Development Fund. 2001. "SROI Methodology." San Francisco: Roberts Enterprise Development Fund. http://www.redf.org/publications-sroi.htm.

———. 2005. *Social Impact Report 2005*. San Francisco: Roberts Enterprise Development Fund. http://www.redf.org/download/other/2005-Social-Impact-Report.pdf.

United Way of North America. 1996. "Measuring Program Outcomes: A Practical Approach." Alexandria, VA: United Way of North America.

———. 2000. *Agency Experiences with Outcome Measurement: Survey Findings*. Alexandria, VA: United Way of North America. http://www.unitedway.org/Outcomes/Resources/upload/agencyom2.pdf.

Wiener, Susan J., Arthur D. Kirsch, and Michael T. McCormack. 2002. "Balancing the Scales: Measuring the Roles and Contributions of Nonprofit Organizations and Religious Congregations." Washington, DC: Independent Sector.

About the Editors

Joseph J. Cordes is director of the School of Public Policy and Public Administration and professor of economics, public policy and public administration, and international affairs. His academic specialization is in public economics and policy analysis. An associate scholar in the Center on Nonprofits and Philanthropy at the Urban Institute, he is the coeditor of the *Encyclopedia of Taxation and Policy,* 2nd edition, and *Democracy, Social Values, and Public Policy.* He has also authored or coauthored numerous articles and chapters in books on tax policy, the economics of nonprofit organizations, government regulation, and government spending. With Evelyn Brody, he contributed a chapter to *Nonprofits and Government: Collaboration and Conflict,* published in 2006.

C. Eugene Steuerle is the vice president of the Peter J. Peterson Foundation and a former codirector of the Urban–Brookings Tax Policy Center. He is also the author, editor, or coeditor of 15 books and hundreds of articles, columns, testimonies, and reports. His latest book is the second edition of *Contemporary U.S. Tax Policy.* Through his column, *The Government We Deserve,* he shares his extensive knowledge of issues concerning the federal budget, taxes, retirement security, health, and other areas of public finance. Among many positions, he has served as deputy assistant secretary of the Treasury for Tax Analysis, president of the National Tax Association, chair of the 1999 Technical Panel advising Social Security on its methods and assumptions. Between 1984 and 1986, he served as the economic coordinator and original organizer of the Treasury's tax reform effort.

About the Contributors

Alan R. Andreasen is professor of marketing and executive director of the Social Marketing Institute in the McDonough School of Business, Georgetown University. Andreasen is a member of several academic and professional associations and serves on the editorial boards of the *Journal of Consumer Policy,* the *Journal of Consumer Research, Social Marketing Quarterly,* and the *Journal of Public Policy and Marketing.* His publications include 18 books and over a hundred articles and conference papers. His most recent books are *Social Marketing in the 21st Century, Ethics in Social Marketing,* and *Strategic Marketing in Nonprofit Organizations,* 7th edition (coauthored with Philip Kotler). A consultant to many organizations, including the World Bank, the American Cancer Society, and the Centers for Disease Control, Professor Andreasen conducts executive seminars worldwide for diverse nonprofit and private-sector organizations and government agencies.

Evelyn Brody is a professor at Chicago-Kent College of Law, Illinois Institute of Technology, having visited at Penn, Duke, and NYU law schools. She teaches courses on tax and nonprofit law. She has worked in private practice and with the U.S. Treasury Department's Office of Tax Policy. A reporter of the American Law Institute's *Project on Principles of the Law of Nonprofit Organizations,* Professor Brody is also an associate scholar with the Urban Institute's Center on Nonprofits and Philanthropy. She served as a member of the Nonprofit Sector's expert advisory group, and, in 2004 and 2006, was an invited presenter to Senate Finance Committee Staff Roundtables. She serves as an advisory board member of Columbia Law School's Charities Law Project.

Harry P. Hatry is a distinguished fellow and director of the Public Management Program for the Urban Institute in Washington, D.C. He has been a leader in developing performance measurement and evaluation procedures for federal, state, and local public and private agencies since the 1970s and has provided assistance on activities related to the Government Performance and Results Act to several government agencies. His book, *Performance Measurement: Getting Results*, is widely used and has been translated into two other languages. He is a coeditor of *Handbook of Practical Program Evaluation*, coauthor of *How Effective Are Your Community Services? Procedures for Performance Measurement*, and coauthor of the United Way of America's widely disseminated report *Measuring Program Outcomes: A Practical Approach*. He is an author and coeditor of a recent series of six guides on "Outcome Management for Nonprofit Organizations."

Linda M. Lampkin is a research director of the Economic Research Institute and heads up the Washington, D.C., office. As former director of the National Center for Charitable Statistics at the Urban Institute, she was responsible for creating a database of the IRS Form 990 information filed annually by charities and managed research projects on the nonprofit sector. She was also responsible for the classification system for nonprofits used by IRS and researchers in the field. Coauthor of the *New Nonprofit Almanac and Desk Reference,* she has published articles and spoken extensively on the nonprofit sector, with particular emphasis on data sources, tracking outcomes, and financial accounting. She served as a member of the IRS Information Reporting Program Advisory Committee and received the IRS Commissioner's Award for her work on electronic filing of Form 990.

Burton Sonenstein is vice president and chief investment officer/acting vice president for finance and administration at the Annie E. Casey Foundation. Burton Sonenstein is responsible for assuring that the foundation's financial resources serve its mission and programs. He oversees investments and the management of the foundation's endowment, and helps program staff with their grant portfolios. His roles have included founder and CEO of United Insurance Management Company, president and CEO of United Educators Insurance, vice president of finance and administration at Wellesley College in Massachusetts, vice president and treasurer at Wesleyan University in Connecticut, and a practicing CPA and management consultant at KPMG Peat Marwick.

Howard P. Tuckman is the dean of the Fordham University Graduate School of Business, dean of the business faculty, professor of finance and economics, and holder of the George N. Jean Chair in Business. Prior to joining Fordham University, Dr. Tuckman served as distinguished professor of economics and interim dean of the Fogelman College of Business and Economics at the University of Memphis, dean of the School of Business at Virginia Commonwealth University, and, most recently, dean of Rutgers Business School, Newark and New Brunswick. A consultant for corporate and government agencies, he is the author of eight books and over 130 refereed journal articles. He has served as a consultant to private, nonprofit, and government entities and is on a variety of nonprofit and for-profit boards of directors.

Eric C. Twombly is a principal research associate and the director of organizational studies at KDH Research and Communication (KDHRC), a public health research institution, where he studies health delivery mechanisms and health literacy programs. He is an expert on the organizational behavior of community-based health and human service providers, and he has been the chief evaluator on several public health projects funded by the National Institutes of Health. Before joining KDHRC, he was a senior research associate at the Center on Nonprofits and Philanthropy at the Urban Institute and an assistant professor in the Andrew Young School of Policy Studies at Georgia State University, where he continues to lecture on public policy and social policy issues.

Christa Velasquez is the director of social investments at the Annie E. Casey Foundation, a private charitable organization whose principal mission is to help build better futures for disadvantaged children and families. She is responsible for managing the foundation's $100 million social investment fund and implements investment strategy, designs investment policies, and educates staff about social investments. She spent six years at the consulting firm Brody-Weiser-Burns, specializing in social investing, community development financing, and business planning for social ventures. A board member of TRF Urban Growth Partners, the American Visionary Art Museum, and Catholic Charities of the Archdiocese of Baltimore, she is also a member of the advisory committee of the Yale University School of Management Internship Fund.

Dennis R. Young is the director of the Nonprofit Studies Program at the Andrew Young School of Policy Studies, Georgia State University, and Bernard B. and Eugenia A. Ramsey Chair of Private Enterprise. Professor Young helped establish the Mandel Center for Nonprofit Organizations at Case Western and was its director from 1988 to 1996. A former president of the Association for Research on Nonprofit Organizations and Voluntary Action (ARNOVA), Professor Young has written many articles and several books, including coauthoring *Corporate Philanthropy at the Crossroads and Economics for Nonprofit Managers* and editing two recent volumes on the economics of nonprofit organizations. He is also founding editor of the journal *Nonprofit Management & Leadership,* which he edited from 1990 through 2000.

Index

adaptation, organizational propensity for, 3–4
advertising collaboration, pro bono, 163–64
aggregation of assets, 135
aggregation test and aggregation proposal, 105–6
alliances with corporations. *See* cross-sector marketing alliances
American Cancer Society, 161, 173, 177
American Council for Voluntary International Action, 260–61
American Diabetes Association, 11, 18
American Express, 156
AmeriCorps, 226, 227
ancillary joint ventures, 103–4
Annie E. Casey Foundation (AECF), 194, 199, 207–9, 212–13. *See also* East Baltimore Development, Inc.
Making Connections initiative, 213–14
arm's length rule, 107
Arthritis Foundation, 176, 178
asset lock, 116
attenuated property rights, 222

Bay Area Equity Fund, 204–5
benchmarks (outcome measurement), 252–53
Benetech, 73–75
blended value capital, 114
board service, 165
Bookshare.org, 39
Boomtown Café, 38, 39
Botanical Garden, 38
brand-building diverse involvements (alliances), 162
business activity, nonprofit, 83–85
  legal framework for, 84
  organizational form for, 85–87. *See also* organizational form(s)
business in nonprofit sector, new modes of, 223–24
business judgment rule, 110

"campaign overload," 181–82
capital. *See* financial capital
cause-marketing alliances. *See also* cross-sector marketing alliances
  taxonomy of, 159–67

cause-related marketing, 157. *See also*
    marketing, corporate cause
Cause-Related Marketing (Adkins), 168–69
CCAF-FCVI Inc. framework for
    performance reporting, 260
charitable activities. *See also* philanthropy;
    potentially charitable outputs
    blending business ventures with, 48, 49
    vs. investment, 115
charitable occupations, change and
    growth in, 58–63
charitable sector, 233. *See also* potentially
    charitable outputs; tax benefits for
    charities
    growth of, 56–57, 241
City Year, 80–81
commercial activity, 224
    taxation and, 94–95, 135
commercial collaborations, 158
commercialism, 224
commerciality doctrine, 94–95
community-centered outcomes, 258–59
community development financial
    institutions (CDFIs), 201–2
community interest company (CIC), 116
community-level fields, 231
Community Reinvestment Act, 201–2
Community Wealth Ventures, 39–40
comparisons (outcome measurement),
    252–53
compensation, 218, 220–22. *See also*
    under labor
    flexibility in, 109
competition
    with for-profit organizations,
        increased, 224–25
    for qualified labor, 226–27, 231–32
consumer reactions to corporate social
    initiatives, 170–73
    types of, 170
corporate executives serving on nonprofit
    boards, 165
Corporate Involvement Initiative, 115
corporate-nonprofit alliances. *See* cause-
    marketing alliances; cross-sector
    marketing alliances

corporate quid pro quo. *See* quid pro quo
    organizations
corporate socially responsibility (CSR),
    10, 30, 157, 172. *See also* social
    investment
cost-benefit analysis, 264–65
cost-effectiveness analysis, 263–64
Crain, Rance, 174
credit-counseling agencies, 85–86
cross-sector marketing alliances. *See also*
    cause-marketing alliances
    and broader issues for nonprofit
        sector, 181–83
    defined, 157
    future challenges, 183–84
    impact, 156, 158–59, 167
        first-order benefits for corporations,
            167–69
        first-order benefits for nonprofit
            partners, 175–76
        positive second-order benefits for
            corporations, 169–72
        possible negative second-order
            effects for corporations,
            172–75
        possible negative second-order
            effects for nonprofits, 177–81
        second-order benefits for nonprofit
            organizations, 176–77
    objectives, 157–59
    problems in, 180–81
    taxonomy of, 159–67
customer surveys, 250

DARTS, 40
Delancey Street Foundation, 69–71
donated funds, 241
donative behavior and worker prefer-
    ences, 220–21
double-bottom-line concept, 199–200
double-bottom-line model, 18, 114
double-bottom-line social ventures, 3, 11,
    50
double-bottom-line venture capital
    funds, 204–5

East Baltimore Development, Inc.
    (EBDI), 209–12
economies of scale and scope, 132
education, higher, 86, 111–12
effectiveness, 247–48. *See also* outcomes
    attributes of, 260
"empire building," 105
employment, nonprofit. *See also* labor
    economic and demographic factors
        and, 230–31
    trends in, 228–30
Enterprise Center, 72
entrepreneurship, social, 54. *See also*
        under social enterprise, alternative
        disciplinary approaches to
    nonprofit ventures and, 72–74
    organizational structure, 74–75
    relation of mission and revenue-
        producing activities, 74
Europe, social enterprise in, 33–34
executives serving on nonprofit boards,
    165

financial capital, raising, 108
financial reporting. *See under* outcome
    measurement
financing. *See also* social investment
    benefits, 206–7
First Book, 79–81
fiscal control in hybrid structures, 140–41
for-profit subsidiaries. *See also* hybrid
        organizational forms; taxable
        subsidiaries
    organizational benefits of creating,
        134–37
foundation financing, 193–94. *See also*
        social investment
"fourth sector," 16
"fragmentation rule," 119n.23
Freedom Wheels, 138

Girl Scout cookies, 39
goodwill-building partnerships, 165
Google.org, 1

government
    competition for labor, 226–27
    shifts in attention toward nonprofits,
        225–26
government policy. *See also* policy issues;
        public policy
    organizational choice and, 64–67
grant-making foundations, 27–28. *See also*
        Annie E. Casey Foundation (AECF)
Green Institute, 73–74
Greyston Bakery, 39

health care industry, projected growth in,
    231
hospitals, 86
housing, development of affordable,
    203
Housing Works, 76, 77
human capital, gaining access to, 108
hybrid identity, social enterprises with,
    35, 37–38
hybrid organizational forms, 16–18, 35,
        41, 43, 130, 150–51. *See also* for-
        profit subsidiaries; structures (of
        hybrid nonprofits)
    concerns with, 142–44
    distribution by mission category,
        147–49
    economic strategies facilitated by
        creating, 131–34
    evidence on the prevalence of, 144–50
    example, 137–38
    with for-profit subsidiaries, advantages
        of creating, 134–37
    future of, 150–51
    public and donor perceptions of,
        144
    reasons for lack of academic study of,
        150
hybrid projects, 35

image management, 78
income tax, 44, 114–15. *See also* unrelated
        business income tax

income tax exemption, federal, 44, 83–84, 90–91, 93–96
"intentional investment," 198
investment-leveraging, 205
investment(s). *See also* program-related investments; social investment
    vs. charitable activities, 115
    social return on, 114, 265–66

James, Estelle, 27
Jenny Craig, 179
job training, 49–50
job training programs (traditional model), 69
    organizational structure, 71–72
    relation of mission and income-producing activities, 71
    types and examples of, 69–71
joint issue promotion (alliances), 162–63, 173, 178–79
joint product marketing, 161
joint ventures, use with private parties, 103–9
Juma Ventures, 70–72

labor, nonprofit, 217, 232–33. *See also* employment
    changing environment for, 223–26
    future directions, 230–32
    importance, 217–18
    new era for, 226–28
        increasing demands on nonprofit workforce, 227
    theories of, 219–20
        changes in organizational form and nonprofit compensation, 222–23
        donative behavior and worker preferences, 220–21
        property rights and nonprofit labor, 221–22
labor force, age distribution of, 230–31

leveraging, 205, 206
licensing, 161, 173, 178
limited liability companies (LLCs), 89. *See also* single-member limited liability companies
    use with private parties, 102–4
Living Faith, Inc. v. Commissioner, 93–94
logic models. *See* outcome sequence charts

Manchester-Bidwell Corporation, 76–78
marketing, corporate cause. *See also* cause-marketing alliances; cross-sector marketing alliances
    history of, 156–57
marketing assistance, 163–64
membership *vs.* share ownership, 89
Minnesota Diversified Industries (MDI), 71, 72
mission-related investment, 195, 196, 198
mixed programs (partnerships), 166–67
money-making projects, 35
"multi-product firms," nonprofits as, 27

New Community Corporation (NCC), 75–78
nondistribution constraint, 2, 17, 47, 48, 53, 87–88, 222
nonprofit conglomerates, 50–51, 75–76
    organizational structure, 76–77
    relation of mission and revenue-producing activities, 78–79
nonprofit corporation codes, 87–89
    affiliated organizations and effect on charitable purpose, 89–90
nonprofit status, when nonprofits forgo, 108–9
nonprofits
    vs. for-profits, 1–2, 6, 15, 239–40. *See also* organizational form(s)
        advantages and disadvantages, 108–9

new demands facing frontline staff of, 227–28
not-for-profit organizational form, 2
advantages and disadvantages of, 6

occupations
change and growth in charitable and noncharitable, 58–63
social services, 231
operational control in hybrid structures, 138–40
organizational arbitrage, 6, 53
organizational boundary associated with nonprofit status, 2
organizational change, internal, 13–16
organizational culture, changes in, 53–54
organizational features and organizational form, 52
organizational form(s)
changes in, 222–23
choice of, 4–7, 48–51
economic factors influencing, 52–57, 64–67. *See also* occupations
future trends regarding, 66–67
issues regarding, 65–66
policy issues, 64–67
continuum of, 52
examples, 52
for nonprofit business activity, 85–87
organizational identity, 5, 31, 34–35
outcome indicators, 242–43, 251–55, 261–62
proxy, 251
outcome management, moving toward, 249. *See also* outcome measurement systems, barriers and obstacles to implementing
outcome margin *vs.* profit margin, 240
outcome measurement, 266–67
and assessing economic and social value, 263
budgeting and, 262–63
current state of, 242–49

external guidance and standards, 247–48
financial reporting and, 243–44
standards requiring reporting on program results, 244–46
modeling of program effects and, 244, 247
pressures for, 240–42
program operations and, 248–49
resource allocation and, 262–66
ways it has helped programs, 248
outcome measurement systems, barriers and obstacles to implementing
attribution problem, 252
contradictory and multiple outcome measurement requirements, 251–52
diverse, confusing, and contradictory terms, 250–51
misinterpretation and misuse of data, 252–54
too difficult and expensive, 249–50
outcome sequence charts, 254
outcomes, nonprofit program, 261–62
standard framework of, 254, 256–59
outcomes framework, developing a common, 254–59

parent/subsidiary structures, 89
participant-centered outcomes, 257–58
Pension Protection Act of 2006, 107
performance evaluation, 15, 242, 266–67. *See also* outcome measurement
philanthropic collaborations, 157–58
philanthropy, 25, 26, 35. *See also* charitable activities; social enterprise
Pioneer Human Services, 70–72
Pioneer Social Ventures, 72
policy issues, 64–67. *See also* public policy
policy marketing, 158
political collaborations, 158
portfolio balance strategies, 133
portfolio management in hybrid structures, 140–41

Posner, Judge, 101
potentially charitable outputs
    defined, 55
    growth of industries with, 55–57
Precision CertiPro Warehouse, 137
"primary purpose" test, 93
Principles of the Law of Nonprofit Organi-
    zations (Brody), 89
private benefit, 100
private inurement, 100, 101
Private Letter Ruling, 115
private parties, use of LLCs and joint
    ventures with, 102–4, 108
    aggregation and controlled
        subsidiaries, 104–7
    when nonprofits forgo nonprofit
        status, 108–9
pro bono advertising collaboration, 163–64
Pro-VenEx fund, 201
program-centered outcomes, 256–57. *See*
    also outcomes
program evaluations, 249. *See also*
    outcome measurement
program-related investments (PRIs),
    12–13, 195, 205–7
    defined, 195
    rationale and history, 196–99
    rise in number of, 197–98
program standards, 260–61. *See also*
    outcome indicators
programmatic opportunity cost, 209
property rights, attenuated, 222
property tax, paying, 109
property-tax exemption, 91–92
    pressures on, 113–14
public perception, 9
public policy. *See also* government policy;
    policy issues
    social enterprise and, 44–45
public policy studies as alternative
    approach to public administration,
    22–23

quality outcome indicators. *See also*
    outcome measurement
    examples of criteria for, 254, 255

quid pro quo organizations, 51, 79–80
    organizational structure, 80–81
    relation of mission and revenue-
        producing activities, 81

reform proposals, 109–10
    broader measures of social benefit,
        114–16
    pressures on property-tax exemption,
        113–14
    reforming tax exemption, 110–12
    reforming UBIT, 112–13
Revenue Act of 1950, 84
Rockefeller Foundation's Program Ven-
    ture Experiment (Pro-VenEx fund),
    201
Ronald McDonald House Charities,
    166–67

sales-related transactional partnerships,
    161
second-order benefits, 158–59
selective incentives, 26–27
set-asides for nonprofit organizations,
    85
Share Our Strength, 39–40
share ownership *vs.* membership,
    89
Sierra Club, 183–84
single-member limited liability compa-
    nies (SMLLCs), 89, 102–3, 121
SmartWood, 39
social enterprise, 4–5, 17, 45
    alternative disciplinary approaches to,
        24
    economics, 24, 26–29
    entrepreneurship, 24, 32–33
    history, 24–26
    international manifestations, 24,
        33–34
    management theory, 24, 29–30
    organization theory, 24, 30–32
    defining, 22–23
    importance of clarity in the concept,
        23–24

identity *vs.* form of, 35
  organization-level identities, 36–38
  project-level identities, 38–42
  public policy and, 44–45
social enterprise identities, 35
social enterprise ventures, business
    practices of, 42–44
"social entrepreneurs," business ventures
    as, 26, 54
social impact analysis, 16
social investment, 195. *See also* Annie E.
    Casey Foundation; investment(s)
  approaches to, 200
    direct investments, 200–201
    double-bottom-line venture capital
      and private equity funds,
      204–5
    intermediaries, 201–4
    investment-leveraging and
      syndication, 205–6
  defined, 195, 196
  measuring the impact of, 210, 212–14
    deal-specific impact, 213
    population-level impact, 212–13
  rationale and history, 194–95
  trends, 197–99
social marketing, defined, 157, 163
social mission. *See* mission-related
    investment
social purpose enterprise, 35
social purpose project, 35
social return on investment, 16, 114
social role of corporate business, 25
social services occupations, 231
socially responsible business, for-profit,
    51. *See also* corporate socially
    responsibility
socially responsible investing. *See* social
    investment
societal marketing, corporate. *See also*
    social marketing
  defined, 163
sponsorships, 162
strategic collaborations, 158
structures (of hybrid nonprofits), 129.
    See also hybrid organizational forms
  dimensions of structure, 138

complexity, 142
exercise of operational and fiscal
    control, 138–41
legal form of entities, 141–42
economic motivations to create
    multiple, 131
  demand/revenue, 132–34
  strategies that respond to
    competition, 134
  supply/cost, 131–32
strategy and structure, 130–31
surveys of customers, 250
Susan G. Komen Breast Cancer
    Foundation, 179, 182
syndication, 205, 206

targeting assets to specific groups,
    135
tax benefits for charities, 90–100
  preventing undue benefit to private
    persons, 100–102
tax exemption, 90–91
  reforming, 110–12
tax preferences with indirect value to
    nonprofits, 108
taxable subsidiaries. *See also* for-profit
    subsidiaries; hybrid organizational
    forms
  number and distribution of (by asset
    size), 145–46
taxation, 44. *See also* income tax;
    property tax
Taxpayer Relief Act of 1997, 106, 107
Timberland Company, 80
Toyota, 183–84
"trust attributes," 53

United Cancer Council v. Commissioner,
    101
United Way of America, 261–62
universities, 86
unrelated business income tax (UBIT),
    95–100, 104, 106–7, 109
  reforming, 112–13
Urban Institute (UI), 12, 268n.9

Vehicle Maintenance Service, 40
Vehicles for Change (VFC),
    137–38
"venture philanthropy," 26
ventures, new
    cashing in on and selling, 108–9
Viet-AID, 38
volunteering, 232, 233
    strategic, 164–65

wages. *See* compensation
Weisbrod, Burton, 18
"whole hospital" joint ventures, 103
Win-Win Cleaning service, 38
Women in Community Service (WICS),
    174

YMCA, 92